Praise for *Moby Dyke*

"*Moby Dyke* is a hilarious adventure story, a full-throated love letter to lesbian bars, and an openhearted memoir all wrapped up in one glorious package. Come for the bars and stay for the people inside them."

—Emma Straub, bestselling author of *This Time Tomorrow* and
All Adults Here

"Krista Burton's voice is one of a kind and this is the exact book I've wanted from her. *Moby Dyke* is hilarious and perceptive, expertly weaving cultural and personal history with observations that made me laugh in public. I hope to copy down a drunk thought as eloquently as Krista does, and to read many more books that are this in love with their subjects."

—Tavi Gevinson, actor, writer, and founder/editor of *Rookie*

"As warm, lively, and funny as your favorite regular at your favorite queer bar."

—Rax King, author of *Tacky: Love Letters to the
Worst Culture We Have to Offer*

"This book is a masterpiece—simultaneously a hilarious memoir, rip-roaring travel diary, and thoughtful trip through history. Burton writes with such ferocious personality that you'll feel as though you are right there with her, zipping around unknown cities on scooters and panicking on the highway in rental cars while trying to grasp the last beacons of a vanishing gay cultural touchstone. Engaging, witty, heart-filled and heartfelt—I couldn't put it down."

—Danielle Henderson, author of *The Ugly Cry* and
creator of *Feminist Ryan Gosling*

"A celebration of [the] places that have long served as safe havens for the lesbian community. But Burton's stories about her own life also shine—she brings the introspective and observational humor that made her blog, *Effing Dykes*, so popular."

—Marie Lodi, *BUST*

"Engaging, entertaining, and insightful . . . A fun but thought-provoking book that's a perfect read for the start of summer."

—Jaime Herndon, *Book Riot*

"Burton's keen observations and sense of humor are on full display. . . . An infectious celebration of the joy and resilience of queer spaces."

—*Publishers Weekly*

"A lighthearted, honest narrative . . . Fans of travel memoirs and Burton's zealous personality will delight in this white-whale hunt."

—*Kirkus Reviews*

"A hilarious and affectionate investigation into the past and future of queer gathering spots . . . An accomplished and very funny journalist, Burton is able to track serious issues around queer belonging in a fresh and lively voice. The personal narrative underlying her pursuit of lesbian bars—including her marriage to Davin, a trans man, and coming out to her conservative Mormon family—is as topical and good-humored as the interviews and reportage contained here."

—Catherine Hollis, *BookPage*

"Endearing . . . Easy to read and personal, Burton's story will make any reader want to follow in her footsteps."

—Emily Dziuban, *Booklist*

"Part celebration and part elegy . . . Stirring up necessary conversations about who is welcome where."

—Michelle Hart, *Electric Lit*

"Burton writes in an upbeat, engaging voice that makes you feel like you're chatting with her over beers. . . . [One of] the best queer American travelogues since Edmund White's *States of Desire* was published way back in 1980."

—Jim Gladstone, *Passport Magazine*

Moby Dyke

An Obsessive Quest to Track Down the Last Remaining Lesbian Bars in America

Krista Burton

Simon & Schuster Paperbacks
New York   London   Toronto   Sydney   New Delhi

An Imprint of Simon & Schuster, LLC
1230 Avenue of the Americas
New York, NY 10020

First Simon & Schuster trade paperback edition June 2024

SIMON & SCHUSTER PAPERBACKS and colophon are registered
trademarks of Simon & Schuster, LLC

Simon & Schuster: Celebrating 100 Years of Publishing in 2024

For information about special discounts for bulk purchases,
please contact Simon & Schuster Special Sales at
1-866-506-1949 or business@simonandschuster.com.

The Simon & Schuster Speakers Bureau can bring authors to
your live event. For more information or to book an event,
contact the Simon & Schuster Speakers Bureau at 1-866-248-3049
or visit our website at www.simonspeakers.com.

Interior design by Lewelin Polanco

Manufactured in the United States of America

10 9 8 7 6 5 4 3 2 1

Library of Congress Cataloging-in-Publication Data has
been applied for.

ISBN 978-1-6680-0053-3
ISBN 978-1-6680-0054-0 (pbk)
ISBN 978-1-6680-0055-7 (ebook)

For anyone who's ever walked into a dyke bar and realized they were home.

Contents

What follows is my impression of my visits to the remaining lesbian bars in America. While nearly all bars received multiple visits, certain events have been compressed for brevity. Some names have been changed.

Moby Dyke

Introduction

On a bright summer morning in 2021, I sat on the splintery front steps of our barn-shaped house, coffee in hand. I was eyeing the lawn, which badly needed cutting.

The pressure was on. Our next-door neighbors had just cut *their* lawn, and mowed into ours a little bit, too. In the Midwest, that is a fucking message.

"Jeez," I said to Davin, who was weeding the front garden. "We just mowed last week!"

Davin looked up, streaks of sweat darkening his Faribault Girls Golf Team T-shirt, which he's been wearing since high school. "I think we can do it before it rains."

"Is it supposed to rain?"

"Yeah!" he said, excited. He stood up and leaned back, hands on hips, to look up at the sky. "Big storms tonight! Lemme check the radar."

Davin pulled his phone out and tapped at his weather app, which was already open. "Hooo boy," he said, zooming in on the storm radar. "*Oh* yeah. Comin' right at us!"

He tucked his phone back into his pocket and grinned at me, rubbing his hands gleefully. "Starts at eight, goes all night!"

"*Nice*," I said.

And that's when it hit me.

Right then. That moment.

Oh my god, we're middle-aged.

The signs had been increasing lately; I'd just been ignoring what they meant. But how else to explain the weekends spent picking up primer and caulk at Menards, which we do now so often that I don't even make "caulk" jokes anymore; the somber discussions we have about what we'll do when the truck—a 2002 Ford Ranger with 271,000 miles on it—finally wheezes its last; the second dog who gets his own stocking at Christmas? How else can you explain our new inability to get up from deep sofas without grunting; Davin's shining eyes when we're out with friends and I whisper, "You wanna go home and put on sweatpants?" into his ear; our *sudden shared interest in herbal tea*?

Holy shit, it happened. I never thought it would. We're settling down. Davin and I are middle-aged queers, born in the eighties, two *full adults*, a lesbian and a trans man.

Married.

Living in a small town.

In *rural Minnesota*.

What the fuck.

I went inside and put my mug into the dishwasher. On autopilot, distracted, I stuck my finger into each of the potted plants on the windowsill, testing for dryness.

Middle-aged. My god, we were talking about adopting *kids* within the next couple years.

All the plants needed water. I filled a glass and brought it to each of them, tipping the water gently over their terra-cotta rims.

I was an active participant in my own choices, but I wasn't ready to be this stable. I set the cup next to the sink and found myself thinking, again, about a conversation I'd had a few months earlier.

In February of 2021, I'd been sitting up in our bedroom with the lights off at eight p.m., pillows scrunched behind my lower back and stacked on top of my outstretched legs. My phone was propped on top of the pillow stack, glowing in the darkness; I was having a FaceTime call with two of my friends, Marie and Lola. Outside, under the streetlight, the snow softly, endlessly came down. The vaccine was still a couple months away from being available. We'd all been in lockdown for almost a year.

"What do you guys miss the most?" Marie had asked us both, looking out from under her dramatic cat-eye liquid liner and turquoise-eyeshadowed lids. She'd done her makeup just for our FaceTime, and she looked like she was floating in front of her green screen background. The background was a picture of what *she* missed the most: the kitschy pink restaurant at the Madonna Inn in San Luis Obispo.

Lola didn't even have to think about the question. "I miss going to midnight screenings of *The Rocky Horror Picture Show*," she said. "A hundred strangers in suburban New Jersey shouting out every line of dialogue together in the middle of the night? There's nothing like it; it encapsulates everything I've been missing during the pandemic."

It was my turn; they both looked at me. I paused. What *did* I miss the most? Was it gossiping over brunch? Traveling? Smelling all the discounted vanilla body butters at T.J. Maxx without a mask on?

And then I knew.

"What I miss, more than anything," I said slowly, "is the feeling of being in a packed, sweaty dyke bar, surrounded on all sides by queers so close they're touching me, and then to feel someone with a drink in one hand try to inch past me." I frowned; I wasn't explaining this right. "You know—when the bar's so crowded that your arms are up and held tight to your body, with your elbows tucked in, and you can feel people jostling you from all sides?"

Queers are etiquette masters in this scenario—the person trying to get by always puts their free hand up in the air, leaning backward to indicate they need to squeeze past but aren't trying to touch you; or, if they have to, they put their hand lightly, ever so lightly, on your upper back, enough so you can feel it and understand that you need to move, but not enough so that it feels pushy or threatening. They lock eyes with you, say, "*Sorryyyy, ugh*," with a sympathetic grimace, and slip past you, drink held high above their head, instantly absorbed into the crowd pushing toward the dance floor.

"That," I said. "That exact feeling."

"Jesus, yes," Lola said. "What I wouldn't give."

For weeks after that phone call, I thought about being surrounded by queers on all sides. I daydreamed about it; I lay in bed at night, imagining the feeling of being at a crowded lesbian bar over and over. *It would be like therapy after this year*, I'd thought. *What I wouldn't give.*

And then the vaccine arrived. I got vaccinated that April by a sweet eighty-year-old nurse who had come out of retirement to give people shots. I didn't even feel it. She patted my arm and said, "OK, hun, you're all set," and my eyes welled up with tears. I cried in a Hy-Vee pharmacy next to the rotisserie chickens. I would see my friends again. We all would. I would be able to be surrounded by queers on all sides at dyke bars again. It was happening!

Except it wasn't happening. For the first time in my adult life, and just off the high of getting the vaccine, I was realizing I no longer had an IRL queer community. Most of my closest friends lived nowhere near me; as we'd hit our thirties, we'd all scattered across the country and world—for jobs, for partners, for fun, for fresh starts. In the early part of the pandemic, Davin and I had moved to the house we live in now, in a small Minnesota town, and now it had been over a year of living there and *never* going out and we had befriended exactly one queer person, and she lived across the street from us. None of this had mattered during Covid, but now the facts were waddling home to roost like our down-the-block-neighbor's fat chickens every night: the closest gay bar was a forty-five-minute drive from where we lived; the closest lesbian bar was more than three hundred miles away.

And in the summer of 2021, on the day that I realized I was basically middle-aged, *none* of that seemed right.

Retreating from the porch, I hauled a load of laundry upstairs from our cold basement and began folding it angrily, flipping T-shirt arms violently toward themselves and snapping hand towels open with a crack. I get this from my mom—rage-cleaning. It's a trait of people who get silent and icy when they get mad, who repress their anger; it's something I work on in therapy and also something that feels innate when you grow up in an ultrapatriarchal Mormon community, like I did. There was no acceptable way for Mormon women to express anger (and there still isn't! anywhere! for any woman! wheee), so shutting kitchen cabinet doors *slightly* too hard, lips set in a tight line, is how I saw most of the women I knew in childhood alert others to their resentment. Now I do the exact same shit, fully aware of what I'm doing and also still trying to find my way toward an anger-management strategy that doesn't involve a Mr. Clean Magic Eraser.

I shoved several pairs of Davin's underpants into a drawer. It was me I was mad at. I was suddenly *sure* I wasn't ready to fully settle down just yet. *Middle-aged.* Man, fuck mowing the lawn. Fuck being responsible. I wanted an adventure. I wanted drama. Goddammit, *I wanted gay chaos*. I had missed queers *so much* during lockdown, so much that I had fantasized, daily, about being surrounded by them. What was I *doing*??? Why wasn't I with queers, now that I could be? Why wasn't I laughing my head off at a dyke bar with my friends *right that second*?

A pair of socks in my hand, I scowled. This was my own fault. Sure, most of our friends lived far away, but I was happy with where I lived. There *was* something I regretted, though. Something I thought about a lot.

Five years prior, in 2016, I'd started writing queer-themed opinion pieces for the *New York Times*. Writing for a publication as big as the *NYT* had been a huge deal for me. Especially since I'd gotten my start writing observations and jokes about my own people way back in 2009, on my now-defunct blog about lesbian stereotypes, *Effing Dykes*. The period when I'd been writing my blog regularly was during the still semi-innocent days of the internet. You know: when not many people were writing publicly and explicitly about queer shit, and I didn't yet understand that what you write on the internet will be around forever, even if you're a twenty-six-year-old idiot who likes to make sort-of-mean snap judgments for laughs.

It was easier for me to be judgmental in those days. I was young, and believed everyone was gay exactly the way I was gay, in the reckless, sure-I-was-right way of someone who has really not been alive and thinking critically for that long. When I was first writing about being a lesbian, for instance, the concept of privilege hadn't yet become mainstream. The list of things I'd never given real thought to—because I didn't have to—included being white, being cis, being an American citizen, being raised middle class, being able-bodied, and having a college education, to name just a few.

But I'd grown since the blog days. I'd stopped narrowly defining myself and other people. I'd gotten much quieter, in a good way. With my *New York Times* pieces, I'd tried to talk about queer culture in a way that was both entertaining and thoughtful, and found I liked that better than just being a lesbian joke factory that manufactured snide remarks about Keens sandals on demand.

One of the articles I'd written in 2017 was called "I Want My Lesbian Bars Back." In it, I'd written about how much I loved lesbian bars and how they were vanishing in America at an alarming rate. "Lesbian bars are dropping faster than drag queens on a slippery stage," I'd stated. "Rubyfruit Jungle in New Orleans. Sisters in Philadelphia. The Lexington in San Francisco. All gone . . . I feel like I'm losing something small but precious. . . . How do we find community now?" It was mostly me trying to bring some attention to the phenomenon of the closing bars. I spent my queer youth in dyke bars, so watching them slowly disappear had been feeling almost physically painful to me.

Because of the *NYT* articles, I'd gotten a literary agent, and we'd kicked around book ideas together. One of the ideas was simple: What if I went to every lesbian bar left in America and documented what I found? It would be fun! It would be funny! It would help us all figure out why the bars are closing!

Introduction

We canned the idea in favor of other potential books. In retrospect, I wasn't sure why. Most likely, it was because I hadn't wanted to pigeonhole myself as someone who only writes about queer topics. But I had really liked that book idea; I should have fought for it. I spent the next few years of my evenings after work putting together pitches for other books. Those pitches went nowhere.

Meanwhile, other articles about vanishing lesbian spaces were being published on major media outlets at an accelerating rate. Around the same time I got my vaccine, the *New York Times* had reported that there were only 20 lesbian bars left in America, down from 206 in 1987.

It wasn't just the news media. Projects documenting the loss of lesbian and queer bars had already been done, and more began to pop up. In 2020, Lea DeLaria, one of the stars of *Orange Is the New Black*, launched the Lesbian Bar Project—a fundraising effort to support the last lesbian bars in the country. Later, the group made a documentary, and then a docuseries.

Vanishing lesbian bars were suddenly a hot topic. And I'd missed my chance to write a book about them.

I finished folding the laundry, my anger spent. I went downstairs and ate an apple standing up, idly looking out the kitchen window at Davin, who was now picking up sticks that had fallen from the oak tree.

Then I went out and mowed the lawn.

A FEW WEEKS LATER, MY agent emailed me. An editor I'd previously talked to from Simon & Schuster had seen yet another article in the *NYT* about how lesbian bars were vanishing. He'd asked my agent a question: "What about a book where Krista travels to all these bars and reports what she finds?"

He'd had the same idea. The lesbian bar trip book.

"Maybe it's not something Krista would be into," he said. "But I thought I'd mention it in case."

Are you kidding.

Introduction

Maybe it wasn't something I'd be *into*? The book I'd wanted to write for four *years*?! *WTF WTF WTF.*

I reread the email, feeling shaky.

It all added up.

Covid was receding.

Vaccines were in arms.

Lesbian bars were disappearing. But this time to more public outcry. *I* was desperately missing dyke bars. And in a year and a half, I would be forty.

I still wanted to do it—I wanted to go to every lesbian bar in America, and to write a book about what I found. It was time. Everyone in the country was coming out of a collective public nightmare, and I didn't know about anyone else, but I was emerging from pandemic lockdown feeling . . . dimmer. More isolated. More disconnected to the queer community at large than I had ever felt before. I was way more settled, but had way less radiant, chronically gay energy these days. And hey—when would I be able to write a book like this again? *Especially* if Davin and I adopted kids??

Never. I already knew the answer was never. It was now or never. And not just for me—maybe for the bars, too.

"I'm incredibly interested," I wrote back. Very calm. Professional. Resisting the urge to end the sentence with nineteen exclamation points and three cry-face emojis.

And so it was decided. I would write a proposal for the lesbian bar book, and my agent and I would send it in.

Writing a book proposal takes a lot of energy. I had already done it twice; I knew what I was getting into. But this time, I didn't inwardly panic about the amount of work ahead of me and start thinking of ways to procrastinate. *This* time, I just sat down, opened my laptop, and began. Within a half hour, sitting at my dining room table, I was a wild animal, unhinged, furiously clacking away on my laptop at a speed that scared the dogs, growling when Davin interrupted me for any reason.

Introduction

I was filled with the holy fire of someone who had been given a second chance to work on her dream project—the *gayest possible* dream project—someone who was very concerned that if she didn't *hurry the fuck up*, the chance would be snatched away.

"I am taking the closure of lesbian bars personally," I typed in my proposal. "Bars I loved—bars that raised me, bars that gave me a queer family, historic bars where I've had sex in filthy bathroom stalls and cried on smoky back patios and falteringly asked out women who were way too old for me and 100 percent humoring me—have vanished, leaving *nothing like them* in their place."

I narrowed my eyes at my screen, fingers poised, thinking about possible arguments against this book idea. Sure, there are monthly lesbian nights at gay bars; yes, there are still queer parties and meetups; OK, yes, my god, Olivia cruises are still running. But I live 331 miles from the nearest lesbian bar. Where am I supposed to fucking *go*? In my nightlife ambitions, I want to be practically smothered by as many other queers as possible on a packed dance floor, and I want there to be almost no chance that a straight cis man wearing cargo shorts will also be there. All of my friends, who are almost all queer, also want this in *their* cities. So what exactly was going on, here, with the dyke bar closures?

We all needed answers. "While gay bars catering specifically to gay men continue to thrive, lesbian bars are shuttering across the country, for understandable and not-so-understandable reasons," I typed. That is to say: Of course there's gentrification and community division and lesbians historically having less money than gay men and also there was the pandemic and also everybody lives online 24/7 and goes out less, but come *on*. One in *five* Gen Z adults identifies as queer. One in five! That's 20 percent of the newest named generation! You're telling me that *20 fucking percent* of Gen Z adults are never going to know what it's like to win a sparkly glitter dildo at dildo bingo night at a dyke bar while surrounded by eighty other furious queers, all screaming at the bingo caller that the game is rigged?

Introduction

The thought brought tears to my eyes. "This is our future," I typed. "Our future *needs* to win glitter dicks at lesbian bars. And each sad closing announcement on social media of yet another perfect, dark, slightly sticky, lesbian-centric space feels like a dagger aimed directly at my heart."

The proposal took weeks to finish. I'd polished it for hours after work every day. Attaching the final version in an email to my agent, and feeling strangely calm, I hit Send.

A FEW WEEKS LATER, I opened my inbox and saw my agent had written. Simon & Schuster wanted the book.

My shriek was so piercing Davin hurried in from the other room.

"THEY WANT THE BOOK."

"*No!*"

"YES."

"That's amazing! And can you please never scream like that again unless you want me to call 911?"

"Sorry."

"You get to go on a lesbian bar road trip!"

"OH MY GODDDDDD!!!"

Pacing up and down the living room, I began plotting, making mental notes, feverish.

OK. I had already decided that this book would not be a history book. Other people had already written about the history of lesbians and bars, and done a much better job than I could ever have done. My book wouldn't be academic, either, but that was by default—I have zero degrees in queer theory and no patience for inaccessible academic concepts and language.

And the book would need to have rules. Rules would make the visits to each lesbian bar fair and consistent. So far, the rules I had come up with were:

Introduction

1. I would only visit bars that self-identified as lesbian bars, or that had historically always been lesbian bars.
2. Each bar would get two or more visits on different days, so I could get a good feel for it. That way, too, a bar could have an off night without being reviewed on only an off night.
3. I would contact the bar owners and try to interview them, settling for an employee or a regular if the owner couldn't be reached.
4. I had to approach and speak to at least two strangers at every bar.

Rule number 4 was scary to me, but I knew if I didn't make a rule forcing me to speak to strangers at lesbian bars that I would never do it, and then the visits would be boring. The problem was twofold: First, I am not shy at all, *unless you put me in a room full of strangers*, and then I am so shy that you will find me locked in the bathroom two minutes later, taking deep breaths and whispering positive affirmations to myself. Second, because I'd been going to lesbian bars for nearly twenty years, I knew that approaching random folks in the bars would be considered strange. Almost taboo; maybe even creepy.

In general, ~my people~ don't tend to approach one another. It's not done. Queers usually go to lesbian bars with friends; if we do go to the bar solo, most of us don't typically go with the intent of striking up conversations with multiple strangers. It's not like in gay bars, where men are openly cruising. Lesbian bar etiquette is much subtler, and many people are just out for fun and not necessarily looking for a hookup. (Some are! But not everyone.) Because dyke bars are such catchall spaces for the queer community—*specifically* because so many different types of people frequent dyke bars—there's a lot more staring, a lot more checking people out while pretending not to, a lot more sizing one another up. In addition, lesbian bar patrons are, for their own safety, usually wary of strangers.

Talking to people for the book was going to be the hardest part for me. Thus the rule about it.

All right. There were twenty bars. Using the list of remaining dyke bars compiled by the Lesbian Bar Project, I pulled up a map of the United States.

Oof. The bars were scattered all across the country—a cluster on the East Coast, a handful in the South, but mostly there was no pattern to where they were located.

"And no way to do a road trip to all of them, all at once, with the vacation time you have," Davin pointed out helpfully. "And it couldn't be a road trip anyway; I'm guessing all the bars have different days they're open because of the pandemic."

"Shit," I said. I hadn't thought of that. I started checking the bars' websites. Davin was right—they *were* all open on different days. I wouldn't be able to do this in one big *On the Road*–style trip, like I'd hoped. My full-time job was never going to let me take a leave of absence for something like two months.

"You'll have to spend weekends traveling."

"Wait. Wait. That would be, like, twenty flights," I said, suddenly going very still. This book—this brand-new, minutes-old baby book— was going to cost a lot of money. More than the initial part of the advance I'd be paid upon signing the contract, with the rest not coming until *after* I'd delivered the manuscript. "And I'd have to rent cars. And take Lyfts. And, oh my god, what about hotels? And"—here I began to feel queasy—"if I want to go to the bars on the fun nights, Friday and Saturday, I'd have to leave for the airport on Friday *morning*. For *all* of them . . . which work would *never* let me do."

"You're probably going to get fired," Davin said cheerfully.

"I think I am."

Davin was kidding, but I started worrying. We didn't even have a savings account. All extra money went directly toward paying off debt and student loans as fast as we could. Losing my job was not something I could joke about.

Over the next few days, Davin and I strategized. We would get a no-interest-for-fourteen-months credit card and put the trip's expenses on it. When I got my book advance, we'd pay off the credit card. Davin, who *lives* to plan, would book all my travel and keep my calendar up to date.

He began making an Excel doc. Sitting across the kitchen counter from him on a Sunday afternoon, watching him create different tabs—a sheet for expenses, a sheet documenting friends I could potentially stay with in particular cities, a sheet that listed all the hours for each of the bars—I swallowed hard. Writing a book was my dream—it had always been my dream—and Davin hadn't asked me how he could help. He had just started helping. This book was going to take all my time and all our combined money for at least a year and a half, and not once had he brought up how any of this was going to affect *him*. All he wanted was to make sure it happened for me.

He made a new tab in the Excel doc: "People Who Helped."

"This way, we can keep track of who you need to thank at the end of this," he said.

In bed that night, I turned to Davin. He was half lying down, doing a crossword puzzle with a pencil.

"Do you want to come?" I asked. "On the bar trips?"

He looked up. "No." A pause. "I mean, *yeah*, but no. This is a book about lesbian bars."

"Yeah, and you've been hanging out in lesbian bars your whole life."

"I'd feel weird. This is your book. And it's about lesbian spaces. I don't want to take up space that isn't meant for me."

"*I'm* a lesbian, and I'm *also* married to a trans man," I said, annoyed. "These bars are for you, too."

Introduction

"Together, we look like a straight couple. No one will talk to you."

He had a point. I'm a femme lesbian, which can mean a lot of things, but, for me, means I dress in a traditionally "feminine" way that's difficult for other queer people to read as "obviously gay." Femme is a queer identity—a straight person cannot be femme—but that doesn't mean that other people read me as queer. I wear tight skirts, big earrings, lipstick, shirts tied at the waist, animal print. Straight people perceive me as straight; so do queer people, unless I'm on the arm of someone who looks queer in a way they understand. And Davin? He has a big red beard. He doesn't get recognized as trans by other queers unless he's wearing a faded old black tank top that says THIS IS WHAT TRANS LOOKS LIKE in huge white capital letters. When Davin goes to dyke bars with one of his best friends, Rae, a trans man who identifies as femme, people think they're a gay cis male couple. When Davin and *I* go to dyke bars together, we look like a couple who's looking for a third.

"But that makes you the ideal person to go!" I said, excited now. "You being there will bring up some questions I want to ask!"

"Like what?"

"Like who's welcome in lesbian bars these days? Who's not? Why is that? How have queer spaces evolved? How have queer *people* evolved?"

"I dunno, cutes."

"Come," I said. "Come to half of the bars. Here's what we do: we go to half together, and I'll go to the other half alone, and I'll compare how we get treated together against how I get treated when I'm alone."

Davin sat up, his crossword sliding off his lap. "Really? It won't mess your book up?"

"I think it'll make it better."

"Well, shit! OK!"

All through the rest of that summer, you couldn't tell me anything. I was gone, in a daze, daydreaming about the trips I was about to take, more excited than I had ever been in my life.

I thought back to that deep-Covid February night, when all this had just been a fantasy I talked about with my friends. It was real now. Queers were going to slip past me on packed dance floors, their hands held high in the air, Rihanna and Britney blaring. I was going to see huge numbers of homos again. Somewhere, probably on the patio of a dyke bar at one a.m., I might even see someone drunkenly trying to introduce the concept of ethical nonmonogamy to their girlfriend at *exactly* the wrong moment. I couldn't wait.

We would start in San Francisco.

San Francisco
Wild Side West

• • •

Just because you *can* rent a scooter doesn't mean you *should* rent a scooter.

I had been seeing them in the Mission all morning—electric blue mopeds zipping past, two young people giggling on them, the person on the back holding a frantically sloshing iced coffee in one hand.

"I think those are rentals," I said, pointing at another one going by up the hill, this time ridden by twinks in matching checkered Vans slip-ons.

"No," Davin said. "They can't be."

"I'm gonna look it up, maybe they're not stupid expensive?"

We sat down on the steps of a pink-and-lavender house and checked on our phones. They *were* rental scooters, you could totally rent them; there was one parked right in front of us, and . . . wow, they were a *lot* cheaper than Uber or Lyft. Cheap was important; Davin and I were just coming off breakfast at Tartine (which is a famous bakery and which I'd of course never heard of, because I have a cold-shoulder dress I still think is kind of cute in the year of our lord 2023) and this *bakery breakfast* had been forty-three dollars!! For food you eat out of waxed paper!

Davin and I were quickly remembering that that's how everything is in San Francisco: whatever it is, it's just going to cost so much more than you think it will. After studying the glass case at Tartine, we'd ordered two croissants, one bite-size caramelized Bundt cake, one little tart with glossy lemon cream, and one small cold brew. At the register, Davin had

16

been so startled by the price that he had coughed into his mask while handing over his credit card.

"Here you go," he croaked at the barista, turning to bug his eyes at me. Forty-three dollars will buy you a ten-acre farm in Minnesota.

The barista passed me our cold brew over the counter. It was in a clear, biodegradable plastic cup, with a kind of mouth opening I had never seen before. It was like a sippy cup that you flipped back the top on. It felt incredible when you put your mouth on it to drink—so smooth, much better than a straw. It was what I imagine sucking on a dolphin's dorsal fin would feel like. Davin and I were both impressed. We kept taking tiny sips as we walked, just to feel the mouth of the cup. "Ooh," we said each time, smacking our lips. "Wow."

And honestly? That's one of the nicest things about having moved to the middle of nowhere. Everything in big cities impresses me so much now. It's impossible to be jaded. In my real life, I live in a cornfield, but that weekend, I was standing on a busy street, holding cold brew trapped in a container designed to *melt into the earth*. We were *decades* behind this shit at home!

I don't really live in a cornfield. I just live surrounded by them. Northfield, Minnesota, where Davin and I now live, is a town of twenty thousand people that's forty-five minutes south of Minneapolis and St. Paul. It's home to the headquarters of Malt-O-Meal, the makers of those giant bags of off-brand cereal you see piled in wire bins at the grocery store. You know—Toasty O's instead of Cheerios; Marshmallow Mateys instead of Lucky Charms—knockoff cereal that tastes exactly like the name-brand kind but is half the price and comes in "body pillow size" instead of "family size."

Northfield is also home to two private liberal colleges, Carleton and St. Olaf, which means that the town is a little progressive bubble encircled by Trump country for at least twenty miles in every direction. The colleges also mean that, for nine months of the year, there are slouches of spoiled teenage girls in ripped jeans perpetually standing in front of the register at my favorite coffee shop downtown. They all want a matcha latte with oat milk, even though there is clearly only one person making drinks and that shit needs to be hand-whisked for several minutes per drink. Sometimes the line backs out the door. Only the most unflappable baristas are scheduled for Saturday mornings.

Northfield's motto is "Cows, Colleges, and Contentment," and we live there because Davin tricked me. I didn't know it, but he was playing a long game, years in the making. Davin grew up in both Northfield and Faribault, the next-nearest town, and when we both lived in Minneapolis and were dating, he used to take me to visit Northfield on the weekends. "Just to get out of town," he'd say. "Have a little trip."

Northfield is cute. Aggressively, in-your-face cute. It is the real-life version of Stars Hollow from *Gilmore Girls*. All the parking is free. All the buildings downtown are historic. Everything is walking distance from everything else, and nothing costs very much when you get to where you're walking to. The Malt-O-Meal factory makes the air smell like Coco Roos (Coco Puffs) or Fruity Dyno-Bites (Fruity Pebbles), all of the time. I had never been to a town that looked like Northfield that was *not* devoted to cutesy twee tourism, but Northfield was dead serious. This was a real, working town, and as someone who had lived her entire adult life in big cities, I was fascinated. On our weekend visits, Davin would show me around, smiling a serene cult-member smile. *This* is the town square, he'd explain, gesturing to a tiny park with a working old-fashioned popcorn wagon staffed by cheerful, thick-suspendered senior citizens. *This* is the dam, where generations of families fish off the bridge. *Here's* the café that looks and feels like 1995, down to the last detail (they just started taking credit cards!); *there's* the impressive independent bookstore, stocked with the kind of books you'd never expect to find in a small town. Hey, did I know we could go tubing down Northfield's river? Had I seen all the gay flags on people's houses? Look, there's another one!

I sensed what Davin was up to. I loved Northfield, but I wasn't having any part of it.

"We are never moving here," I'd warn him, licking a two-dollar maple ice cream cone and crunching my way through the red and yellow leaves drifting across the town square.

"OK."

"I mean it. Never," I'd insist, drinking an excellent eight-dollar cocktail at Loon Liquors, a distillery bizarrely located inside an industrial office park.

"Has anyone ever asked you to move here?"

"No," I said, watching the light filter through green leaves swaying overhead in the Big Woods, a lush, waterfalled state park ten minutes from Northfield. "But we're not going to."

Four years after I first saw it, we moved to Northfield.

Davin has never once said "I told you so," but I can tell he thinks it daily.

BREAKFAST AT TARTINE WAS ABSOLUTELY worth forty-three dollars (the lemon tart alone was), but Davin and I had arrived in San Francisco only the day before, and we'd already burned through the bulk of our budgeted funds for this trip.

So when we saw the cheap rental scooter, it looked like a good option for us. It would be a fun way to get around, and we could afford it.

All I had to do to rent it was watch a seven-minute video on my phone and take a quiz. And that was it: I was putting on the included helmet and trying to be OK with the fact that the inside of it smelled strangely sweet and fatty, like honey and dirty hair.

Now, I drive a scooter at home, so I was feeling confident, even if the streets of San Francisco are steep and crisscrossed with tram tracks that look like you shouldn't drive on them. Straddling the scooter, I switched it on and turned to Davin.

"I'm going to take this around the block to make sure I feel comfortable before I have you hop on the back."

He nodded, silent with admiration at how butch I was.

I twisted the scooter's handle to give it some juice and crept up the street toward the Castro. Cars flowed behind me and around me. Careful, *careful* . . . oh, OK, this was easy.

A baby could drive this, I thought, revving the scooter up to its maximum 30 mph and cruising through a green light. This was great! The wind in your face, a cloudless blue sky, the perfect pastel houses terracing up and up! No more Ubers for us—we were scooter people, now!

At a red light, I looked left. And there it was: The steepest street I'd seen all morning. A street that was practically vertical.

I turned the scooter onto it.

"Let's see what this thing can do," I muttered under my breath, narrowing my eyes at the hill, suddenly the lesbian main character in a private *The Fast and the Furious* spin-off. I gunned the engine.

OK. Before we go any further, I need to explain that I'm clumsy. Not *ha-ha-isn't-that-cute-she's-always-adorably-tripping* clumsy. No. I am life-threateningly clumsy. Accident-prone, in a *someone-call-an-ambulance* kind of way. I have dislocated my shoulder falling out of a hammock. I have dislocated my shoulders *three other unrelated times*. I have broken my toes, my ribs, and both my arms twice. I have broken my nose by turning and hitting it against a doorframe. My tailbone is ruined from when I ran down a wooden staircase in new socks, slipped, and landed on my ass on the floor with my feet straight out in front of me. (Did you know your chiropractor can adjust your coccyx by sticking her fingers into your asshole? Did you know she can delicately suggest this procedure so that you'll agree to it by calling it "an internal manipulation"? It's true.) Two years ago, at a work dinner in an upscale San Antonio restaurant, I pulled a heavy bathroom stall door closed against my foot while wearing sandals, and my big toenail just *popped off*. It happened so quickly I didn't even feel it; I looked down in confusion to see blood pouring down my sandal and pooling in a dark circle on the floor. My big toenail dangled by a thread of skin off to the side of my foot, like a press-on nail.

"Uh oh," I said faintly. I made a split-second decision: I'd run at top speed back to my coworkers to get help. I'd be moving too fast to get blood on anything.

Friends, I sprayed that restaurant in blood. Ruby droplets flew through the air. Sandals clopping, a trail of gore spattering across white marble floors, I ran past tables full of startled couples about to tuck into plates of scallops. Across the restaurant, in slow motion, the hostess covered her mouth, watching.

What I'm saying is: I hurt myself constantly. Sensationally. I have no concept of my body in space. I had *no business* trying to see how well a scooter I'd never driven handled the steepest hill I'd ever seen.

And yet there I was, gunning the electric engine and murmuring "*c'mon . . . c'monnnnn*" as the bike began climbing the hill, already juddering with the effort. Ten seconds in, I knew it was a bad idea, but I'd already committed. I *wanted* to climb that hill. I *wanted* to not know what would happen. I'd wanted to do this lesbian bar road trip for four *years*, goddammit, and now I was getting the chance to do it, and I was going to say yes to new experiences, no matter how ill-advised they seemed. I was all in, twisting the scooter handle as hard as I could, eyeballing the distant summit of that hill. *Let's go.*

Midway up, the scooter started slowing.

Dramatically.

My god. How was this hill even legal? I was basically parallel to the street, the scooter straining. I mean, the pedal was on the *floor*, and we were *crawling*, inching up the hill, the bike shaking like it was going to come apart.

No one was behind me. Houses passed at walking speed. A man with huge calves pushed his garbage out to the end of his driveway. I smiled and made eye contact, trying to make it look like I was OK and it was very normal to be seated on what felt like a small, rearing horse, trying not to topple backward at two miles per hour. He looked at me, expressionless, and walked back inside.

The scooter and I were nearly there. We were going to make it. And then—shuddering, gasping—the scooter crested the very top of the street. We'd done it!

Triumphant, I turned around to see how far up I was. San Francisco spread out beneath me like a dream city, the hills vanishing into hazy smoke from forest fires in the distance.

My god. What a view.

Overcome with relief, I relaxed my grip on the brakes.

The scooter started rolling backward.

"*SHIT*," I whispered. I had two choices: roll backwards with the scooter and die, or flip the handlebars to the left as hard as I could, which would crash the bike.

I flipped the handlebars. The bike crashed to the ground and threw me off.

And somehow, twanged awake by the possibility of death on a mighty cement mountain, my body's survival instincts took over. My arms wrapped themselves around me, my chin tucked into my chest, and I rolled over and over, partway down the hill. I was a log, tumbling. A log wearing cheetah-print overalls.

I popped up on my feet, breathing hard, fists clenched, adrenaline shooting through my body.

Nobody had seen me. There were no cars. No pedestrians. It was just me, alone near the summit of an empty, sunny, steep San Franciscan street lined with small stucco houses, whimpering "*oh my god oh my god oh my god*" and taking shaky breaths. I walked back up to the scooter, abandoned on its side in the middle of the street, mentally checking in on all my body parts.

OK. I'd scraped my foot. My left arm hurt. Gritting my teeth, I squeezed the length of my arm without looking at it, bracing myself to feel something new and unwelcome, like a bone poking out of my shoulder, or a pinky drooping at an odd angle.

No exposed bones. No free-range fingers.

I took a deep breath. There was no reason I should be unhurt, but I was. I picked up the fallen scooter (not a scratch on it!) and realized Davin was still waiting for me. I would have to drive to him. No way was I trying to go back *down* that hill, though, so, grabbing the scooter's handlebars, I pushed it, slow and heavy, all the way back up to the top of the street, feet sweatily sliding in my sandals. I would drive around until I found a less steep hill to go down.

Ten minutes of circling later, I found an acceptably pitched hill and scooted back to Davin.

There he was, still standing on the corner.

"Where *were* you?"

I got off and told him what had happened. He gave me the kind of look you can only give your partner when you've spent years of your life filling out forms for them in the ER. He prodded me all over, poking suspiciously at joints and major bones.

"Do you think you could be bleeding anywhere inside? Like internal bleeding?"

"I don't think so."

Satisfied, he shook his head and climbed on the back of the scooter, wrapping his arms around my waist. "Let's try to avoid hills, OK?"

WE WERE IN SAN FRANCISCO for one reason: to go to the very last lesbian bar in the city. Contrary to popular queer belief, there still is one. It's just that nobody under fifty seems to know about it.

When I asked several Bay Area queers about San Francisco lesbian bars, they solemnly told me there weren't any left—that the Lexington Club, which closed in 2015, was the last.

"The Lex closing still haunts me," said my friend Shay, who's lived in the Bay Area for fifteen years. "I get pangs in my chest when I pass by."

Moby Dyke

"There aren't any more lesbian bars in San Francisco," said my friend Seven, who spent their twenties in Oakland and recently moved back there. "When the Lex closed, it broke my heart."

It broke lots of sapphic-leaning hearts. Mine included. The Lexington Club was a divey dyke bar in the Mission. Founded in 1997 by Lila Thirkield, who later went on to found Virgil's, a popular queer bar that closed in 2021, the Lexington Club was a landmark—a lesbian bar that never charged a cover, in the area surrounding Valencia Street. That part of town had attracted lesbians for decades, since it was close to the Castro, San Francisco's gay district, but had cheaper rent. (And cheaper rent + gay-adjacent = lesbians. Always. Landlords, pay attention: This is the scientific formula for attracting lesbians, *the greatest tenants of all time*. Get yourself some lesbian tenants, and within weeks, that mud pit you advertise as a yard will be transformed into a bountiful garden. We're talking raised beds, butterflies flitting, free tomatoes showing up in a bowl on your front porch, the whole thing. The shitty, splintered wood floors in your building will be refinished; every cracked wall you're charging up the ass for will be spackled and painted a restful pale lavender. Want long-term tenants who make pickles and regularly go to bed at ten? Give some thought to lowering your rent slightly, dummies.)

The Lexington Club was the first real lesbian bar I ever set foot in. My first girlfriend, who I'd met while at college in Minneapolis, had moved to San Francisco for her job. I was twenty-one, newly out, completely in love with her, and selling my eggs to pay for my tuition and life. Flush with cash from my own ovaries, I would visit her in San Francisco regularly; sometimes twice a month. We would go to the Lexington Club. The first time I walked in there, I just—I couldn't believe it. I had been to gay bars before in Minneapolis, but *this* was *different*. A whole bar, *full* of people like us? A whole bar full of people *who probably also for sure liked women*?!

Wild Side West

On Friday and Saturday nights, the Lexington Club was always mobbed; there would be a large crowd of queers standing outside, smoking, making out against the walls in the dark, fishing their IDs out of their back pockets, fighting under the streetlight—either fully yelling or in that tense, whispery way that dykes in relationships fight when they're out with their friends and one of them has just done something that needs to be Talked About Outside. You know: your basic talking laughing loving breathing fighting fucking crying drinking situation going on. Inside the Lex, there wouldn't be space to move. The crush surrounding the bar was hopeless, three layers of people thick before you could come anywhere *near* the bartenders, who were unfairly cute and tattooed and would take your drink order with the indifferent expressions of the chronically hot and hit on.

A few years later, after my first girlfriend and I had broken up, I got a job taking the authors of educational books on weeklong seminar tours. I'd get sent to San Francisco often. I'd regularly end up at the Lex at night after work, powerless against the magnetic force that pulled me toward older butches with strong jawlines, muscled arms, and a wary look in their eyes. If none were available to stare hopefully at, I'd just sit in the bar, happy to be there and envious of the other queers surrounding me.

These gays live *in San Francisco*, I'd think, eyeing the shaved heads and piercings and complicated-rag outfits of the dykes walking through the front door. *They're not just tourists. They can come to the Lex whenever they want.*

Even then, circa 2008–2010ish, San Francisco was so expensive that the only way most transplants could live in the city proper was to be either *really* rich or *really* broke (and thus OK with living in a shithole with seven other queers). No one I saw coming into the Lex looked remotely wealthy, though, and since most queers are not wealthy, in general, I knew the majority of the patrons had made a choice. They wanted to live in the gayest city in the world. Full stop. They were willing to be uncomfortable, to pay shocking rent, to live in busted, code-violating, closet-size rooms, just to be in the same vicinity as lots of other people like them. Just to have the Lexington Club be their neighborhood bar. Just to have access to a queer community, right outside their door. Even then, I knew I was unwilling to make a choice like that, and so I envied their commitment to the ~homosexual lifestyle~. I wanted a queer community, but I also wanted to remain unsure of what a bedbug looked like.

The Lexington Club was a legend; one of the last of its kind.

But not the very last.

The very last was right in front of me, at 424 Cortland Avenue in Bernal Heights. After parking the scooter, Davin and I walked up the hill from our Airbnb toward the wooden sign, which said:

THE WILD SIDE WEST
SINCE '62

The Wild Side West is the oldest (and only) lesbian-founded, owned, and continuously operated lesbian bar in San Francisco. Opened in Oakland in 1962 by two out lesbians, Pat Ramseyer and Nancy White, the bar was originally just called the Wild Side, after the film *Walk on the Wild Side*, starring Jane Fonda and Barbara Stanwyck. Opening the bar was a wild act in itself—the *San Francisco Bay Times* reports that in California, in 1962, it was illegal for a woman to be a bartender, so two women *owning* their own bar? It was a big deal. A few years later, Pat and Nancy moved the Wild Side to San Francisco's permissive, Beat-movement-famous North Beach neighborhood. They renamed it the Wild Side West. Sailors, artists, and musicians hung out in the bar. Janis Joplin is said to have played pool and music there.

But Davin and I were standing in front of the Wild Side West's third and most permanent location, a tall, cream-colored, Victorian-looking house with purple trim. Pat and Nancy moved the Wild Side West to this Bernal Heights location in the late seventies; the bar's been there ever since. Billie Hayes, the Wild Side West's current owner, runs it now. (I'd tried calling the bar multiple times to see if I could get ahold of Billie, but no one had ever answered the phone.)

Looking around, I had a feeling that Pat and Nancy had bought property in Bernal Heights at the right time. The neighborhood had maybe gentrified *just* a tad since the seventies. Cortland Avenue was lined with bougie-looking restaurants and cafés stretching as far as I could see in both directions. Two doors down from the Wild Side West, a flower store's windows displayed the kind of hand-selected, exotic-bloom, artisanal bouquets you only buy when you've *really* fucked up. Next door to the bar, a bicycle shop was selling $4,000 electric bikes.

Eeesh. Good thing Pat and Nancy had owned the property. The rent on a bar in this location in Bernal Heights now would be unthinkable.

I had never been to the Wild Side West before. I turned to Davin, nodding toward the bar's facade. Wooden siding covered almost its entire front, where the windows should have been.

"Wonder what goes on in *here*," I said, bouncing my eyebrows. I love bars without big front windows; they make me feel daring, like I'm about to step into a situation where privacy might be required. And this was *San Francisco*. A gay paradise! A city known for its tolerance and sexual diversity and leather bars! Maybe this bar was actually, like, a known place for anonymous public lesbian sex. Maybe we were about to walk into something like a gay bathhouse! Maybe no one under fifty had ever mentioned the Wild Side West to me because this bar was on the down-low in San Francisco—something you had to go looking for and discover for yourself!

Heart pounding, I pulled open the front door.

Oh. It was just a bar. No anonymous public lesbian sex happening, as far as I could tell.

But it was a strange bar. It looked . . . it looked kind of like a brothel? In a movie? It looked like an old western brothel, like Mae West was going to rustle around the corner in a corset and ruffled skirt any minute. It was fairly dark inside, but I could already see that the Wild Side West was, like so many dyke bars I've known and loved, painted dark red—walls and ceiling, everything. (Y'all, why is this a thing? Is it because red light is flattering on all skin tones? Is it a subtle, old-school nod to the mystery of the yoni? What is it with queers and blood-colored semigloss paint?)

A pool table dominated the front room. There were Pride flags and pennants for San Francisco sports teams everywhere; I saw a poster of Obama as a proud centaur, holding up an HRC logo and a pink triangle and wearing a rainbow tie on his top, human half. The walls were hung with porcelain masks and ornate mirrors and large paintings of women in various stages of draped, artistic nakedness. An old-fashioned barber chair sat near the front, the obvious king of all the mismatched chairs in the Wild Side West. A brick chimney ran up through the middle of the room, sharing space with a life-size, carved wooden figure of a Native American (yikes) standing next to it.

It felt dusty in there. It wasn't that it *looked* dusty. It was just something you could feel in the faded hanging fabrics, in the old framed photos, the sheer amount of memorabilia in the space. This place had been lived in, and it had been loved, and it was old, now.

Davin and I headed for the wooden bar, where the bartender was polishing glasses and joking with a small knot of elder queers. We sat down. The bartender looked up at us. I held my breath. Here I was with Davin, a trans man with a beard, at the oldest lesbian bar in San Francisco. Would they be rude to him? Refuse to serve us? Throw him out?

The bartender's eyes passed over us without seeming to register us.

"Vax cards and IDs, please," they said.

Oh. Right! I loved San Francisco for this. You couldn't step into a store or restaurant—you couldn't even get a cup of coffee—without proving your vaccination status. It was such a relief, especially coming from Minnesota, where, just the week before, I'd seen a skinny teenaged Kwik Trip employee quaveringly ask a barrel-chested man at the store's entrance to please wear a mask. Without breaking his stride, he'd said, "Make me," and headed toward the bathrooms.

No one cared that Davin was there. No one seemed to even notice us, which was actually a little odd. I'd never been in a dyke bar, or any queer space at all, really, where people weren't surreptitiously checking out who was walking in. Queers are fucking nosy—we *have* to look and see each other. But here, it was like we were ghosts. No one but the bartender had so much as glanced at us.

The door burst open, and three young, boisterously drunk queers stumbled in.

"It's Emily's BIRTHDAY!" one of them, a gangly gay in a crop top, crowed.

Emily grinned at the room, swaying gently. "My birthday," she explained to us. "Today."

The bartender didn't blink. "Vax cards and IDs, please."

"We want SHOTS!" one of them cried.

"BIRTHDAY SHOTS! For HER BIRTHDAY!"

"Vax cards."

There was a tense pause. Then, suddenly meek, all three of them hunted through their pockets and produced their vaccination cards.

"Shots?" the gangly one asked.

"Let's do it," said the bartender.

There was an open door at the end of the bar, light spilling out of it. Another room, maybe? Davin and I walked through it.

And stepped out into a magical fairy wonderland.

You guys. Wild Side West has a garden. It's not just a garden. It's . . . this is the reason to go there. This garden is *beautiful*. And secretive. And green and dense and singing with crickets and twinkling with tiny sparkling lights, woven into falling-down trellises and around rotting wooden benches and heavy stone tables. The garden is so different from the inside of the Wild Side West that it's bewildering—it's a completely separate, hidden-away place.

This shock of a huge secret garden being where you do not expect a huge secret garden to be is one of the things I like best about San Francisco: it's so full of surprises. It's such a closed-off-to-the-street city; all the buildings are colorful, sure, but they have a hard look to them, with serious, twisting metal grates guarding their entrances. But then someone unlocks the grates and lets you in the front of a building and holy shit, here's a sweet little courtyard with padded wicker chairs and flickering lanterns, and it's all hidden from view on the street. Or maybe from the outside, the crumbling stucco on a house makes it look like an unlicensed vein removal clinic, but oh my god, look through the slots in the front fence and you can see an enclosed private terrace, overflowing with magnolia trees and bougainvillea. That's how the Wild Side West is—the outside of it gives you no indication that the bar even *has* a garden, let alone that the garden will be enormous and glorious.

"Whoa," Davin breathed, looking around.

The fully fenced-in garden sounded full of people, but because there were so many private areas to sit, it was hard to tell. Laughter floated into the night from unseen sources. People came down the patio steps, found their friends, and were swallowed whole into the foliage. We sat down at a table with a fraying rattan screen and wobbly wooden seats and took in the view. Lights wrapped around the trunks of trees. A headless mannequin stood creepily in a corner; faded plastic rocking horses guarded a flowering trellis. There were wrought iron chairs and statues and pots full of plantings, iridescent gazing balls, and succulents. A fountain trickled.

The garden is special partly because it feels so hidden, and partly because of how it got its start. When Pat and Nancy bought the place in the late seventies, neighbors welcomed them within days by throwing a broken toilet through the front window and dumping piles of household trash in front of the bar. They didn't want a lesbian bar in their neighborhood. Pat and Nancy boarded up the front windows and picked up the trash. Early proponents of recycling, like all queers, they hauled the thrown objects down to the garden behind the house and used them to decorate. "Pat's Magical Garden" is what the Wild Side West calls it. They literally made flowers grow from hatred and garbage.

To my right, partially shielded by the leaves of a huge monstera plant, two queers looked like they were on a first date that was going well. They were both dressed head-to-toe in black, and their hands were close but not touching across the top of their table. They were gazing into each other's eyes, earnestly discussing their birth charts, and that's so stereotypical I wish that I was making it up, but I'm not. While I watched out of the corner of my eye, one of them—the one wearing a big silver necklace—asked for the other's Venus placement. *Psssh*. It was all over. They were gonna fuck tonight.

A group of what looked like young gay guys sat at a stone table, laughing and yelling and causing a ruckus. They were dressed to go out, and since it wasn't super late, I guessed that Wild Side West wasn't their final destination. One of them had a porn 'stache; they were wearing short-shorts and a baby blue satin jacket they were obviously proud of and kept smoothing.

A cluster of what looked like older lesbians was hanging out under a wooden shedlike structure near the patio, and they were causing the biggest ruckus of all. They sat in a semicircle, and it would be quiet for a second as someone spoke, and then they'd all break up, hooting and bellowing and slapping their legs. They had the appearance of having known each other for decades. It was clear they felt at home in this bar.

Watching them, I felt a pang of longing.

"We gotta get our shit together," I said to Davin. He nodded. He'd been watching the older dykes, too, and knew what I meant. Someday, assuming climate change, nuclear war, or another plague doesn't end the world as we know it within our lifetimes, Davin and I both want to live on a piece of land with all our queer friends. A bunch of little trailers, or maybe tiny cabins. It would be like a gay-ass summer camp that never ends, you know? "Beaver Gap," we'll call it.

Moby Dyke

But if you want to have queer friends you grow old with, you have to all agree on the place where you'll do that, and none of us will commit to a location. We're in Minnesota, Scotland, Chicago, Raleigh-Durham, New York, California . . . and we're mostly settled. And while I appreciate the freedom to live anywhere we want, and I love visiting those places, I do feel a sharp sense of loss knowing I can't see the people I consider my queer family on a daily basis. That is: I don't want to see my loves once a year. I want to see them every day; enough to be sick of them. I want to rummage through their fridges, talk shit on their porches, tuck their plant cuttings into my pockets to bring home. I want them to let themselves into my house with their own keys; I want them to borrow so many of my books that my shelves look spaced and slanted, like a mouth full of crooked teeth. Watching the lesbians in the Wild Side West's garden, gray-haired and laughing so hard they had to get thumped on the back—that's it. That's what I really want. That's the goal.

But maybe they didn't all live here. Maybe they were having a reunion. Or, if they did all live in San Francisco, who's to say those older queers don't envy what younger generations of queers have? Maybe they were all raised in San Francisco, and grew up in a time when there were far fewer options for meeting other lesbians. Maybe they'd lived in San Francisco by necessity, and were here because this community was what *they* had. And now this bar, the Wild Side West, was the last of its kind in the city, a last holdout as times changed.

I climbed up the patio steps to get two more bottles of Peroni, the only drink Davin and I could easily afford in San Francisco at this point. Inside, the birthday girl and her group had left. There were only two people at the bar, both elder queers. One of them, a butch with thick-rimmed black glasses and stylishly swooped silver hair, looked extra comfortable sitting there, almost proprietorial. Oh my god. Was this Billie, the owner??

I approached, hesitant.

"Excuse me, but . . . are you Billie?" I bleated. Jesus. I *had* to work on approaching strangers. This was embarrassing.

The older butch looked at me steadily for a second.

"No," she said. "I'm Lisa."

"Oh," I said, dejected. "Because I'm writing about the last lesbian bars in the US, and I was hoping to talk to Billie about this place. I couldn't get in touch with her."

"Billie's great. She's not here right now. But this is a great bar. I've been coming to this place for—let me see—thirty-one years now," said Lisa.

"Really?" I said eagerly.

"Yeah!"

"Would you mind if I asked you some questions?" I flipped open my notebook. "Starting with how you spell your name, and what your pronouns are?"*

A smile flickered across Lisa's face. "I go by 'she.'"

She settled back in her chair. "This bar was different back in the day, of course—the bar scene and the bars were all different then. There were more of them, for one thing. Now there's just this one."

"Why do you think that is?" I asked. *Oh my god. I was doing it! I was having a spontaneous conversation with a regular!* "Why do you think lesbian bars are closing?"

Lisa took a sip of her drink. She looked thoughtful.

---

* These were the two questions I asked everyone I spoke to. If someone is quoted in this book for longer than a couple overheard sentences, they have been asked for their name and pronouns, and been made aware I was writing a book. When I use a pronoun for someone specific inside the bars, I have either directly asked for it or heard it used in reference to the person in question. Additionally, inside the bars, if I wasn't sure of someone's pronouns because they weren't confirmed, I use they/them pronouns when writing about that person.

"Well . . . in my heart of hearts, I think it's because we're integrating into society; it's way more acceptable now to be a lesbian," she said. "I mean, there are a lot of reasons the bars are closing, from us earning seventy-nine cents to every dollar men make, to us fighting among ourselves about who can go to our bars. But honestly? I think it's because we're so adaptable." She paused. "Yeah. We're good at surviving. Our bars are closing because we don't need them the way we used to. Society's changing; we're all changing. And I think that's a very good thing."

I blinked. What a cool answer. Especially from someone who could have, just as easily, been bitter or angry about the loss of lesbian spaces in San Francisco over the years. I thanked Lisa, and she waved me away, turning her attention back to her friend, who she'd been chatting with.

Conversation over, I pointed my camera way over the top of the friend's head to take a picture of the art on the walls at Wild Side West. The friend looked at me, thinking I was taking a picture of her, and said, "Hey. Fuck you."

"I'm sorry," I said. "I wasn't taking a picture of you. I was taking a picture of the bar." I gestured to the masks along the wall.

"Fuck you," the friend said again, pointing at me. Aggressive.

I looked at her uncertainly and took a few steps back. Was I about to get into a bar fight with a lesbian thirty years my senior?

"Hey now," Lisa said.

"I'm kidding," the friend said, spreading her hands open. "I'm kidding. I make jokes. That's what I do."

"Oh," I said.

"I'm funny," she continued. "That's why I'm putting together a one-woman show." She pointed at me again. "You should come. I made a whole show because I'm funny."

"That sounds fun," I said. "I'll be right back."

Beers in hand, I escaped to the patio. If I've learned anything as an adult, it's that if someone feels the need to tell you something like "I'm funny" or "I'm really good in bed" or "I don't believe in drama," it's because the opposite is true.

Down in the garden, Davin and I leaned into each other, sipping our beers quietly. A woman in a pretty red flowered dress came over and asked to use the ashtray at our table.

"Sure," I said.

"D'ya mind if I sit?" she said, surprising me.

"No, of course! Sit down," Davin said.

She sat down and sighed, tipping her chin up and away from us to exhale her smoke.

"I love this garden," I said. "This is our first time here."

"Oh really?" she said. "I've been coming here my whole life."

"You have?"

"Oh, yeah. My whole life. I've always lived in this neighborhood," she said. "I've been coming here since I was a little kid. My parents used to come here. Pat used to give me a soda at the end of the bar while I waited for them."

"Wow," I said. I explained what I was doing at the Wild Side West, and asked her if I could use her name.

"Not if it's going in the book!" she laughed. "I hate being quoted. You can write down what I say, though."

"Thank you," I said, scribbling madly.

She nodded. "This is a community bar," she said. "One of the best. I've never known another place like it. Did you know, this bar used to hold holiday parties for dogs? They'd play music and hand out treats to dog regulars during the holidays. Yeah. They do less of that stuff now. But dogs have always been welcome here. Everyone has. I'm not sure this bar should be on your list; it's not really a lesbian bar. I mean, it is, but everyone's welcome here. Neighborhood people come here. It's way less 'just lesbians,' you know?"

"It feels that way."

She took a final drag of her cigarette and stood up. "Well, it was nice talking to you both. You two have a nice night."

She walked back up the garden path, toward the patio steps.

Davin and I looked around. The garden leaves rustled gently in the night breeze. The astrology queers next to us were comparing hand sizes. It was time to go.

We headed back inside, where someone was leading a scarred, muscled pit bull on a leash through the front door. The people who had trickled in and were sitting at the bar turned to her and cheered; she was clearly a friend of the bar, and a good girl, too—she sat down politely and thumped her tail against the floor while regulars gathered around to pet her.

As we left, I glanced back at the bar a final time. I could see why the Wild Side West was loved: it had survived so much, and it was so distinctive. I could also see why no one my age or younger had ever mentioned it to me: the inside of the bar felt a bit like a time capsule, a relic of what had already happened in queer history.

But that *garden*. Imagine living in the most famously gay city in the world and taking your crush to a garden like that. Imagine linking your fingers together while talking about your rising signs, completely hidden behind a giant potted fern, surrounded by magical gay trash.

The first bar of the trip had been a success. There were nineteen more lesbian bars to go. This was maybe going to be the best year of my life.

Davin and I walked toward our Airbnb, the evening air warm and smelling like a mixture of night-blooming jasmine and weed from the open windows of parked cars. The scooter we'd left in front of the apartment was still there, shining under the streetlights, a bucking blue bronco stabled for the night.

"Tomorrow, we can scoot all over," Davin said.

I looked at him. "After what happened today?"

"You won't crash it again."

Wild Side West

In the morning, we scooted all over San Francisco, the pavement glittering, the gulls wheeling overhead. On my own, I would never have rented another scooter again. Sometimes, though, all you need is someone warm at your back as you size up the next hill, yelling into your ear that you should go for it.

New York City
Cubbyhole and Henrietta Hudson

◆ ◆ ◆

The plane was about to land, and my seatmate was creeping me out. We were slowly circling above New York City in the late-afternoon sun, low enough to see famous landmarks clearly. The Statue of Liberty raised her arm, a teal, molded-plastic figurine. The Manhattan skyline drew nearer, the new World Trade Center building narwhaling into the air. All around the plane, my fellow Minnesotans were craning their necks at wild angles, trying to get a good view of the city, *ooh*ing and *ahh*ing and *look at that, babe*–ing.

But my seatmate, who had a prime window seat view, was not looking.

She was staring straight ahead, actually. No headphones in, no phone, no book. Just staring.

Maybe she lives in New York, I thought, squinting over her to see a big bridge. (I don't know what bridge; I live inside a hut hacked out of prairie sod!) *Maybe she has to do this flight twice a month for work.*

But it was eerie. Even if you live in New York, even if you fly there for work all the time, even if you're an extravagantly bored incognito celebrity who is constantly on a plane to La Guardia, flying into New York City and seeing it close up is exciting. Every single view of its skyline has been filmed from every imaginable angle. It's just so famous, and so I think it must give even jaded people a tiny, shivery thrill to see that skyline from the air in real life, no matter how often they might see it.

Cubbyhole and Henrietta Hudson

Not my seatmate, though. I sneaked another look. She was lasering holes with her eyes into the locked tray table on the back of the seat. Not blinking. Floating past her was a fish-eye-lens view of the biggest city in America, an all-you-can-eat view *buffet*, but she never wavered from staring at the seat back. It was like she was trying to levitate it.

Now, OK. She might have been terrified of flying. She might have been on a lot of Xanax. But listen, I'd never seen anything like it. Abandoning all pretense of not looking at her, I turned and fully watched her for a moment. The hairs on the back of my neck started to rise. She looked uncannily like a large doll, strapped unmoving to her seat, big blank eyes open and unblinking. The more I thought about it the more I couldn't stop looking at her, and the more I looked at her the more freaked out I got.

Never have two people been on such opposite ends of the looking-out-the-window-excitement spectrum. I was pretty much vibrating out of my seat, since I'd spent the entire flight watching *The Old Guard*, during which I'd realized that any movie where Charlize Theron fucks men up while wearing tight outfits is my actual favorite movie. I was hopped up on plane ginger ale, checking and rechecking my purse to make sure I had my good pen and a brand-new notebook, *thrilled* to be going to New York with Davin to go to lesbian bars.

Ordinarily, there are three lesbian bars in New York—Cubbyhole and Henrietta Hudson in Manhattan, and Ginger's in Brooklyn—but Ginger's had closed during the pandemic, and when I visited New York to do research for this book, there were rumors about the closure being permanent.* I was distraught about it. Firstly, Ginger's was a great bar, period. And secondly, Ginger's had been an excellent bar for spotting sporties, for whom I have an inexplicable and unshakeable attraction. (And if you don't know what sporties are, please understand that they

---

* Ginger's has reopened! You should go right now!!

are basically queers who are athletic in some way, or who strongly identify with team sports, and that I cannot help myself or be trusted to return back to my own friend group at the bar when it comes to muscley long-hair butches [LHBs] in little striped matching rugby shirts.)

After we landed, Davin and I took the subway to our hotel in Chelsea, which was called Dream Downtown. It was trying very hard. The shower curtain in our room was made of chain mail. Just, like, ten straight feet of chain mail, suspended on a rod from the ceiling far above us. The shower itself was separated from the bedroom by a shared glass wall. It was the kind where your silhouette shows up, fuzzily backlit, against the glass as you soap yourself up, usually a sure sign that a hotel uses the word "edgy" somewhere in the copy on its website.

We went out onto the street. And whoa. New York City! Here it was! There were people everywhere, actual *throngs* of people, people going out to dinner and heading home after work and walking together and stopping at little silver kabob trucks, and it had been so long since I'd seen crowds at all that I just kept gasping and whispering, "Look at those shoes, those are so *cool*," and "Dav, see the dog? The bubble backpack. *Look!*"

Davin was the same way, stunned, his mouth open, watching the trail of a long silk scarf fluttering behind a tall person in a well-cut jacket. Man. Everyone was so stylish! My *god*, I'd missed seeing people who get dressed every day. People who put *outfit*s together. Fucking pandemic! I'd forgotten what it felt like to try to look good, and to see other people trying to look good. These days, in Minnesota, if I wear anything fancier than a pilling oversize sweatshirt and tinted lip balm to someone's house, they *will* open the door and say, "*You're* dressed up," in an accusing tone, their eyes daring me to walk across their floors without taking my shoes off first.

It was early on a September evening, and it was hot out. Manhattan felt alive, electric, people streaming from all directions like cells off to do their jobs inside a giant's body. No one would make me take off my shoes at a fancy party *here*, by god. I'd missed this kind of energy.

Cubbyhole and Henrietta Hudson

Ever since we'd gotten home from San Francisco, Davin had been ramping up his role as the planner of the lesbian bar trips. He'd finish his job for the day—working remotely as a legislative assistant for the Minnesota Senate—and then hunch over his laptop like a gnome, comparing travel deal websites; his main tab open to the complicated Excel master trip spreadsheet, a pop-up window of our shared, color-coded Google calendar in the corner of the screen. In this state—a physical calendar laid out next him, a pencil in his hand, and a look of intense concentration on his face—Davin was at his most blissful, immune to time passing, unable to hear basic questions asked of him about whether or not he wanted a big salad for dinner. He was *loving* being in charge of the trip organization, and that was really great for me, because I, without exaggeration, would rather have dislocated both my shoulders again and simultaneously than have had to plan out the year of travel I was facing.

Thanks to Davin's ~~obsessive~~ meticulous planning, our hotel in New York was a ten-minute walk to both Cubbyhole and Henrietta Hudson. We headed for Cubbyhole first. We'd both been there several times before, but were lured by a years-old memory of its outstanding happy hour. Cubbyhole had also made a recent Instagram announcement of a new patio space built because of the pandemic, a charming thatched-roof area off the sidewalk called Cubby's Hut.

And there it was, just like I remembered it: a little green-painted bar on a cobblestone street corner in the West Village, its awning spelling out CUBBYHOLE in rainbow letters. Cubbyhole opened in 1987. It used to be called DT'S Fat Cat until 1994, when its original owner, the late Tanya Saunders, bought the name Cubbyhole from another lesbian bar. Cubbyhole is an institution; most queers—even gay men—I know have at least heard of it. Whenever I told anyone about the premise of this book, Cubbyhole was usually the first bar they asked if I'd be visiting.

Before arriving, I'd spoken over the phone with the owner of Cubbyhole, Lisa Menichino, about the bar. At the time, she'd owned Cubbyhole for three and a half years, but had worked there for almost twenty-one years. Tanya Saunders left the bar to Lisa when she died.

"I always say we're a lesbian bar with a little asterisk," Lisa said. "We welcome everybody."

Interesting. Typing as she talked, I noticed that Cubbyhole, like the Wild Side West, took pains to identify as a lesbian bar that welcomed everybody. Of course this is how they identify; it's the only way for a lesbian bar to stay in business these days. It's kind, and it doesn't exclude anyone. And while I get it—pigeonholing yourself as *only* a lesbian bar is a great way to alienate other people who might spend money in your bar—I also am not sure, then, why gay bars aren't this, as well. Why have gay men's bars been able to pigeonhole themselves? Why haven't their bars been divided by queer politics and infighting? Why are lesbian bars almost solely in charge of being inclusive? Why don't gay men's bars have regular neighborhood types wandering in, feeling completely comfortable there? Is it society's overt homophobia toward gay men? Or is it something a little more insidious—that some gay men's bars have actively worked to keep other people out, including the rest of the members of the queer community? Maybe a little of both?

I didn't know it at the time of my conversation with Lisa, but her exact statement of welcoming everybody would become such a theme on these trips that we should probably make a drinking game out of it now. Take a shot anytime someone says a variation of "We're a lesbian bar but everyone's welcome," folks at home who drink!

"Cubbyhole's the kind of place that feels friendly, like a small town dumped into a crowded city," Lisa said. "We're open three hundred and sixty-five days a year because Cubbyhole is special to this community. We stayed open through 9/11, through Hurricane Sandy, through blizzards, blackouts ... even if we could only be open a few hours a day, we wanted to be a beacon for people. Somewhere they could go."

Covid was hard. "March 16 [2020] was the first time we ever shut down, and I felt like I'd let Tanya down somehow," said Lisa. "I started to get messages from people about how so many of them had had momentous occasions here, messages like, 'I had my first kiss here'; 'I met my partner here'; 'I came out here.' I would come check on the bar once a week and people would leave little notes for me, like, 'Hi, do you remember that little lamp on the third table? I loved it and I stole it. I'm so sorry, please open'; or 'Hi, remember when your sink clogged during Pride six years ago? That was me, I should have told you. I really miss this place.' I loved those little notes. They really showed me how much the bar meant to the community. I knew I had to reopen when I could. As soon as we were able to open our doors, everybody came back. On weekends, Friday and Saturday, because we have a capacity, we can only get around seventy-five people in." She was quiet for a moment. "There are so many places people can go, but they choose to come here—in the rain, heat, in the snow, during a blizzard. Sometimes I'll go out and hand out free-drink chips to the line on the weekends. There are something like twenty-seven thousand bars in NYC, and people wait to come in here, and we're so grateful."

Running Cubbyhole, Lisa once saw a sight she'll never forget. "During Pride one year, one person got into an argument and was distraught. She went into our bathroom, and she *ripped the toilet from the cement*, flooding the bar. Maybe it was the grief from the breakup giving her extra strength. The wildest thing was, she came back the very next night like nothing happened."

She thinks there's more of a need for spaces like Cubbyhole than ever. "The younger generation hasn't had an experience where spaces are exclusive. That's not part of their stories. A few older people have a problem with us being so inclusive because they feel like it's invasive. But most people are happy everyone's welcome."

Lisa was touching on an ongoing issue. Queers want dedicated spaces where they can go and have everyone around them be queer. That's because that shit is fun. And it's such a relief, not to mention so much safer, for us all to be able to be together. But most of us also want each and every version of queerness to be welcomed in those spaces, and who gets to decide who's queer and who's not? Who gets to take up space in our bars, the only dedicated places we have left? It's a bit like Pride—*yes*, we're all thrilled that being queer is so much more acceptable to society, and also, *my god*, there are so many straight people and corporations at Pride, *the only large-scale event by, for, and celebrating queers*, that lots of queers no longer even go to it. There are also definitely lesbians who want only cis women to be allowed at lesbian bars and events, and who don't accept that trans women are women, and believe that trans men are gender traitors. Those lesbians (and other people who believe this) are called TERFs—trans-exclusionary radical feminists. TERFs cause a lot of fights, especially when it comes to their trying to gatekeep lesbian-centric spaces. (For the record: Fuck TERFs.)

Lisa just wants everyone to *come* to her bar. She believes the only way to keep lesbian bars open is for people to, you know, go to them. "There's a cognitive dissonance," she said with a rueful laugh. "People don't realize that their support is what keeps the bars open. I think sometimes a lesbian bar is like an old friend you've spent a lot of time with and then drifted away from. Queers think of the bar fondly, and there's a huge outcry if one closes, but they forget that in order to have the bar, they need to come hang out there. Come and support your local lesbian bars!"

That's just what I intended to do.

At Cubbyhole, a fresh-faced young person in a billowy Hawaiian shirt checked our IDs, and then, more carefully, our vaccination cards, before waving us in. Cubby's Hut, the patio, had been full outside, and inside it was just as busy; at six thirty p.m., every seat was full. Now, Cubbyhole is a small bar—less than six hundred square feet—and one look through the front door tells you it's doing everything it can to appear even smaller.* It's pleasantly dark in there, even in the daytime,

---

* Cubbyhole has remodeled since my bar visit.

and the ceiling is *low*. That's because the ceiling is covered—absolutely bananas covered—in hanging, rainbow-colored paper lanterns, piñatas, umbrellas, and fabric lawn ornaments, the kind made of windbreaker material, fashioned to look like hot-air balloons and whirligig butterfly wings. If you've ever been to the House on the Rock in Wisconsin (and if not, please go, take an edible, and then call me), Cubbyhole looks like it's cut from the same cloth, as if a voguish gay hoarder with a taste for tchotchkes and color theory were asked to design a place to drink. It is—like a lot of other lesbian bars, and like the Wild Side West, where we'd just been—cluttered, but in an inviting way.

Like I do for all gay topics, I have a theory about why our bars are so often cluttered. It's because queers are sentimental as fuck. Hang on, don't get mad at me; just think for a second. Have you ever met a queer who didn't just love a li'l memento? Who *didn't* want a tiny item chosen specifically because you were thinking of them? Do you know many queers who *don't* maintain a collection of mugs that have funny or dirty sayings on them? Or any queers who aren't still hanging on to at least one item given to them by an ex?

I rest my case.

At Cubbyhole, patio lights and dangly chandeliers twinkle; a glowing, heart-shaped neon sign near the door reads LOVE in cursive letters; light-up bunches of rubber grapes drape fatly over mirrors. Except for the polished wooden bar itself, there isn't a surface that's not covered in stickers or pictures or posters for upcoming shows. A sign hanging over the bottles of liquor announced that we could get an Uncrustable for ten dollars, which: Are you kidding me? An *Uncrustable*? At a *bar*? I immediately tried to order one, before we'd even ordered a drink, but the bartender said they were all out. He looked at me thoughtfully after that, though, as if I might be someone to keep an eye on.

Davin and I had last been to Cubbyhole in the fall of 2017, when we'd gone together. We'd found an almost stupidly cheap flight to New York and gone for a weekend trip. We were still fairly new then, as a couple—

we'd been sleeping together, on and off, for about a year, but hadn't made it official until late that summer.

We'd actually known each other for years, though. Davin and I met when we both lived in Chicago. We were each in serious relationships with other people at the time, and he and I became friends because we invariably seemed to be at the same parties. I was always relieved to see Davin in noisy group settings; he was such a calm, steady presence. I liked how he listened to everyone like they were the only person speaking in a crowded room, and I liked how he was constantly doing things without being asked—chopping vegetables with a towel over his shoulder, offering to grab drinks from the cooler, quietly vanishing out back doors toward the alley, a bag of recycling in his hands. He *radiated* queer-Ron-Swanson-from-*Parks-and-Rec* energy. So butch he was almost camp. All Davin's clothes looked like he'd been born in them, like they were worn flannel extensions of his own skin, and he laughed a lot, comfortable with himself and at ease in big groups. I thought he was cute, and that was the extent of it—he was off-limits, engaged to someone else, and I was in the middle of regular drama with my partner, unable to get off the high-and-low roller coaster of our relationship.

Both our relationships were going badly, actually, and Davin and I were both trying and failing to save them. Davin's partner eventually ended their engagement. I finally realized I needed to get out of *my* relationship, but didn't know how; our lives felt too intertwined. Months went by like this. Davin and I were both depressed—sad sacks, faces ashen or splotchy from crying, our phones clutched in our hands, ready for the shaky adrenaline rush of the next text-fight with the person we each used to love. Sometimes I would drive my scooter to Davin's Chicago apartment, where we'd sit on opposite ends of his couch in our respective filthy sweat suits and watch episodes of *Roseanne* without speaking.

Davin moved away from Chicago. Emotionally wrecked, he was going to spend a year going on what he called his "Eat Pray Love" trip, a journey around the country in a custom wood camper he'd built on the back of his truck. And that's what he did. He spent his days driving, working as an art preparator at museums and gallery shows, and doing odd carpentry jobs. He spent his nights alone, staring into campfires, weeping to Gregory Alan Isakov songs, and trying to figure out who he was and what he wanted to do next. In between his months on the road, he lived with his dad in Northfield.

Just a twenty-nine-year-old living in his dad's basement, he joked over text.

Meanwhile, I broke up with my girlfriend. After the relationship ended, I moved from Chicago back to Minneapolis, the city I've treated as a home base since college. My friends Tawnya (aka "Sweetpea" or "Pea") and Seven offered to let me live with them in their house. Right before I moved in, Seven had called to ask what color I'd like my room painted.

"White," I'd said listlessly. "Stark white. Like a nun's cell."

I was convinced I was never going to date anyone ever again. I would lie in my bed and stare at the ceiling. Every few months, Davin would swing into Northfield and call me, the only person he knew in Minneapolis, to hang out. We would go get tacos, pick through used record bins, walk along the Mississippi. All platonic.

After I got used to this routine, during another brief period when he was in town, Davin told me he liked me. We kissed. For a second, I was shocked at how it felt to kiss someone with a beard. I hadn't kissed anyone with a full beard since I played Rizzo in *Grease* in high school and had to make out with a boy onstage. (I got hives from the product that boy used in his beard. I was allergic to him, an early gay warning sign!!)

As I kissed Davin, though, I decided I liked the beard. A lot. I liked *him*. He was kind, and he was hot, and he was trans, and I didn't know what that meant for *my* identity (spoiler alert: it meant nothing but an expansion of my identity), but that was all just details.

In between Davin's visits, I was dating someone else, but that didn't work out, in the end. Davin finished his trip, moved back to Minnesota permanently, and that was it. We were in love.

Moby Dyke

The inside of Cubbyhole hadn't changed much since our last visit in 2017. At the time, we'd spent a late Saturday night in there, pressed against the back wall by throngs of queers, all of whom seemed to know each other, all of whom were dancing and hollering and flirting. The crowd had shoved a drunk lesbian wearing a pastel polo shirt into us; she seized this as an opportunity to wave her beer emphatically while explaining to us why long-distance relationships were good in theory and bad in practice, especially for her and her girlfriend, who lived in France.

Two people at the bar got up and left. I lunged forward and sat on one seat, throwing my bag onto the other so Davin could sit. Two startled nearby queers tried to pretend they hadn't also been heading for the seats; they hadn't realized I'd been watching the bar with the kind of cold intensity and focus normally reserved for professional athletes on game day.

There was a reason Cubbyhole was so busy: its happy hour is legendary, with half-price well drinks from four to seven p.m., Monday through Saturday. I had a gin and tonic for $3.50 and couldn't believe it. The people next to us looked just as pleased, their heads bent over $2.50 beers as they discussed what sounded like a seriously toxic boss at their nonprofit in low voices.

A young queer kept coming through the door with a tray and joking around with the bartender, whose name turned out to be Mitch. He was extremely friendly. When I asked, he said he'd been working at Cubbyhole for ten years.

"Ten *years*!"

"Yep, and I'm not the employee who's been around the longest," he said, pouring a vodka soda as he talked. "There's Debbie, who's worked here for eleven years, and Geeta—been here for twenty-two years—and Lisa's the owner; she took this place over from Tanya three years ago. I was a regular for four years before I started working here."

When I asked him why he'd been there for a decade, he smiled and shrugged. "Working here is fun. The employees are really close and the people who come here are the best."

"The money must be good," I suggested leadingly, interested in any-one who liked their job enough to stay there for more than a *few* years, let alone ten. The way *I* make money is copywriting. I've been a copywriter/staff writer since 2010, when I first moved to Chicago and Groupon was still a startup. They hired me to write jokes about Brazilian waxing deals and discount colonic hydrotherapy sessions, and I worked there for five years before I figured out that I didn't have to, that other businesses also needed writers. Copywriting is the only way I know how to make a living wage—it's my only marketable skill. I've spent the last twelve years working mostly contract jobs at different companies, where I always do the same things: send politely bitchy "per my last email" emails, avoid khakied bros in the hallways, huddle in body-shape-concealing cardigans under florescent lights, and write copy for newsletters and ads and scripts and mobile apps and web pages. At the time of this writing, I am the editor in chief of a corporate magazine for plumbing, HVAC, and electrical businesses. Sometimes I fly to different cities to interview the owners of these businesses for the magazine. I don't know that much about plumbing and HVAC, but I do know how to write, and that's what puts special gluten-free bread and goat cheese from the co-op on the table at *our* house.

Mitch laughed. "The money's good!" he said. "We've been busier than ever since we reopened [in April 2021]. There's been shitloads of babyqueers lately. I was thinking maybe it's because of the pandemic; maybe people have realized spaces like these, where you can be yourself, are really important."

There's an old stereotype that lesbians don't tip well, so I asked Mitch about it. "Any experience with that?"

"Oh hell no," he said, wiping his hands on a towel. "Not here. Not at all."

Good. I hate that stereotype, but I've heard it so often from friends who've worked at gay bars that I know there must be lesbians *somewhere* who are tippin' with dimes. A dyke bar employee once told me a joke that I can easily remember, because it bugged me:

Q: What's the difference between a lesbian and a canoe?
A: Sometimes canoes tip.

Mmph. And all right, I *do* notice a ton of queers drinking the ab-solute cheapest beer at bars, but I know *that* has to do with what Lisa, the butch at Wild Side West, had mentioned: lesbians tend to make far less money than cis men. But everyone I know tips well. And why wouldn't we? Almost everyone I know has also worked a service job. Being poorer in general *can't* be the entire reason lesbians have been labeled cheapasses at the gay bar.

At seven p.m. on the dot, Mitch turned the music volume dramati-cally up and down, and the chatter in the bar quieted.

"OK, listen up everybody!" he bellowed. "Happy Hour is over, so we're gonna do a round of free shots together, as a family."

He began filling little plastic sacrament cups on a tray with what looked like whiskey and passing them around to everyone sitting inside.

"Now, don't you drink your shot right away when I've poured it," he scolded as he passed them out. "We're gonna drink it *together*; some-body always forgets." Two young queers, their cups already halfway to their mouths, set them down guiltily.

Britney's "Work Bitch" suddenly blared out of the jukebox.

"OK!" Mitch called out. "Thank you all for being here, today, right now, with us. No matter who you are, or where you come from, we're a family. All of us."

No one spoke for a second. He raised his little plastic cup, and we all lifted our shots and toasted one another. I cheersed the queer next to me, and we both knocked our shots back. Holy shit, it was peach schnapps! I spluttered, laughing, and looked over at Davin, who was also laughing with a group of people, his mouth full of sticky peach schnapps. What a lovely moment, to be made to feel at home in the middle of Manhattan, cozy and homey in this tiny bar filled with so many strangers. We *were* family. I loved Cubbyhole. I loved Mitch. I loved . . . uh-oh. I loved every-one in the bar.

Crap, I was tipsy. The half shot of schnapps had put me over the edge. I'm a lightweight; I almost never take shots when I go out, because I cannot handle them. It takes exactly 1.5 normal drinks for me to be-come the kind of person who says shit like, "You have the most *invisible pores*, your skin is *unreal*" to people I don't know. I looked at Davin, my eyes aglow. He had the reddest beard in the *world*.

Britney's "Toxic" came on, and Davin took a sip of his beer. "Did you hear about the end? Of her conservatorship?" he asked.

"Britney? Oh, mm-hmm," I said, suddenly distracted by how many gorgeous gays were in the bar. Had I just not noticed them before? Was *everyone* in New York good-looking?

"She's engaged now," Davin said.

"I *know*," I said, tearing my eyes from a masc-presenting person in a black tank top. "You think she'll be OK?"

"What do you mean?"

"I mean she just got her freedom back, and now she's engaged, and it's happened so fast, and I'm just worried, is all. Like, who is this guy? What if he's taking advantage of her?"

"She's a grown woman," Davin said. "We don't know her life."

"I know."

"She's *older* than you. She can make her own decisions."

"Yeah . . ."

"You're trying to do exactly what she just got free from!" he said, pointing at me. "You're trying to control her life. And it's her life. That's the thing. It's her life."

I opened my mouth to argue and stopped. He had a point.

Ravenous, Davin and I walked across the street to a sidewalk seat-ing area at Cafe Cluny, a place that had looked, from Cubbyhole's win-dows, like it might have burgers. As soon as we were seated, though, we realized we'd made a mistake. Everyone at Cafe Cluny was clearly far, far wealthier than us. The restaurant did have a burger. A plain burger, without cheese or fries, for twenty-six dollars. Over the tops of our menus, Davin and I shared a guilty look. We were trying to budget on these trips!

But we were already seated and our waiter was already pouring water and it was too late. To hell with it. Always one to live a little when faced with no other choice, Davin ordered a yellowfin tuna burger, rubbing his hands like a cartoon fox about to sneak up on a henhouse. On either side of our small table were two-tops, both occupied by people who were obviously in a different tax bracket. The woman to my right was sleekly picking at some fish, a thin gold bracelet dangling off her wrist, her cream-and-gold leather bag perched on a ledge behind her head. Her date was wearing an impossibly white and crisp button-down. They both looked like the kind of people who (a.) had recently been interviewed about their daily routines for *Business Insider*; and (b.) began those interviews with "Five a.m.: Wake up, drink matcha, meditate for thirty minutes" and had, frighteningly, been telling the truth.

Davin and I lost ourselves in people-watching. Two beautiful queers, both exceptionally tall and wearing loose trousers, strolled past us, holding hands. A family with two little girls in school uniforms walked home together, the dad carrying pink and orange backpacks and the mom putting her arm out, lightly, in front of the smallest girl as they waited to cross the street. What would it be like to be a kid here? To be a rich kid? To be used to all this? I couldn't imagine. When I was growing up, my mom had a thin metal whistle that she blew, piercingly, off our back deck when it was time for dinner. You could hear it from half a mile away. When I heard the whistle, I'd grab my bike and race it through the shortcuts in the woods, splashing through the creek and up the hill to my house, where my mom would ask me how long my leg had been bleeding like that and remind me to use the nail brush when I washed my hands. It amazes me when someone tells me they grew up in New York. How? *How did you do that?* I always want to know. I was a danger to myself as a kid. When I was about seven, I got lost in a cornfield near our house and wandered around it in circles for hours as the sunset faded and the sky darkened. The stars popped out, one by one, pinpricks of ice; the identical cornstalks surrounded me, rustling threateningly over my head. I finally just sat down in the dirt, cross-legged, and waited for death. Cold and exhausted, I was only a few hundred yards from our house. I had never called for help. Our dogs found me. Compare that to the similarly aged kids I've seen in New York walking around by themselves after school together, tapping new-model iPhones with their tiny fingers and casually handing over credit cards to pay for bagels, and you can see that this city must produce an entirely different species of child.

After dinner, Davin said he had a little surprise.

"Come on," he said. "You'll like it."

We walked through the West Village, full and happy to be wandering through a soft blue evening with so many other people. It had just been so long since we'd seen anything like this. Everywhere we went, I kept seeing outdoor dining spaces, all with twinkly lights strung overhead, all at capacity. Cutlery clinked on plates; waiters rushed around balancing trays; the sound of laughter drifted over the streets. It all looked so quaint. So welcoming. Because of the pandemic, dining in New York had moved much more out onto the streets. With more pedestrians and fewer cars, the change was striking. I hope they leave it that way. It looks wonderful.

After just a few blocks, Davin steered me to take a right. Halfway down the street, he turned and faced a brownstone.

"Look," he said.

Oh my god. It was Carrie Bradshaw's apartment. There were the steps! And the door! OH MY GOD. Sorry to be such a loser, but I was thrilled. During the deepest part of winter pandemic '20–21, when vaccines were just an optimistic medical rumor, when we couldn't go anywhere or do anything or have anyone over, ever, Davin and I had rewatched the entirety of *Sex and the City*. That show was the opposite of being stuck in the house in rural Minnesota. All anyone on *Sex and the City* does is go out to crowded restaurants and bars, shop for belligerently pointy shoes, and fuck lots and lots of awful dudes, and the series—no matter how old, no matter how badly the episode with Samantha and the trans sex workers outside her apartment had aged— had helped us get through that winter. I was *delighted* to see Carrie's apartment in real life, embarrassingly excited, like squealing-out-loud excited. Even if the steps had a petty little chain drawn across them telling us we had better not even *think* about climbing them. *This was a private house, OK?*

Well, fine. But it was also Carrie Bradshaw's apartment, and it was satisfying to think of the owners having to step over their own chain every time they left the house.

Do you know what's right by Carrie Bradshaw's apartment and never once gets mentioned in *Sex and the City*? Stonewall. The fucking Stonewall Inn! Two blocks away!

If you don't know what Stonewall is, I'd be curious to hear why you're reading this right now, but! In case you really, genuinely have no idea, The Stonewall Inn is both a gay bar and the birthplace of the modern gay rights movement. That's because on June 28, 1969, the bar was raided by police and . . . the patrons fought back. Hard. Before that night, for decades, gay bars all over the country and their patrons had been subject to regular, sanctioned police violence and harassment, just for serving the community and being themselves. At the time, there were all kinds of bullshit laws concerning gay people. It was illegal to serve gay folks alcohol, for instance. It was illegal to dress in drag. Women had to be wearing at least three items of "feminine" clothing or they could be arrested. It was illegal for gay people to even dance together, for fuck's sake. And not just in New York; laws like these could be found all over America.

So! When the police officers raided The Stonewall Inn and tried to arrest its patrons that June night in 1969, a crowd gathered, and the gay people they were trying to arrest did not go quietly. Now, the internet and the queer community *love* to argue about who fought back first against the police at Stonewall, but because no one recorded what happened on their cell phone that night and interviews with those present are conflicting, no one has the definitive answer about who did what right then. We do know that trans women of color and lesbians were the first people to fight back. After that, accounts vary. (For instance, Marsha P. Johnson and Sylvia Rivera, both self-identified drag queens, are frequently credited with starting the Stonewall riots, but Marsha P. Johnson was open about not being present when the riots began, and no one is sure if Sylvia Rivera was there that night, though both were hugely influential in the uprising during the next few days and in the gay liberation movement overall. Miss Major, a Black trans woman activist, was there, however, and was hit on the head and arrested.)

Shit hit the fan. As the night went on, the crowd outside The Stonewall Inn grew bigger and angrier. People started rioting; more police arrived. By the next night, the news about the riots at Stonewall had spread, and thousands of people gathered on Christopher Street, smashing shit, lighting fires in trash bins, and throwing things at the hundred new cops who'd been sent in to contain the riots. The night after that, thousands more people were there, fighting a street battle against the police, which they won. That's how Pride began. The first Pride was a riot. (And that's why there's a constant fight about whether or not cops should be allowed at Pride: because Pride began with queer people finally pushing back against the enforcers of systematic oppression, the cops who had pushed them around for so many years. Pride is literally antipolice, and so allowing cops at Pride feels wrong.)

Knowing a little bit about the history of The Stonewall Inn is different from actually standing outside The Stonewall Inn while a doorman politely asks you if you want to come in. *Did we want to come in!* To hallowed ground? To gay church? I'd never been there before, and suddenly

I had no idea why I hadn't specifically sought it out, *demanded* to go. I fumbled for my vaccination card with shaky fingers, hyperventilating when I couldn't find it right away in my wallet. I NEEDED TO GET IN-SIDE GROUND ZERO OF GAY PRIDE OH MY GOD.

I found my card. It was examined carefully, and Davin and I were ushered in. Inside, another person bustled toward us, waving us over to two seats at the bar.

"Hi, babies, come on in," they said, talking very fast. "You can sit here or here or at a table or in the piano bar, up to you, babies."

We sat at the bar. It was dim and moodily lit; Pride flags hung from the stamped-tin ceiling. There was a red-felted pool table behind us, set in front of mirror-lined walls. A written history of Stonewall ran across the mirrors, and the back room had pictures of Marsha P. Johnson and other Stonewall legends. Most of the seats at the bar were taken, but it wasn't as busy as Cubbyhole had been. Nobody else sitting there looked like they were trying not to pass out from sheer excitement; everyone just looked like they were having a normal weekday night. *I've made a huge mistake*, I thought, glancing around. *I should have moved here in my early twenties like I'd originally planned in high school so I could be blasé about meeting a friend for drinks at the frickin' CRADLE of GAY SOCIETY.* A burly, bearded bartender poured us moscow mules, and Davin and I sat and sipped and looked at all the regular queer people still having cocktails at Stonewall—which was just a normal bar—all these years later.

The host prowled up and down the bar. "OK, babies, everyone pick a song for the jukebox," they said.

They stopped in front of a skinny young queer. "You. What's your song?"

"Um, Justin Bieber," the kid said. "A song called 'Sorry,'" they added.

"Justin *Bieber*?"

The kid looked embarrassed but stood firm. "Um, yep. Justin Bieber."

The host looked at the kid, their eyes softening.

"OK baby, we'll play it for you, I'll turn it on."

When it was my turn to request a song, I requested Britney's "Work Bitch" because I panicked and it was the only song I could think of. We'd just heard it at Cubbyhole, but hey—Britney is a uniting force for queers, universally loved, part of the soundtrack to all gay bars. It's not our fault—queers are irresistibly drawn to sexy chaotic energy. Britney's like Dolly Parton for us. We *love* a tragic backstory, a timeline of struggles and triumphs, a rhinestone-bedazzled lace-up top threatening to burst open during an interview.

"OK, Britney, you got it, baby," the host said.

When "Work Bitch" came on, Davin and I clinked our glasses together. I looked around again; Stonewall looked like any other bar. My eyes suddenly welled with tears. It *was* like any other bar. But it also wasn't. Here I was, an out gay woman, sharing a drink with my out transgender husband, who I was *legally married to*, at Stonewall, the place that had made all of that possible. The place where it all began.

"Sweets, are you crying?" Davin looked concerned.

"No."

"Yes, you are."

"It's just—" I gestured to our surroundings, trying to articulate how I felt. Davin put his arm around me.

"I get it."

We paid and left. Just out the door, people—lots of them gay men— walked quickly by in twos and threes, dressed to go out, talking about where they were going or people they knew. Most hardly glanced at The Stonewall Inn, its neat, red-lettered neon sign glowing from the window. We could all go anywhere, now.

IT WAS STILL HOT THE next day, and so, so humid. Davin and I walked all around Manhattan, during which time I learned that:

- There is no limit to the number of ludicrously flopping pizza slices I can eat, regardless of the temperature outside and my own previously determined definitions of "reasonable";
- wearing shorts under a skirt to prevent thigh chafing is a great idea until your shorts are completely soaked with crotch sweat and there's no way for them to get dry, since they're *trapped under your skirt*; and
- new sandals that you think are "pretty broken in" will land you in a Midtown Walgreens three hours later, sweatily searching with wide, panicky eyes for those Band-Aids that have little blister cushions on them, while a strange man with a comb-over stands just a liiiiittle too close behind you.

Back at the hotel that afternoon, I got a disappointing email. The Lesbian Herstory Archives, which is located in Brooklyn and which I'd very much been hoping to visit, didn't have any in-person appointments available. It was Covid's fault. I sulked, frowning out the window of Dream Downtown. The Lesbian Herstory Archives, according to its website, "exists to gather, preserve and provide access to records of Lesbian lives and activities." It's basically a living lesbian museum and library, one that holds events and has cool educational programs, and I had wanted to go so much! Along with having a name that sounds like an SNL parody of a lesbian museum, the LHA has a glorious Instagram filled with pictures of dykes back in the day, as well *the* best collection of historical lesbian-themed T-shirts, posters, pins, and dyke bar merchandise on the planet.

The person who wrote to me from the LHA was very sweet and apologetic about the lack of appointments. They also had a suggestion: There was a documentary called *All We've Got*—about the importance of social spaces for lesbians, queer and bisexual women, and transgender folks—being screened that very night, for one night only, at the

WOW Café Theatre in the East Village. There would be a Q&A with the director afterward. It started in . . . shit, it started in forty-five minutes!

I whooped and tossed my phone onto the bed, which woke up Davin, who'd been stretched out dozing. I knew I needed to see this documentary. It was exactly the kind of thing I wanted to do on this trip!

"Oh," Davin said when I informed him of our evening's plans.

"You don't want to go."

"I'll go," he said.

"You don't have to go."

"No, I'll go."

It was too late to walk, so we grabbed an Uber. I knew Davin didn't want to go to this movie, so I spent the ride assuring him that it was completely fine if he didn't come, he would have more fun by himself, and no, I didn't care, please go and have fun, *yes* I was sure, oh my *god*. Sometimes, being two queers—both indecisive Pisces—who were *both* raised in the passive-aggressive Midwest is fucking exhausting to navigate.

The WOW Café Theatre has a confusing address (how can something be located at 59-61 East Fourth Street? am I dumb?) and a clear mission—it's a collective that promotes the empowerment of women through the performing arts. Historically, it was a lesbian-majority space, but they welcome all women and trans people. They got their building from NYC for one dollar (you're shitting me) decades ago, with the promise that they would bring it up to code, which they're still working on, via donations. At the door, a serious-looking person studied my vaccination card intently before waving me inside. I took a tiny, rickety elevator up to the fourth floor, where WOW has a small theater.

As with nearly all queer events, walking into an event at the WOW theater means that every single person in the room turns to look at you. There were metal chairs set on wooden risers leading up from the floor of the stage, and to have my entrance watched by so many pairs of eyes looking down at me was slightly intimidating. Almost every chair in the theater was occupied by what my friend Lola calls an "obvious community member." A lot of older butches and multiple young radical queers were in attendance.

I found an empty chair a few rows up into the risers and sat down. We had a few minutes before the movie started, so I futzed with my notebook and pretended to look at my phone while the room filled up.

The emcee of the evening's screening stepped to the front of the room. "Welcome to WOW!" they said to us all.

Then it happened.

My chair leg got caught in the crack between the wooden risers behind me. The chair started tipping over in slow motion.

I was going to fall. There was no stopping it.

"Ohhhhhh noooooooooo—"

My voice came out in a baritone, comically low, my arms and legs flailing in the air as the chair tipped, a lobster on its back, waving its claws. I was no longer in control of my body; I was a large Hefty sack filled with wet sand. I slid out of the chair and flopped heavily onto the wooden risers. People gasped. There was a brief pause, and then my body continued its downward descent, rolling down two more steps toward the stage, unstoppable.

"Are you all right?" The emcee was standing over me, looking worried. "We must have set the chairs in a bad spot."

I stood up. You could have charged your phone from the heat coming off my face. "I am one hundred percent certain it is my fault," I said, addressing the room. Everyone laughed. It was a relieved laugh, though. A tension-breaking laugh. The fall must have looked bad.

"We got a nice view," cracked an older butch. Someone else cackled. *They all saw right up my skirt*, I realized. I reseated myself carefully. *Everyone here has seen my ass.*

The movie started, thank christ. It was really interesting—it covered a journey across the United States to document several queer spaces that were surviving and thriving, even as other queer spaces across the country closed their doors. From the film's director, Alexis Clements, I learned the magic formula for keeping a queer women's space open for decades:

1. The queer women must own the space, not rent or lease it. (Landlords sell buildings to condo developers; leases get renewed at a landlord's pleasure.)
2. There must be a strong intergenerational community. (Young people need to grow up near the space, associate adults in their lives with the space, go to events there, and feel a sense of ownership and community there.)
3. The space must have an aligned political agenda. (Infighting can destroy spaces and whole communities. Queers, did you hear that? *Infighting can destroy spaces and whole communities.*)
4. There must be an ongoing need in the community for the space. (High population = a queer space is needed. Or maybe the place is in a small town but becomes a destination, since it's the only welcoming spot for queers for four hundred square miles. Either way, if people need it, a queer space is in business.)

The documentary felt happy, like a celebration. Sitting in the dark, listening to the audience laugh and cheer when they saw black-and-white pictures and videos of dyke marches and now-vanished lesbian spaces, I got excited, thinking about how many more lesbian bars I'd visit before the year was out. I still had eighteen more to see!

"So much of the documentation about women's spaces documents their failure," explained Alexis after the lights went up. "I wanted to bring joy to the movie."

"You did. That's how it was," an elder queer said, nodding at the screen. "All that joy. It was just like that."

Others—older folks—nodded, agreeing. Some of their eyes looked far away, like they had just heard a song they hadn't heard in years, but somehow knew all the words to.

DAVIN AND I HAD BIG plans that night: we were going to an *L Word: Generation Q* watch party at Henrietta Hudson, the second lesbian bar on my list for New York. We'd already been to Henrietta Hudson a few nights earlier for a reconnaissance visit, and it had been a quiet early week-night, with just a few pleasant bartenders waiting on a couple clusters of friends. But now it was Friday night, and we'd heard Henrietta Hudson's watch parties had been so packed that they couldn't guarantee a spot for people who didn't reserve tables or come early.

It would be hard to overstate how excited I was for this night's event. An *L Word* watch party!! I used to go to watch parties for the original *L Word* when I was a babydyke, just learning to navigate being an out homosexual in society. My girlfriend at the time and I would go to gay bars so crowded for the watch parties that everyone stood with their shoulders touching. We'd watch each *L Word* episode with all the lesbians in Minneapolis, my girlfriend standing behind me and wrapping her arms around my waist protectively, which was adorable and also ridiculous, because she was a good six inches shorter than me and couldn't see anything that way. Davin *also* used to obsessively watch *The L Word*, but as a high school student in Faribault, Minnesota, when his mom wasn't home. And now here we both were, years later, doing it all again, getting all revved up to go to a watch party for a show that we knew couldn't possibly represent the entire lesbian and queer community and would therefore be both something that almost everyone would watch and enjoy *and* something that would be torn apart on Twitter.

You have to understand: The original *L Word*, which ran from 2004 to 2009, was a wildly unrealistic soap opera. We (the gays) all knew that, even then. We knew it never accurately showed what most lesbians were like and portrayed trans characters badly; we knew a lot of the actors were straight; we knew that—no matter what *The L Word* wanted you to think—it took more than 1.2 seconds to make someone orgasm when you went down on them for the first time. But we didn't care. We watched *The L Word* anyway. WATCHED it. Back then, it honestly didn't matter what happened in a show. If it had gay characters, we watched it. All of us. At the time, it was *amazing* to see a show about lesbians on TV at all. Back then—just, like, fifteen years ago!—it was all we had.

Times have changed. Now there are so many movies and TV shows with queer characters that I legitimately can't keep up, and don't even bother trying. (All I really need is *Carol*, over and over again, playing silently on a loop in my head. That and *Moonlight*. Ooh, and *Call Me by Your Name*. And *Tampa Baes*. And *Work in Progress*! That show is so good!) Whatever. The point is: we queers don't necessarily need *The L Word: Generation Q* anymore. But I was prepared to watch the hell out of it, anyway.

Davin and I walked over to Henrietta Hudson, a West Village landmark in a brick building on a corner. Henrietta Hudson is the oldest lesbian bar in New York City. It refers to itself, technically, as "a queer human bar built by lesbians." It's *also* hard to miss, especially on a Friday night right before a big event during Covid. There was a huge, white-tented patio space out front with Pride flags rippling in the breeze, and there were people everywhere, queers spilling out onto the sidewalk, flashing their vaccination cards at the door, yelling to one another from the patio, and trying to worm their way to the front of the bar for the preshow trivia contest. Holyyyy cow. A few days ago, I had tried to reserve a table for this event and the OpenTable website had basically laughed my laptop shut. I'd guessed this was because on the previous week, Shane and Alice (Katherine Moennig and Leisha Hailey), characters from the original *L Word*, had *stopped by* Henrietta Hudson for the watch party. Just showed up! (Yes, I would have done anything to have been there, and *yes*, I cried blood when I found out I'd missed them by *one week*.)

Moby Dyke

It was pandemonium at Henrietta Hudson. Apparently, Dani (Arienne Mandi) from *Generation Q* was supposed to be there that night. I rubbernecked frantically, trying to get a look at everyone at once. We should have gotten there earlier. The bar was mobbed, and every person in the room had had their vaccination card checked. I was delighted; I even felt fairly safe. Just like in San Francisco! What a wonderful city New York is, to mandate vaccines for anyone going into bars and restaurants. And what a turnout for Henrietta Hudson, and in the middle of a pandemic!

Henrietta Hudson is owned and run by Lisa Cannistraci, who opened it with her business partner, Minnie Rivera, in 1991, after the original Cubbyhole (the one the current Cubbyhole bought its name from!) shut down. It's a beautiful bar, and it's recently had a makeover.

Two queers in line for drinks were surprised by HH's new look; they hadn't seen it yet.

"It used to be kind of dark and divey," one of them said, looking around. "Now it looks like a country club."

Their tone was appreciative. Henrietta Hudson now looks . . . polished. Unexpectedly polished, for a dyke bar. It has a kind of Pinteresty midcentury vibe going on; think white paint with pops of color, giant tropical leaf wallpaper (like Blanche's bedroom on *The Golden Girls*), gold fixtures, and white-tiled, fresh-smelling bathrooms. At the bar, you could get frozen margaritas. Shit, you could get charcuterie plates now! This was so classy!

Both the front and back rooms of the bar were full. The crowd was young, and people were super, *super* into wearing jumpsuits. It was a parade of jumpsuits. I saw two! identical tomato-red Wildfang jumpsuits. In the same *room*! Completely understandable. Wildfang (a clothing company that designs clothes that transcend gender norms) had just had a big sale, and I had added and subtracted that very same tomato-red jumpsuit into my shopping cart five or six times before realizing that there was no way I could buy *any* kind of nonstretchy pants, at all, without trying them on first, regardless of whether or not they were special gay pants.

Two people wearing *The L Word: Generation Q* T-shirts milled around, passing out *L Word* swag to everyone. They had stickers and cool little enamel pins to give out, and they unloaded them into every open hand they saw. Ooh. I wanted those! I fought my way toward the swag people. Oh no. They were heading out the door! I panicked and began pushing through the crowd, nakedly, degradingly desperate to get a free *L Word* enamel pin before they left.

I made it.

"Can I have two?" I panted at the swag people. They handed the pins over.

"Yesss! Thank you!" I cried, pumping my fist full of pins madly in the air. What a score!

Across the bar, Davin was looking at me as if he was realizing who he'd married for the first time. Together, we posted up against the Blanche's-bedroom-leaf wall, trying to occupy as little space as possible. Queers pressed in on all sides. While waiting for the episode to start, the hosts from the podcast *Dyking Out* were telling jokes and running trivia across the screens set up in both rooms.

"What's the most unrealistic plot point of *The L Word: Generation Q*?" one of them asked the crowd. "This is for a prize!"

People in the audience considered the question. Was it the fact that everyone on *The L Word* was rich? Was it that Bette Porter hadn't aged a day? Was it that none of Finley's friends had yet offered a recommendation for their own therapist?

"The lack of pets!" hooted one of the hosts, and the crowd cracked up. They were right! Not one of the *L Word* characters had horrible, spitting cats that lurked around corners and attacked overnight guests. No one on the show had three rescue pit bull mixes named Ace, Mama, and Mr. Pinky, each with their own separate, special speaking voice. So fake!

Moby Dyke

I was eavesdropping on a group of twentysomething queers standing near me. One of them asked a person in a denim jumpsuit how their girlfriend was, and they said, "Oh, well, tomorrow's our two-year anniversary, so we're going to look at rings."

A silence fell over the friend group.

"Aww!" exclaimed the person who'd asked the question, a beat too late.

"Awwwww!" echoed the rest of the friend group, taking their cue. Significant eye contact was shared among those cooing. There would definitely be an in-depth discussion about this later, in a separate group chat thread.

I was standing directly behind two beautiful giraffes, both of whom knew they were blocking my view of the trivia screen and both of whom were helpless to go anywhere else—it was just so crowded. They kept turning around and sweetly apologizing to me. One wore oversize glasses and the other sported a pink Fiorucci angels halter top. They were very stylish and very young and they very much wanted to be touching each other at all times. I guessed they'd been together six months or less. They had that recognizable new-couple energy that other people can see from space and that you never realize is conspicuous when you're one of the people in the couple.

The beautiful giraffes had an irritating circuit queen–looking friend with them who was *also* close to six feet tall, also blocking our view, and who never apologized, which did not surprise me in the least. Circuit Queen kept pulling up used designer coats on eBay on a phone set to maximum brightness, asking, "Honestly, do you think I'd look good in this one? Should I bid on it? You know what, I'm going to bid on it," in a ceaseless, running monologue. CQ's beautiful friends would glance at every proffered screen and murmur that they liked each coat, but this person didn't seem to really be either talking to them *or* listening to their replies. Circuit Queen was talking to the air.

The lights went down inside Henrietta Hudson at last, and the episode began. All eyes were on the screen; it was suddenly so quiet in the room that I could hear the keys on someone's carabiner clinking as they shifted their weight. It stayed that silent for most of the episode, except for when characters kissed. Then the bar erupted as everyone watching *The L Word: Generation Q* screamed, together and spontaneously. Just: "*AHHHHHHHHHHHHHHHHHHHHHH!*" like it was 1964 and we were teenagers seeing the Beatles exit their hotel.

Bathed in the blue light of Shane and Tess finally kissing, I smiled. I was surrounded by queers, our shoulders all touching, in a dyke bar, and I was very happy.

We may not all need *Generation Q* like we used to need *The L Word*, but you know what? It's good we don't need it like that anymore. It means things have changed.

After the episode, I looked for Dani, who had shown up, but never saw her. The staff at Henrietta Hudson opened the doors between the front and back rooms, and suddenly we were in the middle of a dance floor, with what felt like hundreds of queers ready. to. *grind* on each other. Jostled and bumped on all sides while babygays jumped and screamed "I! DON'T! CAAARE!" to Icona Pop's "I Love It," I looked nervously at Davin. It felt too early, too scary, to be on a packed dance floor. Breakthrough Covid cases existed. I wasn't ready.

"You wanna leave?" he shouted, pointing at the door.

"Yeah!" I shouted back.

We pushed our way through the door and staggered out onto the sidewalk. The night air felt nice and cool now. New armies of queers were queuing up to get inside Henrietta Hudson, a fresh parade of jumpsuits ready to dance. Davin took my arm and we walked toward our hotel, just two middle-aged gays lucky enough to have been around for the first *L Word*, and ready for bed after seeing the second one.

SUNLIGHT WAS SNEAKING THROUGH THE crack in the blackout curtains at Dream Downtown. The light looked bright white, hot. It was going to be a sunny day. I shut my eyes. I wouldn't look at it.

Wait.

"Dav, what time are we meeting Jess?"

Davin groaned and rolled over. "Ten. Why?"

"We have to get up."

Jess is Davin's fabulous high-femme friend; they met through one of Davin's best friends, EmJ. I met Jess at a party when I lived in Chicago and she was visiting from New York. I was immediately smitten. Jess is funny as shit and wears huge gold earrings and a lot of leopard print and bright red lipstick and tells great stories, and we were supposed to meet her and her wonderful partner, James, at Washington Square Park. I was not about to be late.

Already sweating through our clothes, Davin and I speed-walked through the park to find Jess and James sitting in the shade under a tree, waiting for us.

"Hiiiiiiii!"

They hopped up and hugged us. Jess and James had brought us coffee and doughnuts. Nearly all the doughnuts had little sneaky bites taken out of them, which was so endearing I couldn't handle it.

We chattered, catching up with our respective lives.

"How's the book going?" Jess asked, offering me the precious last bite of a salted lemon doughnut.

"It's good!" I said. "I mean, I get to go to dyke bars and write a book about it, so it's great! Even if it's hard to write a book about lesbian bars, ya know?"

Jess squinted at me. "Why?"

"Because it's 2021 and, well . . . what's a lesbian bar, exactly?"

Jess laughed. She got it right away.

"I'm serious, though!" I said. "And even if I'm going with my definition of a lesbian bar as 'a bar that was created by lesbians or has historically called itself a lesbian bar and currently still identifies as a lesbian bar (even though everyone is welcome)' . . . what's a lesbian, even?"

I warmed to my subject. "How should I write this book? How should I talk about lesbians? Is a lesbian a cis woman who only sleeps with and is interested in other cis women? Because that's not me, and that's not a lot of the people I know who identify as lesbians," I continued, the words tumbling out of me. "I identify as a dyke, but my husband is trans, and I'm interested in all queers who are not cis men, so maybe? that might make me less a lesbian and more like . . . an exceptual."

"A what?" Jess sipped her iced coffee calmly.

"An exceptual. It's a word I made up. I'm attracted to everyone *except* cis men, get it? An *exceptual*."

"That's hard to say."

"I know. It's not very good. I need a better word."

Jess understood what I meant, though. Her partner is also trans, and she'd also been going out for years in lesbian and queer spaces. She mentioned that she'd seen a resurgence of lesbian identity pride lately, both in queer spaces and online. While it had the potential to be exciting, she felt a bit cautious, because she was unsure about what it specifically meant. Who's a lesbian? What exactly does that mean? Is the resurgence of lesbian pride trans-exclusionary in any way? Because if so, we agreed, fuck that.

Hyper from caffeine and sugar and keyed up from our conversation, I got to my feet. I needed a bathroom. Lord, what would porta potties on a hot day in a crowded public park next to NYU be like?

"Oh!" Jess said. "No, there's a real bathroom, it's right by the dog park over there. They're really nice. Flushing toilets and everything."

She was right. I walked into a shady little stone hut of a bathroom and waited behind two others for a stall. An older woman who appeared to be experiencing homelessness was washing her hair in one of the sinks, fraying bags and a wheeled suitcase set at her feet. There was no hand soap in the park bathroom's dispensers, and the woman, bent forward in the sink, was offering her own personal soap, which she was using to wash her hair, to everyone who came over to wash their hands. After I came out of the stall, I went over to the open sink next to her. The woman offered me her soap. It was in a pink plastic bottle shaped like a unicorn. I pumped it once, thanked her, and felt like I might cry. She had offered to share what she had with all of us—me holding a nitrogen cold brew coffee and worrying about queer labels, and the shiny-haired teenager behind me carrying a Louis Vuitton purse that didn't look like a knockoff. I walked out the bathroom and into the sunshine with clean hands, ashamed of myself.

It was going to be our last night in New York. Davin and I were meeting Lola and her spouse, Jo, at Cubbyhole, so we went back to the West Village. We walked to Cubbyhole, but it was absolutely packed. There was a line snaking around the side of the bar. An unmoving line.

Spying some folded-up chairs leaning against the patio space, we opened them and sat down in a circle in the street, eyeing the bouncer warily. It was obvious we should not have been sitting there, and in a minute, a Cubbyhole staffer came out and politely asked us to move.

Lola looked at the line.

"I can't," she said.

I couldn't, either. I'd been to both Cubbyhole and Henrietta Hudson three times each in four days. No honest part of me had any enthusiasm left for mixed drinks or gaywatching or the rustle of cotton Wildfang jumpsuits swishing past me. I'd had my fill.

We walked to the piers on the Hudson River and sat down on a bench, looking at the lights. This was a special pier, apparently—Lola told me that the pier where we were sitting was featured heavily in *Paris Is Burning*. When I said I hadn't seen all of *Paris Is Burning* yet, just bits and pieces (I know! I'm sorry! I will watch it!), she gave me a profoundly disappointed look.

"You have to watch it."

"OK. I will."

"Krista."

Cubbyhole and Henrietta Hudson

"I will!"

We looked out at the water. We were surrounded, in New York, by queer history; we were *sitting* on it, even. There's just so much there.

I couldn't help but wonder: Would you ever get used to it, living in New York? Would it ever feel normal, having after-work drinks at Stonewall, offhandedly meeting Shane at Henrietta Hudson *L Word* watch parties? It probably would. There would probably come a time when you wouldn't even glance at Carrie Bradshaw's apartment as you walked by. You'd just be used to it all.

I was glad I wasn't used to it. Everything we'd done in New York had felt new, especially after not going anywhere for so long. I looked back at the city. One penthouse apartment, made entirely of windows, frenetically flashed different-colored lights inside. Someone was up there, partying, a view of the entire city spread beneath them.

My ass on queer history, my eyes on the neighborhood where modern queer history began, surrounded by my queer friends, I patted Davin's leg. It was time to go home.

And just like that, New York was done.

San Diego

Gossip Grill

• • •

"ere's your keys," the rental car kid chirped at me, dropping the fat plastic fob into my hand. "You go out these doors and around to the right, and then the spaces are numbered, you should be right there. Red Ford Mustang."

"Thanks!" I said. And then: "Wait. Ford Mustang?"

"Your car wasn't available," she said. "I upgraded you. Hope that's OK!"

She looked pleased with herself, like, *All in a day's work of surprising and delighting our customers!* This was probably her first job.

"Oh! OK," I said carefully. "Thank you."

She beamed at me. *Act normal*, I told myself. *A normal person would be thrilled.* A cool-car upgrade! In California! I crinkled up my eyes to make it look like I was smiling behind my mask and left the counter.

But I was deeply, deeply worried. If renting me a scooter is a liability, consider what it is to rent me a car. Let me be blunt: You shouldn't rent me a cool car. You shouldn't let me drive anything more expensive than the worst available compact car on the market (one Chevy Spark, please), because driving a nice car makes me nervous. And a nervous driver is a bad driver, according to my dad and also all of my combined life experience as someone with a license. If I get nervous, that's it for good driving decisions getting made. You wanna tailgate me in the middle lane for no reason? I *will* speed up for you out of fear, and that means I'll get slightly too close to the dump truck ahead of me, and that dump truck will shit a tiny rock in my direction and crack the windshield. And it will be my fault, because I of course know better than to get too close to a dump truck, but I made a nervous decision, and that's what happens. I once house-sat for two weeks for a rich person at his home outside LA, and he left me the keys to a brand-new Tesla, a vintage, mint-condition BMW, and a late-model Prius. He told me to use the cars whenever I wanted. It took me three days of eating the plain co-op pretzels I scrounged from his cupboards to even back the *Prius* out of the driveway to go to the store. This man lived three minutes from some of the most beautiful coastline in the country, and I felt *zero* percent tempted to go for a joyride. Can you imagine taking *someone else's new Tesla* for a sunset drive along Highway 1 to Malibu? Ha ha ha *i'm shitting bricks.*

In the rental garage, the Ford Mustang gleamed in its spot. Deep cherry red, low to the ground. A muscular car. It looked like it could growl.

I opened the driver's-side door, and an image of a galloping white mustang instantly projected onto the garage floor. I started laughing. Oh my god, a mustang made of light, projected from the door! This car was so expensive! This was such a bad idea!

"I ordered a Kia Soul," I whimpered, trying and failing to squeeze past the steering wheel. The whole thing was slung so low that my head touched the car's ceiling, ruffling my part and creating static every time I turned my head.

And so I set out into San Diego.

I was there to interview a plumbing company for work, but I was also going to squeeze in a lesbian bar visit that night. I had never been to San Diego before. What was funny was that in three weeks, I'd be back again to attend a big outdoor lesbian wedding. To go from never having set foot in San Diego to going twice in less than a month felt exciting, like I was really going to get to see the city.

I could already tell, just driving in from the airport, that San Diego was gorgeous. The water sparkled in the distance. It looked extra blue. Stucco mansions rose into the hills surrounding the highway. They looked extra luxurious. You never really hear about San Diego, do you? It has a zoo and beaches and perfect weather, and I feel like that's all anyone ever mentions. No one goes there to get famous like LA; it was never a gay-and-flower-child mecca like San Francisco. But people who move there never come back. Now I could see why. Already, San Diego felt like the city equivalent of a fun aunt wearing white shorts and a gold necklace with a flip-flop charm dangling between crepey cleavage. Like it was relaxed and sun-soaked and a good time and not that interested in being cool, because who cares?

San Diego looked great from a distance. It also looked impossible to really get to. Locked in my Mustang on a seven-lane highway with people in white SUVs whizzing past me at ninety miles an hour, I was four lanes away from the exit I needed and doing deep-breathing exercises to stay calm. Californians: What is going on with the traffic situation in San Diego? How can a highway have seven lanes?? How can *four* of them suddenly be exit-only, with no warning?

The car ahead of me braked sharply. I slammed on the brakes. My phone slid off the oiled-leather front seat and onto the floor, taking my directions with it.

"Fuck," I whispered.

"Using the right two lanes, take the exit, and get into the right lane to turn right on El Cajon Boulevard," Siri said, muffled but serene under the seat.

"I fucking *can't*."

"Turn right; then, turn right."

"Bitch! I can't!"

Several exits were missed on the way to my hotel. By the time I checked in, it was time to go meet my friends Michelle and Halli for dinner.

Michelle and Halli were engaged; it was their wedding I'd be coming back to attend three weeks later. Although I hadn't seen her in a couple of years, I'd known Michelle for nearly a decade—we met early into the six years I lived in Chicago. Michelle had always been the best possible person to find on a night out when you weren't in the mood to be out and what you really wanted was for someone to pat your back and nod sympathetically while you told her all about your problems. She was soothing and patient and a great listener. Halli I'd met only once; she moved to Chicago to be with Michelle right around the time I moved back to Minneapolis after breaking up with my ex. Now they both lived in San Diego, ostensibly because they enjoyed things like "sunlight" and "Wrigleyville not existing."

We were meeting at Gossip Grill, San Diego's only queer women's bar. Actually, it's the only queer women's bar in Southern California, which is shocking when you realize that this means *Los Angeles doesn't have one.* (The last lesbian bar in LA, the Palms, closed in 2013.) Gossip Grill opened in 2009, and its owner, Moe Girton, works hard to make it as inclusive as possible. (Take a shot if you're playing the drinking game!) I was looking forward to going. Gossip Grill had a great name, and I'd been told it was located in San Diego's gayborhood, Hillcrest. The pictures online looked good, and its website looked—of all things!—recently updated and professional. The bar had a full food menu and an active Instagram account. It even had a drink menu section called "Dry Hump" that featured nonalcoholic beverages with names like "Bean Flicker" (what a gross name) and "Like a Virgin Mary." Gossip Grill also seemed to have a lot of regular events. They had bingo nights and drag king and queen shows and themed brunches and something called "Finger Me Friday," which sounded like an invitation to date rape but was just a regular dance night with a DJ. I couldn't wait to see it.

I'd talked a bit with Moe Girton about Gossip Grill on the phone before I visited. GG wasn't her first experience with queer bars—she'd run a long-standing lesbian bar in San Diego called the Flame previously, and had turned a Mexican restaurant called Baja Betty's into a lesbian hangout.

Moby Dyke

"When people asked me to open my own lesbian bar," Moe remembered, "I said *no way*. This was thirteen years ago, but more and more, I was noticing that people were not identifying with the word 'lesbian' as much anymore, and with more folks coming out as gender nonconforming and queer and genderfluid, I thought 'lesbian' was too small of a box to put ourselves in. For Gossip Grill, we went with the umbrella of it being a 'women's bar.' Gossip Grill is for anyone, *anyone*, that identifies with a little bit of femininity. If you identify with any part of that, Gossip Grill is for you. We cater to everyone outside of cis gay men. There's two gay nightclubs right on this block if that's what you want!"

Some of the bartenders at Gossip Grill have been there since the bar's opening day. "Gossip has a heartbeat all its own," Moe said. "Employees move away; they come back. It's a living thing that holds you tight and wraps you up and gives you a shot!" She laughed. "When folks come out, they need to go somewhere they feel like they belong, somewhere they can be with like-minded people, somewhere they can be supported and feel welcomed. Gay bars don't offer the same belonging as a women's bar does. We're framily—that's a mix of friends and family—all of us—cis, trans, bi, all of us. It's really that sense of belonging that's so important for us to provide."

I was ready to see Gossip Grill. But Parking in Hillcrest is . . . forget it. I'd been in San Diego less than two hours, and I was already learning that parking anywhere in the city requires out-loud pep talks to yourself.

"I'm going to find one," I said aloud, twenty minutes late already and cruising slowly around the four square blocks nearest Gossip Grill. "I am. I am able to find a spot. I summon it."

It was dark, and the streets in Hillcrest were lined with promising-looking restaurants and bars, many strung with glimmer lights or displaying gay flags in the windows. There was a hotdog place called Daddy's Hot Dogs, which: Yes. This is the kind of name we like to see in a gay district.

A blue Mustang with black sporty stripes pulled up at the light next to me, windows down, blaring music. I glanced over. Shit. Shouldn't have looked. The driver was a guy in his twenties wearing a white backward baseball hat. He revved his engine. I ignored him. Then he *honked* (excuse me) and called, "Hey! Heyyyyy!" He revved his engine dramatically again, wanting our Mustangs to race as fraternal equine twins through the gayborhood. I stared straight ahead at the light, willing the seconds to tick down and the light to change. How dare this happen to me. In the *gay district*!

The light turned green. He peeled out.

I finally parked, lit a fire, whittled a walking stick, and hiked back through Hillcrest to Gossip Grill. The place a few doors down from GG was a gay bar, and it was packed—positively *packed*—with strapping young gay men, all looking fresh in their deep-V T-shirts and little airy short-sleeve button-downs. There were so many of them that a few were leaning, one-armed, off the patio rails, like hot sailors hanging off pirate ship ropes, chatting to the guys inside the bar. Two of them raised their beers and waved at me in a friendly way as I headed toward the Gossip Grill entrance. Based on that gesture alone, I decided I liked Hillcrest.

Walking into Gossip Grill is like walking into a jungle. Not like people are on the prowl; I mean the entrance is jungly, with big covered canopies above your head and leafy plants twining around the gates. Before you even get inside, it's private-feeling. A security guard on the patio checked my ID, but not my vaccination card—you didn't need it in San Diego, but you did in San Francisco, interesting—and waved me through. Huh. I'd thought each state had its own statewide Covid rules, but the rules changed from city to city. *Anyone in here could have it,* I thought, eyeing the people passing me on the way in. *You stay back.*

And: Wow. Gossip Grill is . . . Is this what a thriving lesbian bar looks like? Because Gossip Grill looks like it's *thriving*.

When you walk in, your eyes immediately go to a huge wall on the left covered in leaves, where a big neon sign that says WELCOME HOME BEAUTIFUL in pink cursive is nestled. The bar itself is mostly decorated in black, but—wait a minute, what's happening overhead? There are planets and twinkle lights and big striped umbrellas hanging above you, but *there isn't a ceiling.* I stopped dead a few feet inside Gossip Grill, staring upward, transfixed. This bar *didn't have a ceiling*?? What a fucking flex, San Diego. Can you imagine feeling confident enough that it would not rain or be cold, ever, to build a bar with *no ceiling*??? I feel almost hysterical, here. Patches of stars peeped between the umbrellas. Coming from Minnesota, this felt like unnecessary bragging. I shook my head angrily.

The bar was large and the word CUNT was written in glitter cursive above the bottles of alcohol. Every seat was taken by what looked—to my tired, dehydrated-from-the-plane eyes—like *L Word* lesbians. We're talking queers clearly coming from work, still in full suits and button-down shirts; full-on femmes; soft butches in cargo shorts; sporties with team jerseys—stereotypical, categorizable types of queers, all making a lot of noise and joking with a drag queen who was weaving her way through them. Drag bingo had apparently just ended, and the queen's wig was big and slightly windblown, like she'd really just been through something.

Michelle and Halli waved from a table in the back, set in front of a stage. Ahhh it was so good to see them! Well, actually, it was so good to see Michelle. If I'm being honest, I didn't recognize Halli, because at the party in Chicago where I'd met her five years ago, she'd been wearing a floppy khaki bucket hat low over her eyes, and I'd been so distracted by the hat and my questions surrounding the hat that nothing else had really registered.

The bucket hat was nowhere in sight this time. Halli was stunning, as in *How didn't I notice this last time* stunning, with cheekbones sharp enough shave your legs with and a thick, silvery streak in her brown hair. Michelle looked exactly like she always did, gorgeous, her black, curly hair tumbling, her matching-with-Halli cheekbones soaring cathedrals of bone structure. She leaned across the table, slipped her hands into mine, looked intently into my eyes, and it was like no time had passed at all.

Gossip Grill

Because Gossip Grill is a full restaurant along with being a dyke bar, we got dinner. I had an excellent Beyond Meat cheeseburger. This being Southern California, there were also multiple vegan and/or gluten-free options on the menu. This was all a shock to the system to me, a person who'd flown into San Diego directly from a town where I once asked for oat milk in my latte at the grocery-store Starbucks and the teenage barista said, "We're out of oat milk, but it's OK! It tastes better with real milk," and handed me my drink with a smile.

Halli and Michelle and I talked about their upcoming wedding. It was being held at a high-end resort on a private island in San Diego, which I hadn't realized and was surprised to hear. Their parents were paying for the whole thing, which I was also surprised to hear. I dragged a fry through my ketchup, suddenly quiet. Think about that sentence. Their parents were paying for the wedding. Together. Their mutual sets of parents were paying for this wedding, which meant they were in communication of some sort, even if it was just through their daughters, because this was the arrangement. To offer something like that, *both* sets of parents must know *both* Michelle and Halli and *also* strongly approve of their relationship.

Listening to Michelle and Halli talk excitedly about the wedding details, I got the same strange feeling I always get when I watch one of those YouTube videos where a young queer person films themself coming out to their parents, and it goes really well: I was so, so happy for them, and also filled with an indescribable longing. What must it be like, to feel that your parents accept and love who you are as an adult? To have always felt that? To have them offer their support and approval of your life in tangible ways?

I think it would shape you entirely. I came out to my parents when I was twenty-one, and our relationship was never the same after that. I grew up in a small, strict Mormon family, unshakably certain my parents loved me, unshakably sure we belonged to the one true church on earth. After I came out, something between my parents and me was fundamentally altered, our relationship like a broken bone that reset without a cast. It healed, sure, but in a way that made you careful with it, unable to trust it again, the way you move permanently changed.

Growing up, it was just my mom, dad, older sister Shelley, and me. We had plenty of Mormon community, though—there are Mormons everywhere, even in Green Bay, Wisconsin. And if you're unfamiliar with what it means be Mormon, let me explain right now: Mormons are Christians, but being raised an active Mormon is not like being raised in other, more common Christian denominations.

Mormonism is different. It's a total lifestyle; it's far closer to being in a cult than not-being in a cult. Now, Mormons do not appreciate having their religion compared to a cult, but, as an insider looking at it from the outside, it's honestly like an 8.2 on the cult-scale, with 1 being "getting baptized as an infant into a religion you later don't care about" and 10 being "wandering through the front doors of the Hollywood Scientology building and never being seen again." Mormonism is *right* up there.

When you're Mormon, you believe you were alive in heaven before you came to earth, and that you chose your family before you were born. You call all adults "Sister" and "Brother" (so I would be "Sister Burton" to you), believe in getting baptized by proxy for dead people, and believe that one day, if you are extremely good, you will get to run your own planet. You get a large, built-in community that cares about you, but one of the trade-offs is that you accept that men have all the power in the church and in life and that women have none and also that this is God's will. You don't drink, smoke, swear, fuck outside of marriage, take the Lord's name in vain, drink caffeine, watch R-rated movies, or spend money on Sundays. Church is three hours long.* Your absence is noted.

Mormon adults have astonishingly time-consuming, nonpaying jobs called "callings" within their own congregations, meaning they work for

---

* Church is now only two hours long, but it was three when I was going.

the church for free during their spare time. Additionally, everyone—
everyone—gives 10 percent of what they make at their real, paid jobs to
the church. This is known as "tithing." There are no exceptions to the
rule of paying tithing, whether you're seven years old and get a dollar for
picking up sticks in the yard (put a dime in your tithing jar!), or you're
fifty-six and work two minimum-wage jobs and can't afford enough food
for your family. In 2019 and 2020, several major news outlets reported
that the Mormon church had allegedly amassed more than $100 billion
in assets, all through members' tithing contributions. These funds were
supposed to be used for charity, but, um, they weren't. That's interesting,
because according to church doctrine, you are supposed to pay your
tithing before you pay for food, water, electricity, or medicine. You are
encouraged to go hungry before you skip tithing. I once sat in the living room while a church elder encouraged my dad to "obey the spirit of
the law and not the letter" by paying 10 percent on his *gross*—not net—
salary. I knew we could not afford this, but I watched my dad look down
at his hands, loosely linked in his lap, considering the idea.

That's because as a Mormon, you're either 100 percent in or you're
out, and my family was 100 percent in. You have to be. Mormons believe
that their church president is a living prophet on this earth. To disbelieve
one teaching—to not follow one small rule, such as "don't swear"—is
to show that you don't have total faith in the teachings of the prophet,
and if you don't believe and follow the teachings of the prophet, *who literally talks to God every day*, you can't be Mormon. (The living prophet,
btw, is always an exceptionally old white man without facial hair who
knows for a fact that God is *pissed* about you doing hand stuff with your
boyfriend.) Once every eight to ten years, the prophet dies, and another
very old white man takes his place. They are impossible to tell apart. Seriously, Google image search "all the Mormon prophets" sometime and
see if you don't have to lean in closer to the screen.

This is how I was raised. Mormons are ultraconservative Christians
who believe marriage is between a man and a woman, period. Church

leadership has, in recent years, announced that as a Mormon, you *can* be gay, or "experience same-sex attraction," *so long as you remain celibate for life*. Hooray.

Enter moi, a tiny faggette. I didn't know what a lesbian was until I was fourteen, and even then, my friend Sarah, who everyone said was a dyke, had to break it down for me twice. I remember laughing in her room about it—ew, so *weird*!—and then thinking about it in bed that night. I knew it was wrong—I mean, I was a teenage solider in the army of the Lord!—but lesbianism sounded reasonable, if I was being honest with myself. Why *wouldn't* you think girls were beautiful? Why *wouldn't* you rather kiss a girl, instead of a boy who tasted like Gardetto's and had a tongue like a flopping fish? Wouldn't everyone?

By age fifteen, I *did* really enjoy looking at my classmate Cari's elfin, freckled face for extended periods of time during choir, but that didn't mean anything to me. By age seventeen, though, I'd met a girl, Fiona, who went to school on the other side of town, and: Wow. We began hanging out all the time. All the time. Fiona was beautiful. Fiona had dirty-blond hair that fell past her ass. She was wealthier, cooler, better traveled, and more mature than me. She lived in a big house on the bay. She was into Stanley Kubrick movies. She smoked cloves and got me to play with a Ouija board, which I had been taught was one of Satan's portals into this realm, but which didn't seem to faze her.

Fiona's parents were rarely home. I would primp for hours before going over to her house. (For some reason, it was important to me that Fiona thought I was pretty.) It never occurred to me that I had a gay-ass crush on her. Even though we were taking showers together in her parents' massive, multijet shower. Even though we were kissing. Even though we were sleeping in the same bed together during sleepovers, Fiona just in her underwear and me unable to sleep because I was dying, *dying* to touch her.

Nope, still not gay. We were just two people who were in love, we told each other, but we were not lesbians. Absolutely not. We just wanted to be together. This was pure; the world couldn't possibly understand.

We both went to different colleges, and that was it. Fiona was probably a one-off, I decided.

At eighteen, as a new college freshman at the University of Minnesota, I began going to the Mormon Singles' Ward on campus. The Singles' Ward is a branch of the Mormon church that only young single adults can attend as members. It's so everyone can get married off more efficiently. I hated going. I'd begun having questions about the church; I'd also begun digesting tiny amounts of feminism from my friends. *How am I supposed to learn about the world?* I'd ask myself during church services on campus, sitting on a metal folding chair surrounded by women wearing floor-length corduroy skirts. *All of these people live in a bubble.* Singing along to hymns I knew by heart, I could already see my future laid out for me: If I kept going to the Singles' Ward, I'd be married by twenty-two. I'd have six kids before I was thirty. This was not what I wanted.

I stopped going to church. It was a calm and peaceful decision—one Sunday morning in October, I just didn't go. I never went back. I didn't feel conflicted about it; I felt great about my choice. And it took me a couple of years, but I started dating women. I told my friends I was a lesbian when I was twenty, once I was sure. It was fine.

It was not fine when I came out to my parents. My dad could hardly look at me. He wouldn't discuss my "life choices"; he just quietly removed himself from real conversations with me. My mom was . . . it was much worse. She nodded when I told her, and then went silent. She didn't speak to me for months. Then we entered a yearslong period where she'd send me really awful handwritten letters, or call me to "catch up" and then spend thirty minutes sobbing and bearing her testimony of the gospel at me. Once, on a visit home, I mentioned in the car that a friend of mine had been in an abusive relationship and had just gotten out of it.

Mom's hands tightened on the wheel. Eyes on the road, speaking slowly and distinctly, she said, "Kris."

"Yeah?"

"I want you to know that I would rather you be with a man who beats you than with a woman."

I looked at her. She stared straight ahead.

Even now, just writing this—you have to understand: This was the woman who sewed every item of clothing I wore until I was thirteen, bent over the light of her sewing machine late at night in our chilly basement, hurrying because the *dance was tomorrow* and my dress wasn't ready. When she made apple pies, she'd save the dough scraps and roll them in cinnamon and sugar, baking them for me so they'd be warm after school. She stood up, alone, in the audience of my middle school talent show when I froze onstage, doing the dance moves for me and mouthing the words I'd forgotten. My mother *loved* me. She did. I knew it the way I knew how to breathe.

That was my last casual visit home for a very long time.

I TURNED BACK TO MICHELLE and Halli.

"So, what are you both wearing?" I asked in my best Jonathan Van Ness voice, changing the subject and also betting myself a drink called the "Camel Toe Mojito" that this wedding was going to be a double-dress situation.

"Is this a glamorous white pantsuit occasion?" I continued. "Is one of you in a suit and one in a dress?"

"We're both wearing dresses, but don't tell anyone," Michelle said. "We want it to be a surprise."

Our server stopped by. I ordered my drink.

When I glanced back up at Michelle and Halli, I saw that two new people had arrived and were being seated at a nearby high-top. One of them was talking loudly and with much hand movement to the other, a queer who was wearing a black, snap-crotch, leotard-style bodysuit with ultra-high-cut leg openings and black ankle booties and . . . that was it. As casually as if it was a full outfit. This person was lounging in their chair, legs akimbo, acting fully like someone wearing pants, just talking and laughing with their friend, but they were wearing *no* pants. And (from the looks of it) no underwear. Just a snap-crotch leotard bodysuit and *no other articles of clothing* worn out to dinner. This was a Tuesday night. I was fascinated. Forget giving me the confidence of a mediocre white man—I'll have what that person's having.

Michelle and Halli walked me back to the Mustang and we took turns posing for pictures on it. I showed them the door that projected a horse made of light onto the ground when you opened it.

"I can't believe this car," Michelle said, staring at the horse, wonder in her voice.

"I can't believe you're getting married in three weeks."

"I *know*!"

THREE WEEKS LATER, DAVIN AND I were back in San Diego in October, renting a cute-but-slowly-being-reclaimed-into-the-earth Airbnb with a group of our friends from Chicago. None of us could afford to stay at the resort itself, which looked just like the resort in season 1 of *White Lotus*. At the wedding, Michelle and Halli looked so beautiful, so like two people meant to be together, that every eye in the private little cove of a garden where they were being married was leaking. A waiter had passed out flutes of champagne before everyone sat down, and I'd already had two, so that didn't help, but: To be married to your obvious soulmate! To have the ceremony be performed by your hilarious gay brother! To have parents beaming with pride! Our little queer row of chairs in the garden was filled with snuffles and honks, the femmes riffling through their purses to hand out tissues no one else had thought to bring. It was a perfect day, and it would be a perfect evening, with dinner (seated at a table with only people I knew well and loved and didn't have to make polite small talk with) and dancing (eventually, drunk, to Prince's "Kiss" and, drunker, to Shania's "Whose Bed Have Your Boots Been Under?").

The next day was Saturday, and those of us staying at crumbling Airbnbs with warped, unsettlingly spongy bathroom floors woke up at eleven and sneaked back into the resort to go laze by one of the many pools. It was early, and people were hungover, but I began my campaign. Tonight was the night; Michelle and Halli had already given me their blessing for the evening's activities. "We're going to the dyke bar tonight," I announced, dog-paddling up to my friends and looking at each of them intently. "You're coming?"

"Oh my god. *Yes*," EmJ said from the shallow end. "*We know about the bar*. We're coming."

"OK, because I know Michelle and Halli are having a bonfire on the beach, but it's mostly for their family and it's gonna go late, and they're the ones who told me we should go to the bar. They might come for a bit, too."

"Krikka," EmJ said, invoking my peculiar-to-Chicago-friends nickname. "We want to go."

"OK. You don't have to, though."

"Oh my god."

At nine p.m., the six of us sharing the Airbnb were fighting over the mirrors in the bathroom, getting ready to go out to Gossip Grill under the hum of fluorescent bulbs. RELAX, commanded a HomeGoods wooden sign next to the toilet. FLIP-FLOPS REQUIRED barked another in curly cursive.

I was neither relaxed nor casual. My outfit was notably slutty—a $9.99 Fashion Nova dress, black and don't-sit-down'tight, with a V-shape cut down to the navel and crisscrosses across the tits where the fabric should've been. We were going out, and it was because of me! Had I ever been in charge of organizing a night out in my *life*? I didn't think I had; I'd always just showed up to other people's events.

Gossip Grill

We crammed ourselves into an Uber, those of us wearing makeup regretting our choice to apply lipstick before we put our face masks on.

The last time I'd been there, on a weekday night three weeks earlier, Gossip Grill had been lightly bustling. Now it was ten p.m. on a Saturday night, and it was balls-out slammed, people spilling out onto the sidewalk, spreading down the street like an encroaching puddle of queerness, a stressed-looking security guard checking our IDs and waving us through, the line around the bar impossible to distinguish from the rest of the crowd. Perched on the stage in the back, a DJ was lost in their thumping gay-boy house music, waving sinuous arms to the dreamy part of a song just before the beat drops. There were queers packed into every inch of the bar, adorable boi-types in snapbacks and basketball jerseys who thought they looked tough; high femmes in see-through black mesh and matte fuchsia lipstick; gray-haired dykes in sweatshirts; a statuesque person walking around in all black with massive platforms and a single dangling pearl earring; clusters of babyqueers knotted together in a little seating area with fake grass and a swing I hadn't noticed before. It was mayhem.

"Hiiiiiiii!" Standing in the middle of the bar, taking up a large amount of real estate, drinking and giggling, were my friends—every queer who'd been at Michelle and Halli's wedding the day before. They'd all come. All of them. I teared up immediately. I hadn't seen all of those homos in one room together in six or seven or maybe even eight years—not since the days of messy dance nights at FKA and Slo 'Mo and Beauty Bar in Chicago, when all of our ties to each other were looser, all of us were freer, and all of our lives and futures were open-ended questions.

Looking at them, and at the crowd at large, I could feel that I was severely overdressed. Some things never change, no matter how much time has passed.

"Let's get you a drink!" my friend Claire said, batting my hands away as I reached for my wallet. "Did you see the security guards' shirts?" She pointed as a butch-looking security guard brushed past, on their way to untangle some queers who were yelling at the front of the bar. The guard's shirt said PLAYGROUND MONITOR on the back.

I pulled out my notebook, trying to record it all, everything I was seeing, standing up and pressing it against a wooden column to write. I needed one of those space pens! This was never gonna work! I hadn't yet been to a bar that was so crowded there was nowhere to sit, and while I loved it and was delighted, I couldn't believe I hadn't thought about what I would do if I physically couldn't write while at the bars.

Thomas, my beautiful, bearded, favorite gay man on earth, sidled up next to me. "If Boystown had a lesbian bar, this would be it," he said, gesturing with his drink to a queer trying to climb into another's lap on the swing.

He was right; I suddenly saw it. Boystown hadn't been that much of a hangout for me in Chicago. It was literally a boys' town, clearly not where the lesbians were, a neighborhood full of moneyed clubs where, if you were not physically knocked down by a horde of shirtless, waxed Ken dolls, you needed to resign yourself to the fact that you had no chance of getting a drink, unless you got a gay man to get it for you. Gossip Grill had that same Boystowny feeling—like it was a bar that was taking in a lot of money, and its patrons, who were also doing well, were out to *party*, and you didn't know what was going to happen—only that everyone at the bar felt like they were in *exactly* the right place.

The DJ was going hard, and people were still coming in. I could see, judging by the serious, focused faces of the bartenders up front, that this was it—they were in the zone, hardly speaking to one another or customers, just turning, pointing at the next person, cocking their ear to hear the order, and nodding, whirling around to get the whiskey ginger, vodka cran, and three shots of Patrón.

I looked over at Ashley and Lauren, always first to dance, cracking themselves up while shout-singing the words to Crystal Waters's "100% Pure Love."

"I love research!" Lauren yelled at me from where she was. "Let's do more research for books!"

Ashley beckoned me over.

"I just want to discuss something," she said, pulling me in closer. "Why is it—and I'm not saying this is always the case, but I'm saying it often is—why is it that, in any queer couple where one is more femme than the other, the femme is the tall one? Why?"

She pointed to herself and Lauren. She pointed at me. She pointed at a couple that had just walked in the door. I laughed. I used to feel like the tallest person in Chicago when we'd all go out; I remembered looking around one night at Beauty Bar and realizing I could see the top of every person's head within view. I'm not even that tall. Ashley had a point.

Stephen came over. "Are you looking for quotes for your book?" they asked. "Because I just started my period, and I *love* the bathroom."

"Thank you, Stephen."

"You're welcome."

A sudden deep thump of dance music sounded from the room off the back of Gossip Grill. Davin and I poked our heads around the wall and saw the dance floor filling up, a different DJ bobbing their head, another bartender newly in position at a smaller bar, fighting off a building mob. Thick clouds of fog belched down to the floor, illuminated by flashing red and green and pink and blue lights. Two goth kids in black lipstick were grinding slowly against each other, paying zero attention to the beat, and the members of a bachelorette party danced with one another in a circle, the bride-to-be in a shiny red vinyl jumpsuit, wearing a sash that said THE QUEEN. The bridal attendants' outfits included someone in a schoolgirl getup with a plaid skirt and tied-up white shirt, a flight attendant, and a bikini top ensemble, complete with a stuffed snake. This was a Britney-themed bachelorette. Every Britney in the group was drunk, holding hands and shouting along to Whitney Houston's "I Wanna Dance with Somebody." Off on the sidelines, an older white dude in a khaki jacket was watching them. If you've never been to a lesbian bar on a busy night, please know that there is never *not* a creepy older white dude lurking around the fringes, watching.

It was late. Back in the main bar, our friends were starting to close out their tabs. We all had a wedding bonfire at an tremendously expensive resort to catch the last few minutes of. Ubers were summoned. People hugged. I looked at my friends, all suddenly, miraculously in the same space again after years and years and a pandemic apart, and realized I had no idea when we'd all be together like this again.

It's funny how you take it all for granted—when you're really very young, and have no idea you're so young, and you live in the same city as your friends, and you go out together all the time, and nobody is married, and no one has kids or a job they care about, and everyone rents a shitty apartment.

Looking around Gossip Grill, at the flocks of young queers who lived in San Diego and who were likely having exactly that kind of a time in their lives right now, I suddenly understood something. The lesbian and queer women's bars I was visiting—whether they were dives or slick clubs—were just spaces.

What made them important was the people inside them.

Milwaukee

Walker's Pint

◆ ◆ ◆

Did you ever house-sit for someone who left you a list of instructions so long you muttered "jesus" under your breath and stopped reading after the first page?

Davin and I are those people now. We're your gay mom and dad. Welcome to staying at our house! You're gonna love it. Here are four (!!) double-sided pages of notes, and you need to read all of them, because otherwise how will you know about how to take care of the garbage and the recycling and the compost and our ancient, grumpy pet rabbit and the two dogs—one of whom needs medication and guess what, he hates it, good luck—and when to water all the plants, and where you should order food from in our small town and where you should absolutely not, under any circumstances, order food from? How will you know, say, what will happen, when using the oven, if you press the button on the stove that says Off but forget to *also* hit the button that says Bake, even though that makes no sense? (Hint: the house will fill with gas and explode!)

It didn't used to be like this when we were younger. We used to just throw the dog in the car, lock the door, and leave, randomly texting our friends pictures of palm trees two days later with the words lol i'm in miami. Now, as Davin and I prepared to leave on a twelve-day lesbian bar road trip through the Midwest, we needed to line up two different house sitters, clean the house so it wouldn't be disgusting for the house sitters, change the sheets, hide any sex shit lying around, get cash out for the house sitter who doesn't use Venmo, text our neighbors about spare house keys, do a final load of laundry, pack the cooler for the car, and go around putting little explanatory pieces of masking tape on the remote controls, because they all do different things and they all look exactly the same.

When did this happen? When did I become someone who writes sentences like "If you need anything, Rachel lives across the street, and she's very nice—don't be afraid to text! :)"

It all happened so fast. One minute, I was having sex on bare mattresses with strangers from the internet, and the next, I was writing a note explaining that you can't *water* the orchid, it likes a single ice cube once a week on alternating sides.

WITHOUT ASKING, I KNEW WE were in Wisconsin when we passed a Fleet Farm. Fleet Farm, in case you don't know, is a big-box store that's like a cross between a hardware store, a Target, and an Auto Zone, if that store also sold fishing licenses, horse feed, Carhartt's entire coverall line, cheap gas, off-brand candy, and guns. There are Fleet Farms in Minnesota, where I live now, but Fleet Farm total market saturation occurs only in Wisconsin, where I grew up.

I bring this up because seeing a Fleet Farm along the highway is like catching a glimpse of my childhood home—it's that familiar. Dads—all dads, I'm talking *ALL DADS*—in Wisconsin are obsessed with Fleet Farm, and I spent every Saturday of my childhood inside one, waiting for *my* dad, who is not even slightly handy, to be finished standing in the farm supplies aisle, hands on hips, a discerning frown of concentration on his face as he mentally decided between brands of barn fans for a farm he did not own. We were always supposed to be picking up water softener salt, but we could easily be there for two or three hours. I had a whole life inside Fleet Farm, man. You could wander the aisles at will, bumping into all your friends from school, who were there with *their* dads, and form a feral pack, playing hide-and-seek underneath the round racks of women's camouflage hunting jackets, hands and faces sticky with flecks of circus peanuts obtained under hazy circumstances.

Wisconsin just *feels* different to me. Maybe that's how it works for everyone's home state, but there's something about Wisconsin I understand without trying—a feeling that comes from seeing the rolling green landscapes, the barn-stamped license plates, and the outdated fast-food chains (Rocky Rococo???) flashing past that my eyes grew up seeing. In Wisconsin, the radio plays local used car–lot ads narrated by the wives of the car-lot owners, and their accents are so pronounced (*no-uh* for "no"; *baygh* for "bag") that it's hard for me to believe I once didn't hear the accent at all.

When Milwaukee rose into view, I realized I'd forgotten, once again, how big Milwaukee is. There's a whole big city in Wisconsin, y'all! And it looks a lot like a mini-Chicago! We're talking the same kind of shoreline-along–Lake Michigan drives, the same mix of teeny grandma-style bungalows and three-story houses repurposed into apartments, and the same dedication to ensuring every neighborhood has a bar on every corner called the Y-Not Bar or Ollie's.

One of my childhood best friends, Sarah—the one everyone in high school said was a dyke—had offered to let me and Davin stay with her at her apartment. She wasn't home when we arrived, but she'd left us a key. Sarah had just moved to Milwaukee, and her place was small and stunning—high-ceilinged, filled with books and sunlight and little elegant tchotchkes. The whole apartment was so offhandedly chic that I immediately began poking around, touching everything, trying to understand how someone who grew up precisely where I did could have ended up so refined. I even opened up the built-in cabinet by her bathroom, and all the drawers underneath it, just to see if Sarah was a secret slob like me. Horrifying. It was completely organized. All her extra washcloths were folded; her earrings and backup candles and soaps stood in rows, looking like a store display. I shut the cabinet door. Some people actually live like the smug, smiling women in *Dwell* magazine. I don't think I needed to know that.

What Davin and I wanted was a nap, but the midwestern lesbian bar road trip was on a tight schedule. There was no time for, say, sprawling spread-eagled on an inflatable mattress in Sarah's living room in a battered gray men's onesie, eating tortilla chips and questionably bright green guac from the store around the corner.

"We have to go," Davin said. He was fully dressed, standing over me as I lay on the mattress.

"I'm almost ready." I ate another chip, gazing at the ceiling.

"I don't want to get home super late." Davin sounded tired. He's usually the one who wants to stay out late when we go anywhere, but he had driven the entire way from Northfield, six hours at the wheel. I'd fallen asleep around hour three.

"We won't. All I have to do is put clothes on."

Forty-five minutes later, we left for Walker's Pint.

Walker's Pint is the oldest and only lesbian bar in Milwaukee. It occupies the bottom floor of a green-painted, two-story building that was built in 1885. Set in a busy neighborhood called Walker's Point (ohhh), the bar, which opened in the summer of 2001, has lots of interesting neighbors—there's a "gentleman's club" behind the bar and a gay bar with blacked-out windows across the street. It's called Fluid, which is maybe? the grossest name for a gay bar I've ever encountered, and I've heard of gay bars called Manhole, Ramrod, and the White Swallow. Fluid takes the cake. Wow, there were gay bars everywhere, I realized, turning around to crane my neck. There was LVL Bistro, DIX (ha!), and LaCage NiteClub, all within walking distance.

And that's what people seem to do. It was a Saturday night, and a lot of the people who were at Walker's Pint seemed to be walking to each of the bars in turn, ordering a drink or shot, hanging out for a bit, and then heading to another one. This meant a constant influx of new faces. The parade of queers was so distracting that I forgot to even take notes for the first hour Davin and I were there.

Early 2000s jams thudded across the room—Missy Elliott's "Lose Control," Britney's "Toxic"—queued up by a DJ on a small stage tucked into the front of the bar. No one was dancing. Nearly everyone stood up in tight clusters, a beer in one hand, gossiping earnestly into each other's ears. Gay men dominated the front of the bar. They stood near the door, wreathed in cold air from outside, and left their black leather jackets on. They were ready to drink on the move, pointing and miming their orders to the bartender, who just nodded, disappearing under the bar and then suddenly reappearing with a chilled harvest of Miller Lite and Jäger shots to dole out.

Past the gay men, the bar was crowded. Many, many sporties were present, standing around in packs, which is how sporties roll. They're almost never alone; it's because they've spent their entire lives on softball or soccer or rugby teams. I was happy to see several LHBs, long-hair butches, sitting at high-tops off to the side and looking cute. As I walked through Walker's Pint, checking out the bar and smiling inanely at all the queers, their eyes flickered over me for a second. Then I felt their glances slide right off me, as if I didn't exist, or they couldn't see me anymore, the *exact* same way I look at dudes in public for a second and then immediately can't remember their faces. If the patrons at Walker's Pint noticed me at all, my guess is they likely perceived me as straight.

I'm used to it. It happens a lot. A *lot*. The way I look has historically been an issue for me, gaywise. The crux of the issue is this: I don't dress "queer enough" for my own people to recognize me as one of them—meaning I don't wear any of the classic queer markers. I don't have "queer-looking" (aka short, creatively styled, or colorful) hair. I don't have any tattoos or visible piercings. I don't even own pants. Like, not a single pair of pants. I pretty much dress like a slutty third-grade teacher, almost all of the time, and it doesn't help me at dyke bars at *all*. That night, for instance, I was dressed in a tight black dress with a fuzzy pastel pink cardigan, huge earrings, and high-heeled leather boots, and when you are in a divey dyke bar in Wisconsin, that's just not going to read as "big gay lesbian" to other people. It's too bad, really. The idea that there's only one way to look queer is ridiculous.

Not being recognized or acknowledged by other queers as queer because you're femme is something called "femme invisibility" or "femme erasure"—a problem in the community that stems from misogyny. Queers, particularly lesbians, have traditionally celebrated masculine or androgynous qualities among themselves, associating those traits with strength and dominance. Femmes, who often look more traditionally feminine, are not recognized or celebrated in the same way as masc-presenting queers. Femmes are typically seen as softer, weaker. They "pass" for straight in heterosexual society. So that leaves many of us in an outdated mode of thinking we can tell if a person is queer by how they look and dress. The unspoken assumption is: If you look masc, you're obviously queer. If you don't, you are suspect. (Never mind that gaydar is entirely about reading other people's energy.) Eh. I don't really know what to do about it, but I do know I look completely not-right in jeans, which are also so uncomfortable! Why does anyone enjoy having a stiff waistband squeezing one of the softest areas of their body? I DO NOT GET IT, STRETCHY DRESSES 4EVER.

The ceiling at Walker's Pint was strung with multicolored Christmas lights, which gave the bar a cozy, friendly feeling. It was nice, and it was also troubling—I'd only been to a few bars so far, and already, the way they looked inside was starting to blend together. Had I been to a dyke bar yet that did *not* have twinkly lights? Hmm. Behind the bar, there was a row of small metal fridges, each completely covered with stickers from businesses with dirty slogans. EAT IT RAW at Half Shell Raw Bar in Key West; IF IT SMELLS LIKE FISH EAT IT at Don's Seafood Restaurant in Virginia. Glass doors led to a big patio outside, which I was not about to check out, as it was late November and snow-raining. Patio season closes midautumn in the Midwest; you can't drink outside year-round, like you can at Wild Side West.

There was a room in the back of Walker's Pint for darts. The dartboards, I noticed, were both continuously in action and interestingly placed directly in the path of the still-gendered men's and women's bathrooms. If you needed to pee, which I did, you had to walk into an active game of darts with your hands up, making eye contact with all the players, particularly the one poised to throw a lethal-looking dart with their eye closed and tongue poking out, before proceeding. The players stopped their game to let me through. They stopped again when I came back from the bathroom. Both times, everyone playing darts apologized to me. One of them, holding a dart aloft, even said, "Ope, sorry about that, I don't wanna getcha," as I passed by. Like a caricature of how midwesterners talk.

Safe, I settled back into my seat at the bar. Davin went off to look around and came back flushed, reporting that he'd bumped into a sporty queer and said, "Sorry," and they'd said, "You better be."

"It was a little aggro," he said. He guessed it was because the sporty queer thought he was a cis man, but couldn't be sure. There were plenty of gay men at the bar. Maybe the sporty was just looking for a fight.

I was distracted; I'd just seen a pack of older queers grouped around their bill, which was set out on the bar top. Their bill had a generous number of drinks on it; we're talking at least fifteen to twenty line items; and the bill—I did a double take, just to be sure—was eighty dollars. Eighty dollars! For something like twenty drinks! Big-city people who enjoy alcohol: Have you ever considered vacationing in Wisconsin? One of the queers grabbed the bill to look at it and grandly announced, "I'm tipping twenty dollars!" and two others in the group went, "Wooooo OK!!" like the crowd on an episode of *Maury*.

When the bill was signed, the group started breaking up, shrugging into jackets.

"Thank you, ladies!" the bartender called at their backs, and out they went into the night, clapping each other on the shoulders and rubbing their hands together.

I turned to Davin. "Did you see that?"

"What?"

"How long has it been since you heard someone address a whole group of queers as 'ladies' and have that be fine?"

He thought for a moment. "Ages."

"I feel like that might get you killed in a different dyke bar?"

Davin laughed. "Maybe they all know the bartender. Or they just don't care."

We relaxed into our stools, Saturday night at Walker's Pint swirling around us. One of the TV screens was silently playing QVC with closed captioning, I noted with satisfaction. I love QVC. There's something hypnotic about watching someone with wet-looking french tips stroking a chunky, overpriced, gold-plated bracelet for fifteen minutes while desperately trying to think up new things to say about it beyond "This is a bracelet." It's so soothing. I turn QVC on when I go to hotels alone and drift off to sleep with it playing. *I like this bar*, I thought, twirling the straw in my drink and falling into a stupor as a new host came onscreen and began urging me to sink $400 into a payment plan for a tanzanite pendant. *QVC's always telling me how rare tanzanite is, but they've been consistently selling it for as long as I've been alive. How rare could it be?*

Davin poked me. "You need to talk to people."

Crap. Right. I was not just a regular lesbian bar patron having a night out. I was working! I needed to be interviewing people, chatting, talking about the bar with people who went there all the time.

But I was really, *really* struggling to do it. At the last few bars, approaching strangers had been nerve-racking, as I'd predicted it would be. And because I'd already been to a couple of bars, I was aware of added social nuances I hadn't originally thought about. I now knew I felt super rude interrupting groups of people who were in the middle of having a fun night out. And—I glanced down at my outfit, cursing my inability to fit in, stylewise—I also knew it was unlikely that queers at bars would immediately perceive me as one of *them*.

I looked around. Everyone was in a tight knot of friends. It was intimidating.

"I'm trying to decide who to talk to," I stalled.

Davin smiled at me, sympathetic. He is also very used to being perceived as an outsider in queer spaces.

"You should put in the book how you maybe understand how an anthropologist feels in a foreign land, except you're not in a foreign land; everyone else *thinks* you are," he said.

I smiled weakly. I was psyching myself out, and I knew it. I really liked Walker's Pint, but I was five bars into visiting all the lesbian bars in America, and I was already getting a little wary. In the bars I'd been to so far, most queers were friendly and didn't mind being approached, but some had been lightly or openly hostile to me, a strange person who they likely perceived as straight, coming up to them in one of the only spaces they could call their own. Which I absolutely get!! It's just that: I'm also gay, and sometimes this shit hurts my feelings.

I looked around, worried. I just didn't feel tough enough for it that night. Could I *have* an off night? When I'd traveled here specifically to have an on night?

A butch in an blaze-orange sweatshirt spluttered loudly near me.

"What is this, rubbing alcohol?" they asked their friend, a middle-aged man with a glinting gold earring, handing a small glass back to him. "How can you drink this?"

"It's good!" he said, and tossed the entire glass back, neatly.

"I'm getting the shots next time."

"Yes, you are, hun."

The butch squeezed past, heading back to the bar. "Sorry," they said, hands up, trying not to touch me.

Now. Say something to them now.

I didn't.

"Let's go," I said to Davin, upset with myself. "I'll be better at this tomorrow."

THE NEXT DAY WAS SUNDAY, and a Sunday in winter in Wisconsin means one thing: a Packers game. Growing up in Green Bay, I would sometimes go to the home of Andy Reid (this is sports name-dropping; I am so sorry), the then–assistant offensive coach for the Packers and the now–head coach of the Kansas City Chiefs, to attend my Mormon Youth Fireside evenings. Picture me, sitting cross-legged and wide-eyed with other youths while one of our teachers paced in front of us in the living room, telling us in vivid detail how the world was going to end. (There's going to be a final great war and the moon will turn to blood. Any day now. Don't worry about it.) I knew Brother Reid worked for the Packers, and other kids seemed excited about that, but I don't have words to express how little I cared about the Packers then. Or now. Or about football, in general.

That is . . . that is not the case for Davin. A year into dating, I offhandedly mentioned Brother Reid to him, and Davin moaned in a way I can only describe as "orgasmic." I still can't believe it, but I fell in love with someone who loves football in general and the Packers specifically, and while I believe that this is illegal!!!! behavior for a homosexual, I'm willing to accept it, because Davin sometimes makes huge piles of nachos on our largest cookie sheet during Packers games. I live to sneakily fish out the most heavily loaded tortilla chips in the pile while he's bellowing at the TV about third downs or Hail Marys or some shit.

It was the middle of the afternoon, and Sarah, Davin, and I were going back to Walker's Pint to watch a Packers vs. Seahawks game. Davin was very, very excited.

"I can't believe it," he said, breathless as we walked to the entrance. "A Packers game! In Wisconsin! In a lesbian bar!"

Inside, Walker's Pint was busy, but nothing like it had been the night before. All the bar's TVs were turned to the game, and the atmosphere was reverent, every pair of eyes following the replay of some kind of homoerotic pileup. Almost everyone was dressed in Packers gear. Davin, his eyes glowing, took in the scene, ecstatic.

"See, this is what I mean," he whispered, heading to the bar to get us beers. "Here, you get to be gay, *and* you get to like football. That's such a rare combination!"

The bartender, who was wearing a Packers jersey, grinned at him, and I suddenly remembered Crew, the gay sports bar in Chicago, and Game, the gay sports bar in Minneapolis, and how much Davin had loved them, and how both of them had closed.

"Look how happy he is," I whispered to Sarah. She nodded, incapable of looking anywhere but at the French bulldog dressed in a tiny Packers jersey being passed around the bar. People were losing their *shit* over him.

The Packers scored. The whole bar roared in unison. A different bartender yelled, "Packer shots!" and began walking around with a tray of viscous neon green mini shots in small plastic cups. They were free, and people around us knocked them back with glee.

"I made 'em good for ya," the bartender said, winking at us and passing the tray.

"Ooh. What's in these?" Sarah asked carefully.

"Something good!"

We took the mini shots, equal parts cautious and grateful. I had never seen a potable liquid that color or consistency before, and I am pleased to report that Packer shots at Walker's Pint taste like liquid lemon drops.

I don't know if it was because of the game or the clientele or the free alcohol that kept appearing (the Packers were winning), but it felt much easier to approach people than it had the night before.

At the table in front of us, two twentysomething white queers named Mel and Peyton were dressed in Packers gear and having a great time, giggling over their shots and yelling at the TV. They told me, when I asked, that they both identified as "stems," which meant stud/femme, an identity label I keep seeing young white lesbians on TikTok using. It's kind of a trendy identifier right now, and that's weird, since most of these "stems" don't seem to be aware that "stud" is a Black queer identity that white queers aren't typically welcome to use, and "stem" also falls under that umbrella.

Mel and Peyton told me that Walker's Pint holds popular theme nights, like "Scare-e-oke" and ugly sweater DJ dance parties. When I asked them why they liked Walker's Pint, Peyton said, "Honestly? I just like that there's other gay people here. I like the way it feels. I was here once when there was a lesbian wedding after-party, with both the brides in sweatpants, and it was awesome."

"I like that there's somewhere to go in Milwaukee with people who are looking out for us and on our side," said Mel. I nodded. It's true that lesbian bars often feel like a sanctuary from the outside world. It felt safe in there—small enough, maybe, for the bartender to know your name if you came and hung out even twice.

Two people at the end of the bar—some of the only people *not* wearing Packers gear—saw me chatting with Mel and Peyton and motioned me over. They'd noticed my notebook and wanted to know what was going on. Their names were Kaylin and Sydney, and it turned out they'd just moved to Milwaukee together from Iowa City. This was their first visit to Walker's Pint.

I asked them what they thought of the bar. They said they liked it very much and felt comfortable there. Then I asked them the question I asked everyone.

"Why do you think lesbian bars are closing?"

Sydney said, "I feel like lesbian bars are less visible than bars for gay men." She thought for a moment, then added, "I also don't think there's a defined lesbian 'community' anymore."

Kaylin agreed, and then voiced the feeling I'd had the previous night: "I think there's a weird thing with lesbians: we don't talk to one another."

I snort-laughed, and left them with one of the best pieces of advice for meeting queers that I'd ever received. Once, when I'd been moaning about how hard it was to approach someone I was attracted to, my friend Steffany had casually said, "With lesbians, the best pickup line of all is 'Hi.'"

"That's so true," Sydney said.

"That's so sad," Kaylin said.

At the other end of the bar, I met Ana, a trans woman who'd been coming to Walker's Pint for five years. When I told her I was on a mission to find out why lesbian bars were closing, she patted the stool next to her. I sat.

"I have two theories," she said, and held up a finger. "Theory one: The world's becoming more accepting of gay people, and so the separation of gay bars versus straight bars is not as necessary. People are just going wherever they're going, and the bars aren't as needed."

"OK, got it," I said, writing it in my notebook. It seemed unnecessary to mention that everyone has this theory.

Ana held up two fingers. "Theory two: It's the total opposite of theory one. The age of Trump plus Covid has made queer people more afraid, and they've all gone underground."

"You mean all the lesbians are hanging out without us."

She nodded solemnly, then cracked a grin at me. "Both feel true."

The Packers won. It was dark out now. I had seen that Walker's Pint sold fanny packs as merch, and I'd be damned if I was going to leave without one.

I asked one of the bartenders if I could examine a fanny pack, and he reached one down for me to try on.

"You've been writing all day," he said, gesturing to my notebook. I explained my project.

"That's so cool," he said. "My name's Liam, by the way. I have a nice story about this bar, if you want it." He watched me struggle to adjust the fanny pack straps. They were hopelessly complicated; I couldn't get them to lengthen. Trying a new tactic, I stepped into the fanny pack and pulled it up over my hips, yanking on the straps triumphantly. I'd figured it out!

It fell to the floor. Liam bent down to get it, pulling it up and gently putting one hand on my waist to hold it steady while he tightened the straps for me.

Liam told me he was trans, and that he'd been bartending at Walker's Pint for two years.

"I came out as trans about two years ago, right when I started working here," he said. "I hadn't changed my name yet. When I changed my name, I posted on Facebook about changing it, but I also said it was OK if people called me by my old name. Bet-z, my boss—she's the owner of the bar—saw my post and said, 'No. Your name's Liam. We're calling you Liam. Everyone's going to call you Liam.'"

Liam had his name-change party at Walker's Pint.

"Bet-z [Boenning] is an incredible boss," he said. "I rarely have bad days here. This is a magical place."

Bet-z *is* incredible. When I talked with her on the phone, she was warm and friendly, telling me that she had worked a lot of jobs after college, but found she really enjoyed bartending. She'd worked at a women's bar in Milwaukee called Dish, but it changed into a regular dance club after she'd been there for a year. Then Fannies (a women's bar that had been around for thirty years) burned [and was heavily damaged in 1997, reopening as a mixed gay bar], and that was it for queer women's spaces in Milwaukee.

"I wanted a place I could go if and when I got a girlfriend!" She laughed. "I wanted to have our own space. I had no idea how to run a business, but I knew I was good with people."

Walker's Pint

Bet-z opened Walker's Pint, bought out her business partner after a few years, and made sure everyone was welcome. (Take a shot!)

"I try to make Walker's Pint a safe space. It's open to anyone, as long as you're not an ass. I'd rather be inclusive than exclusive, because I never want people to feel how I felt when I first came out. I hope people feel welcome, and enjoy the events we throw. We—me and the staff, and I have great staff; some have been here nine, twelve, nineteen years— pride ourselves that when we throw an event, it's an *event*."

She knows Walker's Pint is special. "When you're one of twenty-one bars in the country, there's a lot of pressure!" she said. "You don't want to be the one to close. And everybody in the queer community wants to be able to go anywhere, but they also want their gay spaces to be *gay*. That's why we still like having our own spaces—because six out of seven nights, there's going to be people in them who are going to understand what you're going through. And I try to make sure my bar is accessible to everyone. My prices are the lowest in the neighborhood. That's on purpose. Women don't make as much as men."

Davin, Sarah, and I left the bar. I was wearing my fanny pack, and kept demanding that they admire its elegance.

"Aren't you jealous?" I asked. "Don't you wish you'd have gotten one?"

"Yes," said Davin, who thinks fanny packs are hideous. "It's very beautiful. What was I thinking? Can I borrow yours?"

"Absolutely not."

As we snuggled on Sarah's air mattress that night, I lay in the dark, thinking about Walker's Pint. It had been full of surprises—I'd been surprised at how intimidated I'd felt there on the first night, and surprised at how gay the neighborhood had been, and then surprised again at how much fun I'd had the next day, how easy it was to approach people. How open everyone had been to talking with me, once *I* opened up.

I thought, too, of what Bet-z had said about how she felt when she'd come out—how she'd felt excluded. I didn't know if she meant she'd felt excluded from society in general, or excluded by other queers. When I came out in Minneapolis, it was around 2004–2005, and it was at the beginning of a time when it was becoming much, much more acceptable to be openly gay in America. I hadn't felt excluded by society—no part of me wanted anything to do with heteronormative culture. It was honestly a thrill to not belong in "regular" society anymore. But I *had* felt—and sometimes do still feel—excluded by other queers. I know I'm not alone in this. We clique up; we judge each other on how we look. We decide people aren't gay enough, aren't cool enough, aren't young enough, aren't old enough, aren't queer the way we want them to be queer, and we stop talking to each other. I was as guilty as anyone.

But Bet-z had decided to do something about it. Her goal had been to make a place where no one felt like that. She was bringing people in, not keeping them out. We need more people like that in the queer community.

I flipped over and pulled on the blanket, tugging to get some of it back. Davin is a blanket hog, but when you wake up cold in the middle of the night and yank on the covers, he opens his arms, still fully asleep, letting you take as much of the blanket as you want.

I was starting to realize there were reasons I was going on this trip that I hadn't understood when I began. I was going to the lesbian bars, yes, but I was also seeing America at a strange time, and meeting queers I would never have met otherwise. I was reckoning with my past in ways I hadn't expected, and I was discovering what it meant to have "grown up" in dyke bars and now actually be seeing them with my fully grown-up eyes.

Walker's Pint is in the state where I was raised, and by the end of our visit, I'd felt so comfortable there, as if I'd been going for years. Maybe it was because it was the most midwestern bar I'd visit for the book, and I am midwestern to my core, but man, I'd loved it.

You never know what's going to resonate with you, really. I spent my teenage years formulating and refining plans to get the hell out of

Wisconsin and never come back. And now that I was back, decades later, it was almost a relief to be there. I'd missed it. I really love fancy bullshit in all forms—cocktails featuring edible flowers; entrées I can't pronounce at restaurants you have to book two months in advance; confrontationally minimalist shops that sell ambitiously priced bars of soap and, like, specially blessed brass incense burners—but I don't come from anything fancy. I come from a place where the hottest restaurant in town was once the newly built Noodles & Company. A place where the sight of a dripping deer hanging upside down on a hook doesn't make anybody flinch. I'm from a place where three people sitting on lawn chairs inside a garage in February is a party. And it turns out what makes my homosexual heart beat faster is sticky floors, queers in hunting sweatshirts, gay bears in wool hats saying "Ope" as they inch past you on their way to the bar, and a dart game that pauses for anyone who needs to pee—twenty, thirty, fifty times in a night.

Bloomington

The Back Door

• • •

Well, it happened. I knew it had to eventually.

Davin and I (but mostly Davin) had painstakingly planned the midwestern road trip portion of the lesbian bar visits around the amount of PTO I had amassed at my job. Driving was the only affordable way to get to all the bars in the time I had, and the whole trip was one big loop. There was no room for error. The road trip was designed to be a twelve-day whirlwind, with eight nights spent back-to-back at lesbian bars, three days at the end of the trip spent hanging out with friends in Chicago, and a final day spent driving home to Minnesota. We'd specifically plotted our route around the nights and hours the bars were all open, which was tricky, because most bars had different pandemic hours than usual.

And very few of them kept their opening days and hours updated online.

The Back Door, in Bloomington, Indiana, took the prize for being the hardest to pin down. Before Davin and I left on the road trip, I'd spent a remarkable amount of time trying to figure out when the Back Door was open. All the available info conflicted with itself. At the time, the bar's official website said the Back Door was open seven days a week, but their Facebook page said they were only open Wednesday through Sunday. Their Instagram profile info said they were open seven days per week, but Google *also* said Wednesday through Sunday. Their updated-hours-ago Instagram feed was advertising an event on a Tuesday, but—

The Back Door

according to Yelp—the Back Door was closed on Tuesdays. Frowning darkly, I'd tried to call the bar a week ahead of time during hours they should for sure have been open, using the number Google listed. (The Back Door's phone number wasn't listed anywhere on its website.) When I called, there was a clicking sound, then a piercing, white-noise scream. It was a fax number.

And now it was a drizzly, freezing Monday night in Bloomington in November, and we had just driven six *hours* from Milwaukee to be in Bloomington on a freezing Monday night in November, and I was standing outside the darkened, obviously closed alley entrance to the Back Door, staring at the bar's physical sign, which read WEDNESDAY–SUNDAY.

"No," I whispered. Davin emitted a hollow laugh, shaking his head in disbelief. This wasn't happening.

But it was.

"NOOOOOO," I howled into the night, rattling the locked metal patio gate like an angry bear. We didn't have *time* to come back to Bloomington! And all our hotel stays for the road trip were nonrefundable! Each bar got two nights! Those were the *rules*!

"Sweets, it's closed."

"Maybe there's a side door." The Back Door does not have a front entrance, just metal gates that guard the alley entrance. I scuttled down the alley, around to the side of the building, and frantically choked out a doorknob I found with both hands. Locked.

"Noooooooo," I whimpered.

"You can see that it's closed. It's dark in there. C'mon."

"What are we going to *doooo*?"

"I dunno, cutes." Along with a couple of barfy private nicknames Davin has for me, he basically calls me either "cutes" or "sweets," all the time. "Sweetheart" means he's irritated. He didn't sound irritated now, though—just defeated. All his careful travel plans. All his marked-up road trip maps. Ruined.

We walked back through the icy drizzle to our hotel, hunched over in the wind. Rearranging the road trip schedule to accommodate two lost nights was going cost many hundreds of dollars we did not have; I could feel it.

I'm just gonna put it out here: Maybe the real reason lesbian bars are closing is simpler than we all thought. Maybe it has nothing to do with money, or community need, or gatekeeping, or anything else.

Maybe it's because no one can fucking figure out when they're open.

I'M PRETTY BAD AT GEOGRAPHY. I cannot list with any degree of certainty all of the states that touch Minnesota, and I couldn't tell you which way is north, right now, if my choices were "die a painful death" or "drive in the direction of Canada." *Two separate people* I've dated have bought me *two different children's wooden puzzles* featuring a map of the United States as a joke. I have done the puzzles. Nothing helps.

So it wasn't surprising that I had never heard of Bloomington, Indiana, before. I had heard of Bloomington, Illinois, and Bloomington, Minnesota, but that was it. What *was* surprising to me was finding a gleaming little full-on *city* in Indiana, complete with an imposing domed courthouse, appealing coffee shops, and hundreds, *thousands* of college students swarming around, all so young and scrubbed and backpacked that you could have curled right up and gone to sleep nestled in the peach fuzz on the sides of their cheeks.

Without realizing it, we'd booked a hotel inches from the Indiana University campus. You couldn't set foot outside without scattering flocks of teenagers like edgy seagulls off the steps, all of them wearing pastel tie-dyed sweatpants and crop tops in the cold morning sunshine. To midwestern college kids, it is never cold enough for belly shirts or cargo shorts to not be an option.

"Excuse me, what is a Hoosier?" I called after a passing blur of baby-pink and baby-blue sweatpants on the sidewalk. There was a snort of muffled giggling as the pairs of pants speed-walked past, a cloud of fruity vanilla body spray left in their wake.

The Back Door

Downtown Bloomington, which is basically the same as the campus area, has a thrilling amount of good, cheap restaurants. It also has a big bookstore and a gourmet foods store that sells things I had not known existed but immediately needed to have in my pantry, such as a small fourteen-dollar jar of ground spices I was forced to buy because it smelled like saffron and rose petals. Bringing it up to the register, I already knew I'd see it in our spice cabinet and say, "We should do something with this," to Davin once a week for the next two years, and it would finally expire, unused, but that was OK. What you're buying, when you buy something stupid like that, is a belief that you are capable of change. *We'll put it on ice cream*, I told myself. *Soup.*

It was Tuesday, the day that the Back Door had advertised an event on their Instagram page, *even though they were closed*, according to their *own sign* on their *own gate*. After trudging back to the hotel the night before, Davin and I had spent hours squinting at maps, calculating new drive times, and thundering, "SPEAK TO A REPRESENTATIVE" at Expedia phone robots, trying to rework the entire road trip so that we could come back on the way home through Bloomington on a weekend night, when the Back Door was sure to be open.

The Tuesday event advertised on the Back Door's Instagram was a late-afternoon candle-crafting session ahead of Trans Day of Remembrance. It wasn't a night visit, but if the bar really *was* open, we could go make some candles and talk to people and see the inside of the place.

Davin didn't want to go.

"Come with me," I pleaded.

"You go."

"You're trans," I pointed out helpfully.

"Yeah, and I've been to a million of these things. It's going to be, like, three people in a room with craft scissors and it's going to feel really sad."

"One hour. And then we'll get dinner. Somewhere good. You can pick."

"Half an hour."

"Forty-five minutes."

"Done."

We walked through the alley to the Back Door's main entrance. As we approached, it hit me: *Whoa, that's why this bar is called the Back Door. Because the entrance is literally in an alley.*

MacArthur genius grant directors: I await my phone call.

The gate to the Back Door stood open this time, and Davin and I stepped through.

"*Look* at this *patio,*" I said, stopping to do a slow 360. We were still outside, standing in front of a vast pink-painted wooden deck, with tables and chairs set out below it like dinghies on a concrete sea. A giant *Golden Girls* mural dominated the back wall of the building; a mural of pink crystals sprouted up next to the entryway. It was all colorful and big and open, and involved the kind of causal square footage that the Midwest specializes in, the kind that makes people from the East Coast inhale sharply. *Imagine the parties you could have back here,* I thought, picturing what Pride at the Back Door must be like. *You could have fifty queens spraying their wigs out here at once and no one would even get sticky.*

A friendly person in their thirties or forties (how the fuck old are queer people? our community ages *differently*) with a mustache and a half-buzzed head was standing by the door leading inside, letting people in. I studied their face. They looked familiar. Was this possibly Smoove, the bar owner? I was almost sure it was; I'd seen a picture of them online somewhere while researching the Back Door.

"Hi," they said. "Thanks for coming. All the stuff's over here."

They gestured to a table filled with tall white votive candles in glass jars. Beyond it, several other folding tables held glue, glitter, sequins, and paint. There were exactly three people sitting and crafting. The atmosphere was quiet and somber. Davin poked me in the back, an unsaid *told you so* hanging in the air.

"Are you Smoove?" I blurted as we all headed toward the tables.

They blinked. "I am."

"Oh, good!" I explained my book project in a nervous jumble. Smoove listened patiently, nodding.

"That's cool," they said, when I'd finished babbling. "I'm happy to talk to you. Grab a candle."

International Transgender Day of Remembrance is on November 20 each year. Begun in 1999, it honors the memories of the transgender people who've died from acts of antitransgender violence—people who've been murdered because they were trans. We would be pasting pictures of trans people the community had lost this year to violence onto the candles and decorating them so they could be lit in a few days for the actual event.

The stack of pictures on the table was thick. I pulled the first one off the top of the pile. A Black trans woman, Tiara Banks, beautiful, young. The picture underneath her was another young, beautiful Black trans woman, her eyes shining—someone photographed in happier times, maybe by someone who loved her. The next was a young white trans man, wearing a backward baseball cap, holding a pissed-looking cat up to the camera. I gently flipped though the pile, my throat catching. All of these people, all bubbling over with life and energy and personality. All murdered. So many in their twenties. A whole stack of them.

Ahead of me, Davin was sitting at a table with pink, white, and pale blue bottles of paint—the colors of the trans flag. He was pasting the picture he'd chosen on a candle with rubber cement, his mouth set in a line. He kept applying more and more glue, making sure the picture was centered, stroking a thin layer over the front to make sure it would be sealed against rain.

"You OK?" I whispered.

"Yeah," he said, his voice tight. "You need the glue?"

It would appear science has made no advances in glitter paint technology since I was in elementary school—it's still clumpy and chunky, impossible to get the glitter to evenly spread where you want it to go. I finished my first candle and set it up on a railing with the others, then grabbed another. Smoove turned on some music, and the atmosphere lightened up a bit. The queers who'd been crafting when we got there started gossiping about their jobs. Davin and I got faster at decorating the candles, pasting one picture after another, swiftly swirling glue designs and pressing handfuls of loose pink and iridescent white glitter onto them over paper plates. Smoove moved around the room, offering drinks, swapping stories with people, switching out crafting supplies, and telling a series of progressively dirtier jokes. They started with several innocuous dad jokes, then, after appreciative groans from everyone, moved on to, in their words, a "stepdad joke," and then warned us they were going to tell a "guy your mom brought home from Taco Tuesday" joke.

I stopped what I was doing, a baby-blue paint-spattered brush in my hand. Smoove had my attention. The other jokes they'd told had been so filthy I couldn't imagine what they considered an actual dirty joke.

"OK, so what's the difference between a lentil and a chickpea?" Smoove asked the room.

All of us shook our heads. "I don't know."

"I've never had a lentil in my mouth."

It took me a second. Then I gasped.

I loved Smoove. They were busy running the crafting event—people kept trickling in—but we established that I'd be back later in the week, so we could talk then. They did manage to tell me a few stories about the bar, though. Apparently, it was quite common for Smoove and the Back Door bartenders to call an Uber for one of the patrons and pay for it with their own money.

"Your own money?" I said. "Why?"

"I want people to get home safe," Smoove said. "Someone has a little too much, OK. We're going to make sure you get home. This bar—the people who come to this bar are our family. We take care of our family."

"Yeah, but still," I said. "That can't be cheap."

"Well, sometimes it's a lot," Smoove said, grinning. "One time, one of my bartenders got an Uber for someone who was really drunk, and later got a $300 charge on their phone! The person diarrheaed all over the Uber. They got charged a $250 cleaning fee."

"Oh my god."

"I think I'd charge more than that," one of the queers at a table called over.

"Me *too*," I said. "Holy shit. Ha, literally, holy shit, get it?" Davin and I were standing in the doorway of the bar, heading out to dinner.

"It's not funny," another queer said reproachfully. "I drive for Lyft, and that kind of thing stops you from working for the whole night. It's a biohazard."

They looked very serious. I stepped onto the patio. Only Smoove could make potty jokes here and have them land right, I decided. I only hoped, when I came back, that I'd see Smoove dancing, and that I could call them Smoove Move.

"IT'S OK," I SAID ALOUD, my breath puffing into the icy night air. "It's going to be fine."

It was days later, a Saturday night, and I was back in Bloomington, walking to the Back Door by myself. I was going to a drag show there; I'd seen a poster advertising it at the candle-crafting day. I was both excited—my first drag show in two years!! I hadn't seen one since before the pandemic!—and being a little stuck-up about it. Really, my first drag show was going to be in Bloomington? What would *this* be like? Davin and I had sorted all the travel out—we'd shaved a day off our time in Chicago and rerouted the whole road trip. All told, it had, as I'd guessed it would, cost us nearly a thousand dollars we could not spare on the travel credit card to get back to Bloomington.

I was also tired, dragging myself to the Back Door after spending the last four consecutive nights at lesbian bars across the Midwest. Exhausted, Davin had begged off coming with me; he was snuggled under a down comforter at the hotel, watching *Thelma and Louise* on cable. It had been extra hard to put on makeup, do my hair, wriggle into a tight dress, and leave him at 9:45 p.m., a time when my ass likes to be in bed when I'm at home, reading and listening to the conductor of the night train that runs through Northfield absolutely *wailing* on the horn. That train, man. It comes through town a couple of times a night, and I swear to god, every time, it sounds like the conductor has just suffered a massive coronary failure, his lifeless body falling full weight on the horn, the train barreling down on the tracks, no driver. The fucking night train woke me up for a week straight when we moved in.

You get used to it, though. Now I find it soothing.

But yes—it was past my bedtime, and I was so tired, and I also felt nervous to go to the Back Door's drag show alone. And I knew *why* I was nervous: now that I'd already been to Bloomington, I'd seen who lived around there. College students. Nothing but college students. I hadn't yet seen a person over twenty-two years old, unless they owned a shop in town. And while I'm not actually *that* old, you have to understand: in queer culture, especially in the bars, I'm definitely considered an elder queer. I was going to be the oldest person at the bar by a large margin.

And so far, on these bar trips, I'd been OK with the fact that I was thirty-eight and few others were, wherever I was. But that night, venturing out alone, I felt suddenly *almost forty*, which *hits different*, walking with no friends under the streetlights in a dress that was too tight maybe, too dressed up, too not-right. *Almost forty*, I thought, tugging on my dress. *What am I doing here?*

And then, on top of feeling self-conscious and old and inappropriately dressed, I felt bad for age-shaming myself. *There's no such thing as age-appropriate*, I scolded myself as I walked. *It's not a thing.*

Just me and my thoughts, heading to a lesbian bar near you!

People were smoking on the patio at the Back Door. Music thumped from inside. Masked and steeling myself for a sea of very! young! faces!, I walked in.

The Back Door

And there was a mixed bag of people in there! Of course there was! People older than me, younger than me, people about my age. It was also racially diverse, which was a nice change for the Midwest—about half the people in the Back Door were people of color. I looked around, smiling under my mask, suddenly feeling stupid for even worrying about being too old for the Back Door—who the fuck cared? This was a dyke bar. I felt like I belonged there; that everyone in the bar belonged there. I headed to an open back table and set down my winter coat, feeling happy.

The Back Door looks *cute* at night. The walls are spray-painted with black-and-white zebra stripes, and the decor is tacky-on-purpose, all black velvet paintings of unicorns and pictures of Dolly Parton surrounded by feather boas and famous drag queens in glitter frames. It feels homey and DIY, like whoever decorated it (Smoove, I guessed) loves this space and wanted to make it unlike any other place. The bathrooms are spacious, painted pink and black and pale blue. Peeing, I noticed my stall had the word FAGS scratched into the paint in a heart shape. I was home.

Hmm. It was 10:15, but the bar was still half-empty. The drag show was supposed to start at 10:00; it had been on the poster.

I sighed, suddenly understanding. I'd done it again. I am both punctual and gullible, and since I also happen to be gay, this scenario happens to me *all the time*. I show up to a queer event at the time it's advertised, a trusting little fool, and no one's ever there yet. *When* am I going to remember that Gay Time applies to *all* times in queer life and not just parties???

Now, if you're not familiar with Gay Time, the rules are as follows:

A house party that starts "Any time after eight, just come on over!"
The party actually gets going after ten, so best to go at eleven, when everyone will be drunk enough to be loose and fun and still sober enough to remember you came.

Moby Dyke

A dinner scheduled for seven p.m. at someone's house

Dinner is actually at 9:30, because when you arrive at 7:15, there are drinks and gluten-free-certified tortilla chips and hummus (all still in their store containers) set out on the kitchen counter, but the host hasn't even started cooking yet; they're slowly cutting a single cucumber into tiny pieces while avidly listening to the seven other queers standing up in their kitchen gossiping about what Aiden did *this* time.

A dinner scheduled for seven p.m. at a restaurant

Dinner is at seven but they won't seat us because they won't seat incomplete parties and Eli *still* isn't here and everyone's texting them at once and Eli has stopped responding but *did* text OMW twenty-two minutes ago.

The Pride parade starts at ten a.m.

Good luck, this is not happening, the parade will begin moving at eleven thirty under a meltingly hot sun, hungover drag queens struggling valiantly, and it will then be halted for two hours by an antipolice protest. Sunburned children with rainbow face paint will begin crying at 10:03 a.m.

Any other Pride event that starts at any time during the day

No one is coming to a daytime Pride event except the people who organized it and the PFLAG families.

A prearranged eleven a.m. weekend brunch with friends

Fifty-six text messages in the group chat later, brunch is at one thirty and at a completely different location; there's a forty-five-minute wait, everyone's hungover, and holy shit, *someone brought Kaitlyn.*

The Back Door

We were clearly on Gay Time at the Back Door's drag show. I went to the bar to get a drink. They had the best drink names I've ever seen. There was a drink called "Two in the Pink" and another called "One in the Stink," which contained "Skyy Cold Brew Coffee Vodka & Kahlua & Cream." Another was called "Citron My Face." Incredible. There was also a big mocktail list advertised right next to the alcoholic drinks, which I always think is such a welcoming gesture in a queer bar—bars are such a celebrated part of queer culture, but lots of people don't drink!

The place was filling up. The usual drag show suspects took their seats. A large group of sorority-looking students with uniformly long, loosely curled hair came in with what looked like a single token gay boy in tow. Several nervous-looking babyqueers nabbed the last few high-tops. I smiled at one, and they looked startled, and then smiled back bashfully and slid their hand to the back of their hair. Babyqueers are so endearing and so obvious. It's funny to remember how, as a babydyke, I used to think I was so grown up and sophisticated when I'd go out, when really, everyone in the bar could see I looked like a goddamn baby chipmunk in an ill-fitting men's tweed vest from Goodwill.

At ten thirty, a Black drag queen wearing an enormous blond beehive sailed out of the wings. Clearly the emcee, dressed in a tight, champagne-colored, crushed velvet floor-length dress with a matching stole, she began making her rounds, being careful to get to every table, a good sign she was out for *blood* for tips. I love that energy. Nothing like a little warm eye contact and friendly gay chitchat with each table to make every patron feel like they're personally responsible for tipping. She came up to my table and tapped my notebook with her nails.

"You ready to have a good time tonight?" she purred. "No more homework, OK?"

"I'm writing about this show," I stammered, looking at her in the worshipful way everyone looks at drag queens, helpless in the face of a deity on earth.

"OK, honey." Her cheekbones gleamed with gold shimmer high-lighter. She glided to the next table, and I let out a breath I didn't know I'd been holding. The two full years since I'd last seen a live drag show were a long time to wait, I realized. Two YEARS! I'd missed this!

I got myself a Citron My Face to celebrate. A queen, Miss Thang, came out onstage to Rihanna's "Love on the Brain" and the show began. And holy shit, did it feel fantastic to sit in the dark watching a drag show in Bloomington, Indiana. Ten seconds into the song, Miss Thang flipped her high, shiny, black ponytail over her shoulder and slipped out of a fur coat, winking at the audience.

I teared up. It was instant. She was beautiful, lip-synching perfectly, and went around collecting tips, air-kissing people, touching their out-stretched fingers full of dollar bills. Jesus. I hadn't realized how much I'd missed Normal Gay Stuff during the pandemic.

But this drag show wasn't normal, I was realizing. The second num-ber was just as good, and the third was even better, and every seat was full, with more and more people streaming through the door and pack-ing the line at the bar and calling to their friends and cheering wildly for each performer. This was a great drag show!

Most drag shows are pretty fun at their base level. There are always one or two performers who are the obvious stars, crowd favorites, and the filler acts are usually fine-verging-on-meh. But *this* drag show was *different*. This one was seamless, almost tangibly smooth, every per-former a star, each expertly handling the audience. Every song had been chosen with care and exhaustively practiced. Every costume entrance made people gasp.

I'd already had two drinks, and I was pretty excited, and my notes . . . reflect that. Here's what I wrote:

OK THIS SHOW!! These queens are working so hard, this is NUTS.
  Alright they just shined the spotlight on me at my little solo table, and a queen named Kiara Kardash just took my tip and

threw her leg up on my shoulder to thank me, but missed with her aim, hitting my head so hard with her thigh it was like a BELL CLANGING, I saw little cartoon stars. I've been blessed.

Shit, it's the fourth song and I'm already completely out of money! I've never seen an audience tip like this, NEVER, it is RAINING money, is this just because everyone's so thirsty for gay shit from being locked up from covid?? I just went to the ATM, which only! dispenses! singles! and got more out.

Aria Amethyst just appeared in a robe printed all over with dollar bills and stripped down into ripped fishnets and a bodysuit dripping with rhinestones, and I think this gay boy near me is going to actually burst into tears about it. He is clapping with both his fists full of money and screaming at the top of his lungs and Aria swooped over to him and slowly curled her fingers around his forearm while looking lovingly into his eyes and took all his money and if this isn't what meeting God is like, I don't want to do it.

Miss Thang came back out in a bodycon pink bedazzled dress with a slit up to the ass and is doing Beyoncé's "Naughty Girl" and holy shit there is an actual LINE at the ATM!!!

I've never seen queens work this hard, they are working the audience and humping the floor and doing splits and sissy-walking and grinding on people's faces and WTF THIS IS INDIANA, I wish I was rich so I could tip with hundred-dollar bills!

Kiara Kardash just showed up in pasties to Mariahlynn's "Never Bitch," and when she came by to take my tips, she leaned over and smelled like some kind of cotton candy dream. This is the only acceptable situation for supersweet perfumes IMHO— if they're ladled on by the pint by a dancer who is using it to cover the smell of their own sweat, which completely works and then the warmth of their sweaty skin heats it up and projects the smell to the moon, so what you get is hyperrealistic fresh, warm cotton candy. <u>This</u> is what sugary perfumes are for, <u>not</u> for wearing in overwhelming waves of pink sweetness and gassing everyone out of the elevator in the office at eight a.m., take notes, corporate America.

The emcee, Zariah Saint Vontrell, just told a white guy sitting with a whole crowd of friends to come sit on a chair in the middle of the room and when he tried to refuse, told him calmly to "Get your white ass into this chair right now," and he did, looking VERY sheepish, and then she proceeded to ask him his name and then give him an absolutely filthy lap dance to Beyoncé's "Let Me Sit This A$$ on You" and watching his face is incredible; he looks delighted and embarrassed and pleased and horny and confused and thrilled, he's all red and shiny and this is so great.

Sobering up slightly after the show, I knew I needed to try to talk to people, but I am not joking, y'all: the Saturday-night show at the Back Door was one of the best drag shows I've ever seen, and after almost twenty years of being a homosexuelle and going to drag shows fairly regularly, that is *saying something*.

I headed over to a nearby table, where I met a lesbian named Ally, who told me it was her thirtieth birthday. She loved the Back Door. "Having an open and accepting space in a conservative state like Indiana is mind-blowing," she said. Her friend, Andy, nodded. "It's a very safe queer space, and they work really hard at that," he said. "If you go up to any person working here—at the bar, security, anywhere—and tell them that you're having a problem with someone here, they'll take care of it. I love it here."

I went from table to table, asking how people felt about the Back Door, and all the answers were like that. Unprompted. People just loved this bar. I did, too. Especially after I realized I'd drunkenly left my entire unzipped clutch on my table, with forty dollars in ones just hanging out of the front of it, my phone, and all my IDs (including my passport!!!) and credit cards in there, while I chatted with people around the bar for a full twenty minutes, and *nothing happened to any of it*. The money was still hanging out the front of my clutch when I got back to my table, and get in, bitch, we're moving to Bloomington.

I found Smoove, the owner. They were not dancing, unfortunately. It was hot in the bar; we went outside to talk, our breath puffing into clouds in the night air.

They used to work in a corporate setting, which was interesting to me. "Do you love doing this instead?" I asked.

"Sometimes," Smoove said. "Yes and no. Everything has its pros and cons."

"Pros like: you get to hang out with queers for a living, and cons like: sometimes they diarrhea in the Ubers you buy them?"

"Exactly."

The Back Door opened on February 14, 2013. Smoove told me there were three reasons for the name. First, the main entrance to the bar is literally a back door in an alley. Second, the name is a nod to queer clubs in the old days, where you needed a password just to get in. Third, Smoove said, "it's a gay butt joke." They grinned, and I remembered the chickpea joke they'd told a few days ago.

A woman named Deanna wandered down the back patio stairs and hugged Smoove. She was severely drunk, and began telling a long story about someone who'd wronged her mom, and how she would kill to protect her mother.

"I mean it," Deanna said, looking into my eyes and pointing at me. "No one gets to mess with MY MAMA." She looked at Smoove and me. "No one."

I asked her how she felt about the Back Door.

"I love this bar because it's a place I can go and feel comfy knowing I can talk to literally any staff here and tell them I'm uncomfortable and they'll take care of it right away," she said. I nodded. She was the second person that night to say that. What do they get up to at all the other bars in Indiana? Were Indiana bars bastions of being hassled?

"Where do you see this bar going?" I asked Smoove. "What's next for the Back Door?"

"Hopefully, it will just keep going," they said. "It's important to hold space for this community. You can get burnt out at a place, but then someone will come up to you and say thank you. It's a joy boost, to have that happen—this is why we keep doing this!"

It was freezing. We'd been outside for forty minutes, Smoove smoking cloves, no hat, no gloves. Deanna, standing next to us and weaving slightly on the pavement, continued to tell us how we were *not* going to get a chance to mess with her mama, no *way*. I could see why people clearly love Smoove—they're so laid-back and have exceptionally calm, steady vibes. Because we were in the Midwest, they were also *way* too polite and midwestern to ever try to end the conversation, and they just stood there, obviously cold, smiling at me and Deanna.

It was up to me. "Welp, I think I'd better get back," I said.

"I hope I see you again," said Smoove.

"Me too," I said. "Hey, this has been one of my favorite bars so far."

Smoove grinned, heading back inside. "You've got a lot more to go."

Columbus

Slammers

◆ ◆ ◆

When you leave Bloomington, there are lots of signs for Nashville and Columbus on the way out of town, and you get really excited because both those cities seem so close. Then you realize that the Nashville and Columbus that the signs are talking about are . . . still in Indiana. Nashville, Indiana. Columbus, Indiana. All just half an hour away! Along the way to Columbus, Ohio, you'll pass huge black billboards with enormous white capital letters that just say HELL IS REAL. You'll scan the radio, pausing to hear the tail end of Chris Stapleton wailing out "Tennessee Whiskey" on the local Top Forty country station, and then you might find that the next song, for absolutely no reason, is "The Star-Spangled Banner," with a full orchestral arrangement.

Davin and I drove through an unincorporated town called Gnaw Bone, Indiana, on our way to Columbus. It was an overcast, chilly day; ghostly white trees rocked silently in the wind. We didn't see a soul.

"What do you think would happen if the car broke down out here?" I asked Davin.

"They gotta get their name from somewhere," he said, his eyes on the road.

I was very happy when we finally pulled up to our hotel on High Street in Columbus. I love Columbus. It's pretty and not wildly expensive; it's full of gay bars and is *extremely* queer-friendly—there are gay flags everywhere, we're talking flag stickers on the windows of pizza places, laundromats, dog-grooming businesses, *dentist's offices.* (Come get drilled in Columbus, gays!) Columbus has unusual, niche, take-my-money stores, arguably the best indoor farmer's market and food hall in America, good restaurants, and an independent, nook-and-cranny-filled bookstore I love so much—the Book Loft—that has thirty-two separate little rooms, all of which are perfect for hiding in when your partner tells you in an exasperated tone that it's time to leave the Book Loft.

I was on familiar ground. I know all about High Street because I used to regularly spend some of the most stressful days of my life there, scurrying like a rat through the world's largest, worst-labeled convention center, which was steps from where we were staying now. That job I used to have—the one where I would escort educational book authors on seminar tours? That job also involved setting up and running the seminars. The people who came to them—teachers who needed continuing education credits—needed someone to check them in, someone to set up the AV system, someone to monitor the coffee supply, to explain where the bathrooms were, again, for the 426th time in a single morning. In the two years I had that job, I got sent to Columbus constantly. *Constantly.* I could direct you to the nearest bathroom in the Columbus convention center if you set me down inside it blindfolded.

Davin and I walked past it now. It was closed for the day, and empty, but just looking through the windows at its carpet designs made me shiver. My old friend. No matter what, the teachers going to a seminar at the Columbus convention center were going to hate it. The parking wasn't free, the room was always impossible to find, the coffee would always run out, the on-site sound equipment was never going to work right, the room would always be *freezing* ("Can't you *do* something about this?") or hilariously too hot, like cardigans were being *removed*, and the monumentally bored teenagers in polyester vests who worked there, wheeling out carts of Diet Coke to the rabid Diet Coke fiends who teach our nation's children, were never going to do anything about any of it. The food court was closed *every time I had a seminar there*; I mean, it was never open even *once*. If you'd like to know how to instantaneously soak your own underpants with anxiety sweat, let me suggest standing up in front of 132 middle school teachers who had to pay fifteen dollars to park for an all-day seminar they don't even want to be at and tell- ing them that the closest food options for lunch are a block away, *and they're going to have to walk there.*

Until I became a copywriter, I worked a lot of random jobs. It was my seminar-running days, though, that took years off my life.

It felt great to be in Columbus and not have to go to the convention center. Wild, even. I'd never done it. I skipped as Davin and I walked through downtown at night, gleeful to be set loose in such a lovely city for such a gay reason, knowing that never again in my life would I have to explain to grown adults that once the lemon poppy seed minimuffins were gone, they were gone.

I could see at a glance that I would like Slammers, Columbus's only lesbian bar. The gray-painted brick building on East Long Street has a rainbow mural on its side as you approach, gay flags flapping above its facade, and neon signs that say PIZZA and BUD LIGHT in its windows, which always lets you know right away that no matter what you're wear- ing, you won't be underdressed.

Slammers, like the Back Door, and like so many lesbian bars not on the East Coast, was a really big bar—high, tin-stamped ceilings, two expansive rooms, a massive patio outside with a gay flag painted on the concrete. At the end of the long, dark wooden bar, a cluster of young queers was standing up, jackets on, bunched around the bartender. They were leaving, and the bartender was clearly dating one of them, and there was some kind of quiet lesbian drama energy happening be- tween the two as the friend group was closing out their tabs. You can always tell when two queers in a group are having drama because the ones having an issue will continue to speak intensely to one another, but just get quieter and quieter, all the while trying to pretend that ev- erything's fine for the sake of the group while being acutely aware that all their friends are listening and know *exactly* what's going on, but only from their respective preferred friend's side of the issue. Is emotional intelligence a blessing or a curse? None of us know!

It was trivia night, one of the five staples of gay bar event calendars. Drag shows, dance parties, and karaoke, trivia, and bingo nights keep queer patrons coming in the doors every day of the week. Trivia's way more fun at gay bars because there's never a "sports history" category in any round you're playing, unlike at your local Paddy O'McFlannigan's, where your chances of winning trivia are zero, thanks to bro-only teams with names like the Three-Legged Men who get veins in their foreheads when one of the trivia questions involves baseball statistics.

Davin and I were early. After the queers near the bartender trooped out, there were only a few people left in the front room. We pulled up seats at the bar. Slammers has a lot of TV screens, and one of them was showing what appeared to be an endless stream of videos featuring regular people falling spectacularly—off of trampolines, onto each other, off hoods of cars, out of boats, tripping and falling into ponds as they were saying their wedding vows. Davin was sitting right next to me, but one glance at him told me he was gone, unable to focus on anything else, and would be as long as they kept those videos playing. I've never met anyone who loves a falling blooper video like Davin. He never laughs at me when *I* fall, but his pleasure in watching clips of people who've misjudged the capabilities of a golf cart is intense. He was *cackling*, his eyes glued to the TV.

"OHHHHHH!" he chortled, watching an idiot try to walk on thin lake ice and fall in. "Did you see that!??"

"Mm-hmm." A skier spread-eagled into a pine tree.

"Ooooh, THAT'S gotta hurt. Ho-ho. Oh *man.*"

I got up to pee. The bathrooms at Slammers are in the back of the bar and kind of hard to find, as well as undecorated. It was odd; I'd never before seen bathrooms in a dyke bar that weren't HELLA GAY, or that didn't at least feature posters of upcoming drag events, but these were like using the basement bathroom in your divorced dad's new house—wood paneling outside, no decor whatsoever within.

When I came back, the bartender, whose name was Maddie, was chatting with Davin between fatal-looking parkour fails. I asked her if she liked working at Slammers.

"This is the best job I've ever had," she said. So matter-of-fact. "I love working here. Did you know this place has been open almost thirty years?"

I had recently stopped researching the bars before visiting them, deciding that knowing nothing about them when I walked in the doors might help me have a more objective experience.

"I did not know that," I answered honestly. "That's a long time. What's something you love about working here?"

"We've got so much going on here," she said, eyeing a butch-femme-looking couple that had just pulled up at the other end of the bar. "Are you staying for trivia? You should. It's fun. We have kickball and softball leagues, too; we've got something almost every night. There's a drag bar behind us, too—District West; you should go."

"My god, Columbus is gay."

Maddie nodded happily. "It's *so* gay."

Davin and I sat for a while, watching people come in and head directly to the back room, where trivia night would be happening. The couple at the end of the bar was drunk; they were loudly planning their dream wedding. Maddie went over to join the conversation.

"All I'm saying is that it would have to be an *event*, you know?" the butch one said, splaying their fingers in "name in lights" gesture. "I'm only doing this once."

Solemn nods from their audience. I tried to think where I'd heard the phrase "I'm only doing this once" before—it sounded so familiar. Then I realized it's what every male contestant on *The Bachelor* says right before the last episode, when he's forced to choose between two women he's fallen in love with and propose on national TV. "I gotta get this right," he always says, sweating and pacing in his hotel room. "I'm only doing this once."

Trivia was starting. We walked to the back room and were taken aback by how many people were there—we hadn't been paying attention to who was coming in. There was only one small table left, and Davin and I posted up, looking at the crowd. Trivia night at Slammers was obviously a popular event; most tables had four, five, even eight people scrunched around them, all drinking beer, eating pizza, and trading insults with other regular teams. The host, who—in their black skater pants—looked like they knew their way around a Hot Topic, talked fast into the microphone and bantered with the crowd easily, in a way that made me think they (1) were maybe a Leo and (2) were very used to hosting events. Davin went to the bathroom. The host handed me a big green buzzer.

"Pick a team name," they said.

"Um . . ." I said.

"*Anything*," they said, looking intently at me with widened, hurry-up-fifty-people-are-waiting eyes. Then they smiled, to show they were friendly but also meant it.

"Uhh . . . Flapple Bottom Jeans," I said.

The host grinned. "Good name."

I was proud of myself. I can *never* come up with something witty on the fly, but just a few nights earlier, Davin and I had been giggling in bed at home, talking about my new clothing line, which I'd decided to call "Flaps." Noticing that queers seemed to be willing to buy *anything* from an Etsy store with an inclusive sizing system, ethically sourced dyes, and novelty prints (rainbow narwhals, anyone?), I'd determined that the best way to make money would be to quit my job and start selling different versions of two pieces of fabric connected by a piece of string, which you could tighten and loosen as you liked to size. Flaps would sell shirts (two flaps of fabric connected by a string worn over your chest), skirts (this would be similar to a loincloth but *very* expensive), and pants (open down the inseam and on the sides, *so* convenient for peeing at shitty music festivals).

"We could sell nightshirts," I said. "Napflaps."

"Flapjackets," Davin said.

"Raingear: mudflaps."

"Underflaps."

"*Long* underflaps."

"Snapback cap flaps."

"Flapple bottom jeans," Davin said.

"Oh my god."

"Assless chap flaps."

"ASSLESS CHAP FLAPS!!!"

I'd laughed until I cried, tears streaming down my cheeks and puddling onto the pillow. Even now, I cannot even say the word "flaps" without breaking down. We were going to win trivia night. I could feel it.

We lost. We lost quickly and immediately, by an embarrassing margin. It wasn't our fault—the competition was fierce, and there were several tables of gay boys who were *definitely* hitting their buzzers before the host was finished reading the questions out. At the end, when there were only a few teams left, the category was "Famous Cats," and the $500 question was "Who is this cat?" A cartoon black cat with big white eyes flashed onscreen.

The room fell silent.

"Come on, you guys," the trivia host said into the microphone. "You know this cat."

No one knew. Teams exchanged hushed conferences.

"This cat's name has two 'i's," the host prompted. "It's blank-i-blank-i."

Silence. We'd never seen this cat before in our lives.

"Kiki?" a team suggested.

"Mimi?" from another part of the room.

"This cat's name is *my* cat's name!" the host said, sounding exasperated. "Guys, you know my cat, I talk about her all the time! She has her own Instagram!"

Baffled looks. Perhaps the trivia host's cat was not as well-known as they'd thought.

"Jiji," the host said, sounding thoroughly disgusted. "The cat is Jiji, from the movie *Kiki's Delivery Service*. Guys, everyone knows this movie."

The winners—the cheating gay boys—were declared, and trivia broke up. I asked the people at the table nearest us if they lived in Columbus. They all did.

"I can't get over how queer Columbus is," I said. "And I feel like not enough people know about it? I mean, I love it here. But no one's ever said, 'Hey, you should go to Columbus, it's really gay' to me before."

The group at the table nodded in unison. "Columbus is an interesting place," a queer named Berry volunteered. "This city's always been super gay-friendly, but straight-gay, if you know what I mean—it's always been very palatable to straight people. But there's a lot of community here that isn't just the 'G' in LGBTQ. That's why we like it here."

"Here in Columbus? Or here at Slammers?" I asked.

"Both."

The person with Berry, a trans woman named Lina, said she loved Slammers because she felt comfortable there and they had "great pizza, good people, and a great atmosphere."

"Is the pizza good?"

She pointed at me. "Is it good! Do not sleep on this pizza; Slammers is not fooling around. Get the Bobbi—it's chopped bacon, jalapeños, and pineapple. I know it sounds weird but just trust me."

Back at the bar, the Bobbi's namesake had materialized. Bobbi Moore, who's managed Slammers for four years, was there, wearing a Walker's Pint T-shirt and mixing drinks. She turned around and smiled at Davin and me, absolutely radiating good-humored vibes.

Slammers

"What can I get ya?"

"I love your shirt," I said. I explained the book project. "We were just at Walker's Pint a few days ago!"

"Aw, I love that bar! And yeah, a while back, some of the bars had a T-shirt exchange," Bobbi said. "I wear mine all the time."

"Does Slammers have a T-shirt?" I asked. I'd been trying to get merch from every bar I visited, but it had been hard going. Already I was noticing that most lesbian bars either didn't have merch displayed in a visible place, or they *did* have merch displayed but didn't keep varying sizes stocked. This was too bad, as there is nothing happy drunk people like more than buying T-shirts from the place they prefer to get drunk at.

Slammers didn't have any shirts at the moment. Changing the subject, I asked Bobbi what Pride was like at Slammers, assuming that the only lesbian bar in Ohio would have to be unhinged during Pride. She laughed. "We tell new and temp hires for Pride, 'Be afraid,'" she said. "You can't walk, you can't move, we open at eleven a.m. and close at two a.m., but we don't get people out until three a.m., and we just have a *shell* of a bar when everyone's left. We're cleaning till six a.m. and then the bartenders are in at ten a.m."

"Have you ever seen anything wild here?"

Bobbi thought about it. "I'm really good at de-escalating—I used to work in a women's prison," she said. "Anything I do in a situation is to de-escalate it, not to add anything. I try to come at people from a place of compassion; I don't take anything personally. You never know what people are going through."

Bobbi, like Smoove at the Back Door, had a calming presence, taking drink orders expertly and joking with people in front of and behind the bar. She consistently referred to Slammers as "my wife," as in, "Whatever my wife needs, she gets."

Davin and I had been at Slammers for a few hours, and Bobbi eyed us. "You hungry?"

We were.

"Bobbi's gonna make you the Bobbi," she announced. "It's my pizza. You'll love it."

She went back to the pizza kitchen before I could tell her I don't like jalapeños. Clattering noises commenced. A few minutes later, Bobbi was back, carrying a plastic basket with a ramekin in the middle of it. She set it down in front of us ceremoniously.

"Fried pepperonis," she said. "On the house." She pointed at the ramekin. "That's ranch."

Davin stared at the heaped basket of crisped pepperonis, his expression inscrutable.

"You . . . you dip the pepperonis in the ranch?" he asked. "Like chips?"

"Try it!"

He looked up at Bobbi, his face aglow, and I saw that he loved her. She had invented a snack he'd never even *considered*, and it was both chips *and* meat *and* fried *with* ranch. Bobbi was a genius. If I hadn't been there, he would have asked for her hand on the spot.

We ate the fried pepperonis. All of them. When the Bobbi came out of the oven, we ate that, too, and it was cheesy and spicy and sweet and bacony and burned my mouth, and it was so delicious I stopped caring that it was covered in chopped jalapeños. It simply did not matter. It was incredible pizza.

Britney's "Oops" came on. "Look at this," Davin garbled, his mouth full of melted cheese. He jerked his head behind him, where a group of workers dressed head-to-toe in Carhartt—not fashion-Carhartt, but the kind of Carhartt that actually gets used for manual labor—were standing up, sharing beers, and singing along.

"I love the Midwest," Davin said. He looked so happy.

I watched the workers for a minute. Two of them looked like masc queers, and two of them looked like cis men, and the four of them looked like they were good friends. Each one of them was spattered with dried mud and had on battered steel-toed boots, and they were popping their asses to Britney in a lesbian bar in Ohio. Spaces like Slammers are so rare in the Midwest. There are only four dedicated lesbian bars in the region. I did a little Google math, and the combined 2022 population of all the midwestern states is a little less than seventy million people. If 20 percent of those people identify as queer, that means that fourteen million queers were in for *quite a drive* before they could get to a lesbian bar. We were surrounded by hundreds of miles of places where this cute li'l Britney scene could never have happened, and I loved that Slammers was here, providing a place for all queers, in the middle of a gay oasis city.

The next day, while driving to Nashville, Davin and I had the WORST HEARTBURN OF OUR LIVES. Nothing helped. Not fistfuls of Tums, not water, not the single sad gas station banana we were finally able to choke down after a full day of not being able to eat. We drove on and on, discussing the lesbian bars we'd already seen, listening to all of seasons 4 and 5 of *My Dad Wrote a Porno*, the funniest podcast I've ever heard, trying not to laugh out loud, because it hurt so much. Wretched, sick, burning with unbelched jalapeño and fried pepperoni liquid magma, neither one of us had ever experienced heartburn like this before.

And I would like to say this: I would do it again. Slammers is worth it. You should go. Get the Bobbi.

Nashville

The Lipstick Lounge

◆ ◆ ◆

After nearly two decades of inadvertent attention to the matter, I have arrived at the conclusion that there is only one perfect karaoke song, and it is "Goodbye Earl," by the Chicks. Straight men and all those under twenty-five: if you need to pause for a moment to look up "Goodbye Earl," now is the time to do that.

Everyone else, hear me out.

- All people in bars—especially in queer bars—love "Goodbye Earl" and know most of the words (people who choose obscure karaoke songs: do u want to fight)
- "Goodbye Earl" is about murder, specifically the murder of an abusive husband
- It is effective when sung by anyone of any gender
- It can be performed solo or by as many people as can fill the stage
- It's upbeat (why be the person who comes to karaoke with a technically complicated ballad or a personal rendition of "Rolling in the Deep"? no one likes that, everyone's here to have fun, please pick something like "I Touch Myself" and sit down, we're begging you)
- "Goodbye Earl" is easy to sing—no high notes or key changes or unexpected bridges

The Lipstick Lounge

- It taps into queer communal living fantasies—the two best friends in the song buy some land, open a roadside produce stand, and live happily ever after together, without husbands
- You can do jokey cowboy dance moves onstage with your friends the whole time
- And there are no awkward fourteen-bar ::musical interludes:: to surprise you with.

Perfect. It's perfect.

I came to this realization at the Lipstick Lounge, Nashville's only lesbian bar. Billing itself on its website as "A Bar for Humans," the Lipstick Lounge is a purple-and-red-painted karaoke bar in Nashville's East End with a big pair of red plastic lips set out in front as a bench for people to pose on. It opened in 2002 and is co-owned by Christa Suppan and Jonda Valentine.

"Jonda opened Lipstick Lounge, and I was hired as a bartender," explained Christa when I talked to her about the bar on the phone. "I worked there from the beginning and bought a share two months in."

When I asked Christa who the Lipstick Lounge's clientele was, she was firm. "It's lesbian-owned, so there will be no disrespect around that," she offered. "But everyone is welcome here. Everyone. When the bar started, I asked what we would do if someone wanted to come in who wasn't a lesbian, and that was that. You want people to come to your bar! And we all want to be accepted wherever we go; it's not like gay people only go to gay restaurants. That just creates a separation. We're ever-evolving creations. We're a bar for humans; we accept people for how they are when they walk in the door."

Christa owns the building; she bought it in 2003. "We started out with just one night a week of karaoke!" she said. "But in Nashville, ninety-five percent of your audience can sing, or at least rock it out, so it got really popular. Kathy Mac, who also built the sound system for Prince's Paisley Park, built our sound system."

Moby Dyke

Christa believes in the importance of spaces like the Lipstick Lounge. "Places like this, they give you a sense of community," she said. "Knowing you're not the only one in the world. Being able to see other lesbians and queer people surviving and thriving, it's encouraging. And believe me, we see all the people come in when the breakups happen in the fall and the spring!"

"Does that really happen? Every year in the fall and spring?" I asked.

"Like clockwork."

The Lipstick Lounge serves brunch and dinner and has its own upstairs cigar lounge (called the Upper Lip!), as well as a patio. It has a small bar opposite the entrance, backed by a green-striped wall with a disco ball hanging above, and pictures of famous queers like Marlene Dietrich framed in elaborate gold gilt. The Lipstick Lounge is adorable. It is also loud and crowded. It was especially crowded on the chilly, wet Saturday night in late November that Davin and I first walked in, having just had our vaccine cards checked at the door by a stern-faced security guard.

The crowd heaved into us. Practically carried off our feet, we looked around, shocked to suddenly be in the Lipstick Lounge after many hours spent driving through lonely towns with names like Slaughters, Kentucky. It had been a peculiar travel day. Right before we drove through Slaughters, I'd turned to Davin and said, "Do you smell . . . chicken?"

He sniffed the air. "YES," he said, making a face. It was an upsetting smell—raw-rich and thick and kind of bloody.

And then we passed a Tyson rendering plant.

So to find ourselves, hours later, in a rowdy bar overflowing with gay men and bachelorette parties and older lesbian couples who had staked out big tables they were *not* sharing, even though their tables could have seated six (I see you, Deb and Lisa)—to see such a wide mix of people of all ages and races, *and* know that everyone was vaccinated, after a day of being stared at in rural gas stations for wearing face masks—it was a lot to take in.

The Lipstick Lounge

It was late, and the Lipstick Lounge crowd was sloppy and in a good mood. Davin and I got drinks and inched our way closer to the karaoke stage, where a hot queer with a sharp Grace Jones haircut was yelling the words to Alanis Morissette's "Ironic" while gay boys in pastel T-shirts waved their arms and called "YAAAAS!" with their drinks in the air. In front of us, a blond femme in a cream-colored cable-knit sweater turned to face their blond, ponytailed femme partner, also in a chunky knit, and they started *seriously* making out, I mean, hands were *up sweaters*. Imagine Martha Stewart in her twenties in a softcore filmed in Nantucket. That's what it looked like—so many fluffy natural fibers. I couldn't help it—I stared. They looked like they were totally alone in the room, but the bar was so crowded that anyone passing behind them made their ponytails swing. Watching them, I nudged Davin, delighted.

"I know," he murmured, his lips hardly moving, carefully looking above their heads.

"Femme4femme!"

"You're being obvious!" he hissed, bugging his eyes at me.

I couldn't help it. Seeing a femme couple out in the wild is such a rare occurrence! You get to make a wish when it happens! I closed my eyes and wished for more femme couples to bless us all.

Onstage, the opening notes to Radiohead's "Creep" twanged. I groaned. A soft butch clutched the mic, nodding and tapping their thigh, eyes screwed shut, already overcome with emotion. There is always, always a soft butch singing "Creep" and feeling it way too much at karaoke. I focused on the heavy makeout still happening in front of me. Those sweaters. *Did they meet at a queer knitting group?* I wondered. *Do they incorporate yarn into their shibari practice?*

Then it happened. Three giggly-drunk babyqueers who looked like they'd graduated college that afternoon got up on the karaoke stage and began to do square dance moves, like "swing yer partner round and round" stuff. The opening notes to "Goodbye Earl" rang out.

The crowd went *nuts*. The babyqueer in the middle was wearing coveralls (they weren't Wildfang; maybe they were OshKosh B'gosh) and took care of the lead vocals, and their two friends *Na nanana NAAAHHH NAAAH NAAAAAAH*'d with gusto. And the whole bar—*every person but the DJ and bartender, without exception*—joined in. The gay boys, the older lesbians, the *two* separate bachelorette parties that were there—everyone at the Lipstick Lounge screamed "GOODBYYYYYYE EARL!" in unison, drinks slopping in all directions. *Is this the gay "Sweet Caroline"?* I thought, my mouth open. I realized then that I'd never seen someone do this song at karaoke without it bringing the house down, and I've probably seen it performed, at rough estimate, three dozen times, easy.

That's because I am always at karaoke. Please understand: It is never on purpose. I hate karaoke.

I'm sorry. I know everybody else likes it. But karaoke is just something bad that happens to me—a shitty, unavoidable part of my life, like taxes, or being allergic to cats as a lesbian, or chronically dating people who like to describe their dreams when they wake up. If I decide to go to a bar—any bar at all, not just a gay bar—there is a 95 percent chance I will choose the one night of the week that bar is hosting karaoke. And after a great night with friends, maybe a dinner, maybe a party, when a second location is being discussed, it is rare that someone will *not* suggest that we all go to karaoke next, while everyone else lights the fuck up and goes, "Hey, *yeah!*"

It gets tiring, being the only hater in a group. I'm already the person who hates board games *and* card games, and I'd like to have friends. I'd thought, once everyone started to move all over the country, that I'd be free of this plague, but it turns out this never goes away. Karaoke is always suggested as an activity, no matter *where* I live. So for years now, I've gone along to karaoke, even though I never sing, and that's how come I know so much about the kind of person who would choose to sing Garbage's "I Would Die for You" in a dive bar at one thirty a.m. I've seen all the karaoke there is. I'm exhausted.

Which is why I had not been exactly excited to visit the Lipstick

Lounge, originally. It wasn't the bar's fault; I'm just a curmudgeonly dyke who doesn't think she can handle seeing one more person get surprised onstage by the high note at the end of "Jolene." Also, I have lesbian friends who live in Nashville, and their reviews for the Lipstick Lounge had given me zero information upfront.

"It can be really fun! Or not." —Court

"It's kind of one big bachelorette party. But then Nashville is one big bachelorette party." —Bud

"The things I have done in that bar's parking lot." —Heather

I'd been unable to get a read from them on how our bar visit might go, but—I looked around—this wasn't the shit show I'd been expecting from a Nashville karaoke bar on a Saturday night. It was nice, actually. Yes, it was so packed that finding space on the floor for *both* your feet was difficult, but isn't that what we want to see for a lesbian bar? And the crowd at Lipstick was really into each song, shouting encouragement for the singers, hollering with appreciation if someone even *attempted* a dance move. I glanced over at Davin, cupping his hands around his mouth and cheering for the babyqueers as they filed offstage, and felt my shriveled, hardened-against-karaoke heart crack open just a tiny bit. This wasn't so bad.

Tucking my drink against my side, I started clapping, too.

THE NEXT DAY, WHICH WAS Sunday, we explored Nashville. I'd been a couple of times before, but hadn't ever done anything that didn't involve the main strip, Broadway Street, or a Segway tour. Davin and I were staying with friends we'd both known in Chicago together, Court and Caroline. They'd moved to Nashville a few years ago, along with a couple of other friends. Court was newly sober and looked so good and happy and so . . . *there*, in a way I had never seen her be, that I kept tearing up when I looked at her and blinking quickly to hide it. I was just so proud of her. I hadn't understood, in Chicago, that I had been experiencing Court's personality as if it were under a dull, filmed-over glass. Now it was as if she'd had her glass cleaned, so the sun could shine through it, and it was thrilling to discover she had an even dirtier sense of humor when she was sober. Court would have loved Smoove from the Back Door.

While we were wandering around town, I saw something so incredible I need to tell you about it: a cheese train, in the L&L Market, which is a bougie food hall. You know sushi trains? Imagine a sushi train, but instead of sushi, there are little plates of artisanal cheese slowly making their way to you like on a luggage conveyer belt. Tiny wheels of triple-cream brie, a small dish of juicy red grapes, a teensy platter of expensive crackers. Was it the end result of late-stage capitalism in a gentrified neighborhood? Yes! Did I stand at one end of the train with my mouth open like Garfield swallowing a lasagna? Also yes!

There are a lot of intensely groomed women in Nashville, I noticed. So many of them looked identical to me—youngish, wealthy-looking white women wearing either tight jeans, knee-high brown boots, and a cream-colored sweater, or a sort of soft, ruffly *Little House on the Prairie* dress, also with boots. Without exception, these women had a stroller, an expensive bag, or a coffee in hand—sometimes all three—and hair carefully curled into shoulder-length beach waves, a hairstyle originally designed to look effortless but that now just tells me your algorithms know you'll click on a sponsored tutorial for "perfect messy bun." My friend Angela once called the style in Nashville "Hot Girl Christian Autumn," which I thought was hilarious until I found out that "Christian Girl Autumn" was a real aesthetic and that that was its real name, and then I became afraid.

Later, all our friends who lived in Nashville came back to the Lipstick Lounge with Davin and me. Walking in, I sighed with relief—it was much calmer in there on a Sunday night. Onstage, an elder queer was singing the Fugees' version of "Killing Me Softly with His Song" while a person of questionable sobriety danced underneath them, their pants slipping farther with every dramatic arm wave to reveal an astonishingly fuzzy butt crack. As the pants made a full break for freedom, we all split up. Davin and Bud went to get drinks, Court claimed a table, and I headed to the bathroom, because I spend my life either peeing or looking for a place to pee. Next to the sinks, four queers were dividing up drugs. (I don't know what kind of drugs, I was thirty-two before I ever even saw cocaine! These were tiny pills.) "This will make you trip balls," the orange-haired one promised their friend, who nodded eagerly.

I smiled at them while I washed my hands, trying to show that I both knew they were taking drugs and also that that was fine with me. I have absolutely no knowledge or understanding of drugs; as a former Mormon and a soloist in our fifth-grade DARE musical, *Forever Free*, I cannot shake the idea that if I try any drug besides marijuana or mushrooms a single time, I will become helplessly addicted. (I know this is dumb and not true!) Nothing happens if I smoke weed, except that I get sleepy, and since I do not need more reasons to take a nap, it's not for me. The one time I tried an edible, I was at Gay Beach in Chicago, and my friend Jen handed me a cookie that the person she was dating had made, explaining that there was weed in it. Did I want some? Like a greedy possum, I snatched the whole cookie and stuffed it in my mouth, not understanding that I was supposed to break off a small piece and hand it back. I had thought she meant she had a whole *bunch* of cookies, and was asking if I wanted *that* one. She looked at me, wide-eyed.

"Uh-oh," she said.

I remember nothing but flashes from that day. I remember sitting, hours later, in a Chipotle, staring at a steak burrito I would never have ordered (barbacoa all the way, bitch!) and wondering how I'd gotten there. Suddenly, it was nighttime, and I was at my own house, and I was taking off all my clothes in the kitchen during a house party we were somehow having, yelling "HOW DO I STOP BEING HIGH?" at my partner as I twirled in frantic circles on the linoleum. She put me to bed.

Back out on the floor, one sip of my drink explained the butt crack ballet happening up front at the Lipstick Lounge. My gin and tonic tasted like straight gin, like the bartender had poured in Bombay and just passed the tonic in front of my glass. Heather's vodka and Coke looked like extremely weak iced tea. She sucked her straw, her eyes wide. "Whoa."

I was in the mood to approach strangers in minutes, comfortably lit off one-third of my drink. I pulled up a stool at the bar, trying to catch the bartender's eye. Her name, she told me, was Maggie, and she'd been working at the Lipstick Lounge for seventeen years.

"This place gets all types," she said cheerfully. "Everybody comes here."

I wondered if her drinks had anything to do with that. Sitting across the bar from her was Jason, the man who'd been running karaoke at the Lipstick Lounge for years.

"What's it like, seeing karaoke every night?" I asked. "Do you have a favorite song?"

Jason raised his eyes to me, and in them, I saw the profound weariness of someone who's seen 582 intoxicated people perform Missy Elliott's "Work It" in a single year.

"No," he said heavily. "I do not have a favorite song."

I steered us to better territory. "What do you like about working here? To have done it for so long?"

"I like that it's a job I don't take home with me," he said, brightening up. "When I'm here, I'm working, and when I'm off, I'm not thinking about karaoke. We have lots of regulars, too, and that's fun."

A gay man carrying a life-size, mid-nineties-era Mariah Carey cutout crossed to the front of the room, opened the front door, and walked out, Mariah peeking through her hair at us over his shoulder.

"Like that guy?" Jason said. "He's been in the last few nights. Actually, a bunch of nights in a row. He wants to be the first person at Lipstick to sing Mariah's "All I Want for Christmas" this year, but we have a rule here that you *can't sing that song* until December. He's really wants it, though, and tonight"—Jason broke off and smiled like a benevolent genie who grants wishes to fanboys—"tonight I gave in and let him do it."

"Shit! I missed it," I said. "Have people been coming back since Covid?"

"Covid was hard," he said. "We shut down for five months. Then we had a tornado in March of last year—it killed two people in the area— and we were shut down for two weeks. [Note: a tornado hit the Lipstick Lounge in 2020 and caused serious damage.] Then we reopened for a week, and then the second wave of Covid hit. We've been following all the Covid rules, and it keeps some people away."

I'd reached the bottom of my drink, and I could feel my booze-assisted extroversion dissolving into the state I'd soon be in, where I'd try to tell Jason his eyes were the *prettiest* color.

I had one more karaoke question. "OK, you don't have a favorite song, but is there a song you hate? What's your *least* favorite song to see on the lineup?"

Jason smiled grimly. "There is no song I care about seeing performed anymore. I'm no longer capable of feeling shock as an emotion."

I thanked him and Maggie and headed back to our table. The bar had filled up while I'd been chatting; all the tables were full now. A group of young queers was coming in the door, and a bachelorette party was beelining toward the bar in determined single file. Davin and Bud had their arms slung around one another, flannel on flannel; they were laughing uproariously about something I couldn't hear. Court, a glass of club soda in her hand, winked her perfect creepy-sexy half wink at me, a wink where you're never quite sure if she's winking or if she just closed her eye for a second, and gestured to the stage.

"You gonna sing?" she asked.

"Hell no."

Just then, two queers jumped on the stage. A preacher's church organ pealed out a single note. A guitar strummed. The crowd broke out in cheers. "Goodbye Earl" was starting.

"Jeeeesusssss," I muttered, shaking my head. Again! This song, again!

But people gathered below the stage to watch, and we did, too. Couldn't be helped, really. We were all just little rainbow moths drawn to the warm, flickering flame of a joyful song about the defeat of our oppressors, culminating in our collective queer dream of living together with our friends forever. It was only about eleven p.m. The chorus—the *"na nanana NAAAHHH NAAAH NAAAAAAH"* part came, and everyone sang as one, even me, all of us united in our love for lyrics about killing a man with poisoned black-eyed peas and hiding his body with your bestie.

"GOODBYEEEEE EARRRRRL!" I bellowed, my drink in the air, a part of it all. And as I looked around the room, I realized something: I was having fun. I was having fun at karaoke for the first time in my life. I was crunched in on all sides by a lot of people, my shoes were sticking to the floor, I was close enough to a queer's armpit to be able to *taste* the fact that their natural deodorant wasn't working, and it was fucking fun.

The Lipstick Lounge—filled to capacity with queer people, straight people, people who'd wandered in off the street because they'd heard music, and people who wanted nothing more than a stiff drink and a chance to prove they knew all the words to "My Humps" by the Black Eyed Peas—didn't really feel like a lesbian bar at all. It felt like a bar for humans.

Humans who just needed to sing.

Denver

Blush & Blu

◆ ◆ ◆

If you are an Uber driver who is male and over sixty years old, is it a legal requirement that you play top Christian hits during all your rides?

I ask because this happens to me at least once in every city I visit where I don't rent a car. I'll be scanning the street, looking for a gray Honda CR-V, and one minute later, a dad with small glasses will be trying to make meaningful eye contact with me in the rearview mirror of the cleanest car I've ever been in while some husky-voiced weenie on the radio is crooning, "Weary traveler, you won't be weary long."

That was how Davin and I got picked up from the airport in Denver. It was a chilly night in December, a week before Christmas. Upper lip curling under my mask, I listened to the Christian singer warbling that we should all just hold on, because it would be worth it in the end. As we got on the freeway, a floodlit, giant blue statue of a rearing stallion with eerie red laser eyes flashed past my window. What the fuck was that? I poked Davin.

"You see the satanic horse?"

"Hmm?"

He was checking emails on his phone. Had I just seen that? I quickly googled "creepy blue horse Denver" and pulled up the first link, an article called "The Story of Blucifer: Denver's Spooky and Deadly Horse." Apparently "Blucifer" was a local nickname for the giant blue horse sculpture, which had killed its creator by falling on him. Welcome to Denver!

The demonic horse contrasted nicely with the overly earnest Christian music. Pleased, I settled back into the seat, determined to get a look at Denver, where I'd never been. The singer was building up to a dramatic climax. He began to chant. "Someday soon we're gonna make it home. Someday soon we're gonna make it home." Other voices joined him, then more and more. It was a choir! A holy choir! "SOMEDAY SOON WE'RE GONNA MAKE IT HOME! SOMEDAY SOON WE'RE GONNA MAKE IT HOME!" *This song is about longing to die*, I realized. *Holy shit, how many Christian songs are about longing to die?*

I was excited about this trip because I didn't know much about Denver. Or Colorado, actually. Well, I knew people went skiing in Colorado, because it had lots of mountains and snow. I was also pretty sure the "Tap the Rockies, Coors Light" commercials were referencing Colorado. Recreational weed was legal here; I was positive about that. Oh, and Red Rocks. Right. Mention the name of any band and there's an 86 percent chance a straight person will break in and say they saw that band at Red Rocks and it was amazing.

Other than that, my knowledge reservoir was empty. I'm shit at geography, as I've mentioned, but I hadn't even come *close* to knowing where Colorado was on a map. When I looked it up before our trip, it was nowhere near where I'd pictured it to be. In my head, Colorado is where Montana or Idaho is—very far west, kind of up high. And yet there it was, sitting bold as brass in the middle of the country, next to *Kansas*, of all places.

I was looking out the car window for mountains, but it was too dark. All I could see was a vast Outdoor World—a camping and hunting superstore, different from Fleet Farm—all lit up for Christmas. It didn't feel like we were in a snowy white mountain city. It felt like the outskirts of everywhere else in America.

Davin's brother, Cole, and their partner, Jae, had recently moved to Colorado, and we were going to meet up with them for a Saturday night at Blush & Blu, Denver's only lesbian bar. Cole is much younger than

Davin—seven years younger—and *also* trans. Davin jokes that while *his* coming out as trans sixteen years ago caused enormous family drama and the kind of pain that therapy just kind of ~tickles~, by the time Cole also came out as trans, their mom, Denise, just sighed heavily and said, "OK. Sure. Just—just so long as neither of you ends up in prison, I'm good."

Cole now works full time in the weed industry, and has the slow, sweet smile, half-mast eyes, and tie-dyed hoodies of the person you might be picturing when you think of someone who works full time in the weed industry in Colorado. Jae, their partner, who is genderqueer and genderfluid, runs their own cleaning service in Denver, and told me over sushi that they clean Blush & Blu.

I couldn't believe it. "You do not!"

"I do."

"Have you ever cleaned up something . . . serious?"

"It's pretty tame. Sometimes a little barf on the toilet seats."

I looked hard at Jae, certain they were holding out on me. I was a janitor at my college dorm freshman year. People projectile vomit. They shit on floors *right next* to toilets. And the people I cleaned up after didn't even have legal access to alcohol. What would cleaning a lesbian bar bathroom be like after a rowdy Saturday night? I pictured two drunk queers writing ACAB on a stall wall using a dripping tampon like a crayon, and shivered.

We walked over from dinner to Blush & Blu. The bar, which is on East Colfax Avenue, is located next door to a Voodoo Doughnut location. Across the street is a gay sports bar called Tight End, which is a perfect name. Now, I cannot imagine a better placement for a doughnut shop that stays open until three a.m. than *between two gay bars*, and I eyed Voodoo Doughnut with lust, extracting a promise from Davin that we'd go there after we were done that night.

Inside Blush & Blu, it was busy. The bar was crawling with hyper-groomed queers wearing slouchy winter hats, the kind that look cool on other people but make me look like I have a used condom on my head. I looked around the two high-ceilinged big rooms, noticing at a glance that Blush & Blu had a Skee-Ball machine, and an upstairs, and that their bartenders were exceptionally good-looking. The bar was dramatically lit with blue lighting. (Was this where Blucifer came to drink?) Just like at the Back Door, there was also a big drink menu posted over the bar, with a mocktail list as prominently displayed as the alcoholic drinks. We love to see it! You do not have to drink to hang out at the dyke bar!

It was noisy as we went to get our beverages, but through the hubbub, I heard it clearly: a piano somewhere, playing the gentle opening notes of a song I knew well.

"No," I whispered.

I whipped around. Before I could even locate the source, someone was having their Saturday-night solo moment, singing "My Immortal" by Evanescence.

Shit. It was karaoke night. Of course it was.

There they were. Weaving through the bar with a wireless mic, a queer keened out, "THESE WOUNDS WON'T SEEM TO HEEEAL; THIS PAIN IS JUST TOO REEEEAL," throwing their arms wide to the bar. I took a deep breath through my nose. This was fine.

We went upstairs to a private-feeling room that had tables, a pool table, and a balcony, which allowed you to look out over everyone's heads. There was a large group of people down below dressed for an eighties party. At the bar, a sweet-faced babyqueer was celebrating their twenty-first birthday, and I know this because we could hear them shouting about it to their friends between shots. I looked away for—I dunno, maybe thirty seconds?—and when I looked back at them, they were aggressively making out with a femme with neon orange hair, who, even in the middle of frenching the babyqueer, looked like a cat who'd caught a mouse and was playing with it. A thin older man in a turtleneck wandered around the fringes of the bar, touching people on purpose, staring too long at the babyqueer makeout session. I watched him carefully. I'd never seen him before, but I knew him. We've talked about him. This guy is at every lesbian bar. I think I'll call him Solitary Creepy Unwelcome Man (SCUM). I was actually starting to feel like he was following me on the bar trips. SCUM almost always looks the same—white, mid-sixties, khakis, glasses—and he almost always does exactly what this version of SCUM was doing. He walked over to the bar, where he could get a better view of the makeout session, and put his hand too low on someone's bare lower back to get them to move over and allow him to squeeze in. One of the bartenders saw it, though, and the SCUM was suddenly gone, kicked out of the bar with a swiftness that impressed me, shouting as he was ejected. Calm returned to Blush & Blu. The bartender was unfazed.

I made eye contact with a group of friendly-looking queers playing pool up in the balcony room near us. It was time to make a move.

"Hi!" I said, wandering over, cringing inside at how cheesy I sounded. They eyed me warily. "My name's Krista, and I'm writing a book about the last lesbian bars in America! Can I talk to you all for a minute?"

Jesus Krista I would say no to this pitch, how about you be weirder.

"Umm . . . this is my first time here," said the one who'd looked the friendliest. Crap. The group offered me embarrassed smiles—all chatter among them had stopped. It was too late to back up now, though; I was already there. I plunged on.

"Have any of you been here before?"

A woman named Beth said, "I have." No elaboration.

"Oh, cool!" I said, hating myself. "What's something you like about this place?"

"I like that we have somewhere to go," Beth said. "Somewhere we can be ourselves."

"Niiiice," I said, scribbling furiously, pretending I hadn't heard this exact same statement twenty times before, and willing my heart to spontaneously stop beating. "What else?"

"Well . . . sometimes we pregame with all our dogs before we come here."

"Seriously?"

"Yeah, we all get together and bring our dogs, it's fun."

"Awesome!" I said. There was a pause. "Welp . . . I'll let you get back to it!"

And I slunk away, back to our table.

Fuuuuck, that was rough. *But I lived*, I reminded myself, face burning. I had been getting better at being OK with approaching people, and it wasn't usually that hard. Most of the time, lately, talking to strangers at dyke bars had been fine. People had been way more welcoming than I'd expected; most of them hadn't even flinched when I'd taken out my tiny notebook and started asking them to spell their names (suspicious behavior) and tell me their pronouns. Sometimes, though, approaching strangers was still really awful, exactly like the scenarios I'd imagined when lying on my back in the middle of the night, worrying about this book and how many people I'd have to start conversations with to get it written. You just can't ever tell how a new interaction is going to go.

And that's been the thing, I'm realizing: I have no control over how *any* of this goes. I can't plan how it'll be to talk to a stranger. Every interaction so far had been a surprise, and doing research for this book had been helping me to fucking get *over* myself. I mean, I'm thirty-eight years old—my shyness around new people is not going to go away. I was just learning to deal with it, in ways that embarrassed the shit out of me, over and over again. And hey—being able to start up a conversation with strangers is a good skill to have, since you could honestly die waiting for another queer to spontaneously approach you.

Downstairs, someone began singing "Take Me or Leave Me," the lesbian duet from *Rent*. I looked Davin dead in the eye and began mouthing all the words. He hates *Rent*. All musicals, but *Rent* most of all.

He shook his head in misery.

"A tiger in a cage can never see the sun / This diva needs her stage baby let's have fun," I mouthed, making exaggerated faces. I know all the words because I went through a phase in eighth and ninth grade where I was obsessed with *Rent*, to the point of sleeping in a tent with my choir friends outside the Weidner Center, *the* theater in Green Bay, to get rush tickets. As an adult, I also hate musicals, but I do enjoy torturing Davin.

The song finished, and one of the bartenders—devastatingly hot and wearing, as a shirt, one of those cheap black lace corsets you can get on Amazon for twelve dollars—grabbed the mic. They stretched a kind of condom onto the top of it (a microphone condom? Amazing for Covid!) and launched into "All That Jazz" from *Chicago*. Davin moaned, covering his eyes.

"Let's focus on something else," I suggested brightly. "Cole and Jae: Who's cute to you here?"

"I have a Blush Crush on one of the bartenders here," Jae said.

"A what?"

"A Blush Crush. A crush on somebody who works here. They're right there." Jae pointed to a mop of hair wearing a plaid shirt behind the bar.

"Jae. The one that looks like early Zac Efron?"

Jae nodded, laughing.

"That person screwed up my drink," Cole said.

"Me too," Davin said. "This isn't what I ordered."

"Wait, me three," I said. "Mine was supposed to have spiced rum, not clear."

Jae shrugged, still gazing at the bartender, and I understood I'd forgotten what it is to be that young and adorable. You can be absolutely terrible at something and . . . so what? You're so cute, all is forgiven!

We went back downstairs and sat in the room with a stage on one side. A lit Christmas tree sparkled. Two thirtysomething queers with popular-middle-school-teacher energy got up onstage and started in on "I Think We're Alone Now," complete with enthusiastic, synchronized dance moves. On the floor below the stage, an older couple danced cheek to cheek, completely out of rhythm to the song, in their own world. I watched them sway. They looked like they'd been together a long time, one nuzzling into the other's neck, comfortable and familiar.

Cole watched them with me. I assumed he was also all misty-eyed about the older couple, but he turned to me and said, "This song reminds me of my ex. The one who burned all my stuff in a bonfire when we broke up."

"Sorry, what?"

Cole nodded, grinning. "Yup. They posted the video of the bonfire on Snapchat. It was pretty fucked up."

"*Yeah.*"

We turned our attention back to the stage, where a powerfully drunk queer wearing a 40 & FABULOUS! sash was now singing Radiohead's "Creep" and interjecting the lyrics with their own words.

But I'm a creep ("I AM!")

I'm a weeeeeirdohhhhhh ("and it's my birthday!")

They were *horrible* at singing, so bad they could have been hired in a movie as a bad karaoke singer. The crowd loved it. It was like watching Cameron Diaz sing in *My Best Friend's Wedding*.

Karaoke kept going, and I found my mind wandering. I was thinking about that afternoon, when Davin and I had hung out with his aunt Jodi, who lives in Denver. She had driven us around, and I had discovered that Denver itself is flat—the mountains are outside the city, not in it. There was also no snow, and I realized that, prior to visiting, I'd been picturing some kind of Swiss ski resort town when I pictured Denver.

Jodi had taken us to a cannabis dispensary. I had asked her to; I was trying to buy a present for a friend of mine. He loves weed, specifically gummies, and struggles to really relax without them. He has no way of easily getting gummies in Minnesota, so I was on a mission. I would bring him back gummies as a little giftie.

I had never been to a dispensary before, so I was amazed we could just walk into a store and buy pot. "We can just . . . go in?? And it's . . . fine?" I kept asking as we pulled up.

It was. We entered the dispensary and showed our IDs in a special little room, and then were buzzed through another set of doors to where all the products were displayed under glass cases. It felt like being in an upscale 7-Eleven. A skinny guy was working behind the counter. A burly dude was standing against the wall behind him with his arms crossed, carefully not meeting my eyes. This was all very exciting to me. Drugs! We were buying drugs!

"Hi!" I chirped at the guy behind the counter. "I'm looking to buy some gummies for a friend!" Davin elbowed me hard. "So they're a present for someone!" I prattled on gaily. "Oh, and I have to take them on a plane"—Davin's aunt turned to me and widened her eyes, shaking her head subtly—"so I guess I need gummies that are really strong and will look nice and also be OK to take through security!"

The guy behind the counter coughed, but it was the kind of cough that is covering a laugh. His nostrils flared once, but he got it together.

"OK," he said carefully. "Well, you can only buy products for yourself, and you can only legally buy products you'll be consuming within Colorado."

Davin and Jodi were cracking up silently behind me.

"Oh," I said, crestfallen. "So I can't buy anything now, based on what I just told you."

"Based on what you just told me, no."

"What if I told you I also want gummies for me, that I'll eat here?"

"Then you could buy those."

I was quiet for a second.

"OK, I'd like one box of gummies, please."

"For you."

"Yes, for me," I said meekly. "Elderberry flavor, please."

"Great choice," the guy said, hiding a smile. "That'll be twenty-two dollars."

Outside the shop, in the sunshine again, Davin and Jodi burst into scream-laughs.

"Krista."

"How could you do that?! What is wrong with you!"

"How was I supposed to know? You can just walk in like a Walgreens! Nobody told me what I couldn't say!!"

"Why would you tell him all that?" Davin was crying laughing. "God. *God.*"

At Blush & Blu, as I watched a baby butch singing Taylor Swift's "All Too Well," I leaned over and whispered the story of what had happened that afternoon to Cole. He shook his head, saying nothing, smiling that special smile he shares with Davin that means, "How haven't you been hit by a bus yet."

The chords of the last karaoke song died, and a woman began taking down the mic stands onstage. I went up to talk to her. Her name was Monique Guichard, and she runs karaoke at Blush & Blu every week. A warm, enthusiastic woman, she told me why she thought Blush & Blu was special. "Because we're inclusive of everybody—whoever you are, we love you. All humans are welcome here."

"Why do you think lesbian bars are closing?" I asked.

"Colorado is a blue state, but places like this get bullied by red-state people," Monique said. "All the damage that came from Trump—all that stuff was always there, but Trump brought it to the forefront. We have fewer and fewer spaces. Gentrification, too—gentrification hurts everyone. It's the nail in the coffin for our spaces. And apps. Apps make person-to-person stuff much more rare. And the pandemic hurt so much, too."

"So a lot of reasons."

She nodded. "A lot of reasons. But Jody [Bouffard, the owner of Blush & Blu] is the reason we're here. She's fighting for us and has been fighting."

I'd tried to talk to Jody on the phone, but we hadn't been able to get a meeting set. It was like that with many bar owners; I'd tried to talk to them all, but several had been really hard to get ahold of. I understood.

These people were busy! Busy trying to keep the last lesbian bars in America open!

A queer named Robbie, who'd been standing near me and Monique, jumped into the conversation. "Lesbian bars are so great, and this bar in particular is so queer and communicative," they said. "Blush & Blu keeps working on itself, and it does so well with getting everyone together." They smiled then, looking sly. "This is also the only place I've seen where women openly cruise."

"Really."

"Really, I swear to god. It happens all the time here."

I looked around, then, wondering if people had been openly cruising all night in Blush & Blu and I hadn't noticed. Maybe it had been happening right under my nose!

. . . But what would that even look like, though? For queers to be openly cruising, someone would have to boldly approach someone else, a stranger, and *that person would have to understand that they were being flirted with.*

I side-eyed Robbie, suspicious of this claim. It would take an act of god for both those things to be happening at the same time.

Cole and Jae left Blush & Blu for the night, and Davin and I did a final circle around the bar. I liked this place. There were handmade posters up advertising a queer holiday craft fair at Blush & Blu the next morning. The hot bartender in the corset shirt was helping sweep up the dance area, alerting people to cords on the floor so no one tripped. Young Zac Efron was still working, pouring mixed drinks with an ill-advised lack of supervision, but now two twentysomething femmes had installed themselves on stools, dead center of the bar. They looked over at Zac every couple of seconds. Theirs was an obvious, single-minded intent, and I watched Zac run their fingers through their floppy-ass hair, totally oblivious.

Davin and I headed back to our hotel, promised box of Voodoo Doughnuts in hand. It was almost three a.m. We turned on the TV, settling on the bed. The first channel featured a group of men sweating and wiping their brows and whispering in hurried conferences with one another. This was the American Cornhole League Kickoff Battle. It was deadly serious. Teams narrowed their eyes at the cornhole target, preparing to throw a beanbag that could, according to the announcer, "be the turnaround they need to clinch this event." Behind the players, a banner sponsored by Johnsonville Brats declared YOU CAN'T SPELL SAUSAGE WITHOUT USA. Everyone was wearing uniforms that said BUSH'S BEST. (Imagine an athlete being sponsored by baked beans!) In the background, the players' wives and girlfriends sat in the stands, tense, watching the action, hands raised to mouths as their men tossed a small sack of beans into a hole.

Davin and I were so tired, and we couldn't look away.

"What if this was your husband's hobby? And you'd been humoring him for years?" I asked, propped up against the pillows, watching a blond woman in cutoffs jump up and scream when her husband made a good throw. Other women hugged her.

"I cannot," Davin said, transfixed. "I'd get it if this was a joke, but that's not what this is."

"Definitely not." A red-faced man mopped his shiny forehead. It was down to him. Stress was eating him alive.

I had my legs draped over Davin's legs, and I looked at him then, a man who'd come out as a lesbian when he was fifteen and come out as trans when he was nineteen. He likes cornhole. He likes beer and grilling and trucks and wearing camo unironically. On the outside, Davin looks like someone who might be registered to play at the American Cornhole League Kickoff Battle. Instead, he was with me, wide awake at three a.m. in a crappy hotel in Denver, his fingers sticky with mango doughnut puree, traveling to lesbian bars across America.

"You're perfect," I said.

"Should we turn this off?"

"No."

"OK."

We watched the cornhole teams compete for victory, raising their arms in triumph when someone knocked a competitor's beanbag off the board. I snuggled into Davin, grateful to be with him in Denver, a city that turned out to have no mountains and no snow, but plenty of weed, if you knew how to ask for it, and a lesbian bar where we'd felt welcome, exactly as we were.

Seattle

The Wildrose

• • •

I stood outside the Wildrose in Seattle, my heart beating fast. It looked the same. Exactly the same, even though I hadn't stood in that spot in thirteen years. The bar sign, the siding on the building, the Doc Martensed teenagers with shaved heads and thick black eyeliner stomping by—everything was just as if I were twenty-five years old and had stepped out of the Wildrose for a minute to get some air.

From 2008 to 2010, I lived in Seattle, and, because it was the only lesbian bar in the city, my headquarters had been the Wildrose. Now I was back, and it felt like I'd stepped out of a time machine. The only thing different was me. I was thirty-eight now, not twenty-five. Now I wear sunscreen every day, even if it's cloudy, and honestly believe the hummingbirds in my yard prefer *my* sugar water mixture to our neighbor's feeder. Now I do neck rolls before I have sex.

A slow 360 on the sidewalk revealed what I'd hoped: everything was as I'd left it. There was the Unicorn bar up the street, which, because it's circus themed, with carnival stripes, too many taxidermied animal heads, and merry-go-round decor, remains the worst bar in Capitol Hill to get fucked up at. There was Caffe Vita, my public meeting place of choice for screening Craigslist sex-dates in person. (Note for children: before Tinder and even before OkCupid, gay sluts like your Grammy Krista used the personals section of Craigslist to find queers who were

DTF.) On the corner, a crust punk sat, face hidden inside a pile of green army blankets. Nothing had changed.

"Are you coming in?"

The Wildrose bouncer was watching me.

"Oh! Yes," I said. "Just a sec." I fished out my vaccination card and handed it over.

The bouncer gave me a hard look. "You got a mask?"

"Yep, sorry, lemme get it." I put it on.

"You have to wear a mask inside."

"I will."

"Whenever you're not drinking."

"OK."

"Even if you're just walking."

"I will wear a mask," I said evenly, enunciating and looking the bouncer directly in the eye. *Did I look like a Covid denier?*

"Go ahead."

It was a chilly Friday night in February. It was 2022 now. The big Omicron wave had died down to less terrifying levels; I hadn't traveled in almost two months because of it. The Wildrose was clearly still being diligent about following Seattle's strict vaccine and mask mandates, which was good—they'd lose their license otherwise.

It had only been seven weeks spent riding out Omicron at home, but Seattle felt like my first lesbian bar trip in ages. It was also my first solo trip. Davin was back at home, working fourteen-hour days while the Minnesota State Senate was in session. Davin's a political gay, a distinct type of high-energy queer who gets fired up about great causes, like abolishing terrible trans bathroom legislation, but who *also* gets excited about really boring things, like going to zoning committee meetings. If you've never met a political gay, all you need to know is that political gays hang out with other political gays, and they *really* want you to agree to come door-knocking. I am convinced that the way they all find each other is by emitting a high-pitched noise, inaudible to the rest of us, when they're speed-walking to get cold brew. Davin ran for the Minnesota State Senate in 2020. He lost, but was quickly snapped up by the jaws of left-leaning organizations who were *quite* excited to put him to work. As I write this, he's working for a current state senator, managing the campaign of someone who's running for state representative in *our* district, and running for Northfield City Council. His phone goes off so much that, even when it's turned facedown, the notifications make it look like a tiny, silent disco is happening on the table beneath it. We have a lot of yard signs.

Give or take a bar, I was on my own from here on out and feeling a little apprehensive about it. Don't get me wrong: I love to be alone—to eat at restaurants alone, to go thrifting alone, to spend whole days by myself when I can, just napping and reading and walking around—but going out to a dyke bar? Alone? When there wasn't a show or anything? With no plans to even meet anyone? Except for the drag show in Bloomington, it had been *years* since I'd done that.

I walked into the Wildrose. There it was, the front room, just like I remembered! The bloodred semigloss walls (surprise, it's another lesbian bar painted red, specifically Pantone #8a0000, if you need a reference), the long bar stretching off to the back, the scuffed black wooden floors, the twinkle lights wrapped around the two front windows and the mirror behind the bar. I smiled, elated. There had been some cosmetic changes, but the front room of the Wildrose looked basically the same. It was full of people, and I blinked, my memory garnishing the scene in front of me with the times I had sat in *that* corner, and stood *there*, and met my friend Kelly over *there*.

Wow, actually, it was *really* busy. There was nowhere to sit. At all. Every table was full, and the stools were missing at the bar—they'd been removed. Weird. *Probably for Covid*, I thought, but I hadn't seen that in any other bar I'd been to. I poked my head into the other room, where the dance floor is, and gasped. It looked totally different. MAJOR CLUB VIBES back there! I stared, uncomprehending. Could this be the same room where I used to dance with sweaty homos, shouting my name into gauged ears weighed down by industrial metal piercings? If I squinted, I could see the ghosts—the middle of the dance floor, where a bike punk who'd flung her arms around my neck smelled so strongly of BO that my eyes had watered; the red neon sign shaped like a bare ass hung close to the ceiling, under which I'd once made out with a skinny boi who kissed like they were starving to death.

Everything in the back room looked great, but the changes felt like a personal loss. I'd frozen the Wildrose in time in my head, and the memory I'd preserved of the dance floor was very much linked with how Capitol Hill in Seattle in the late aughts felt—well used, kind of dirty, and a bit banged-about.

Now there was a mural of huge red roses on the back wall, and sleek red lighting ran around the room, bouncing off the faces of sharply dressed queers packed together on a big black leather couch. It was like the old dance floor had never existed. There was nowhere to sit in there, either.

OK, I was alone, with no friends and no spot where I could stand without hovering over someone's shoulder. People looked up from their tables—which were surrounded by empty chairs—knowing I was looking for a seat, eyeing me coolly. I went up to the bar, hoping that, since there weren't barstools, I could just stand there, leaning, with a drink, but the nice and apologetic bartender told me that wasn't allowed. Covid rules—you get a drink and you go sit down.

That's when I did something sad: I panicked and pretended I was waiting for my friends. I know, I know—I'm a grown-up gay lady, by now getting used to approaching strangers, but *man* it felt like the first day at a new school, looking for a seat in the cafeteria. I just felt *lonely*, too, being back at a bar I'd loved so much in the past and suddenly finding myself a stranger. I also felt a little dumb. What had I actually expected? To have the Wildrose look and also *feel* exactly the same? That doesn't happen. You can never go back to a place you loved during a formative period of your life and find nothing's *really* changed. Even if the physical place is the same, you've changed. So has everyone else.

When I ordered a drink and the bartender told me I couldn't stand at the bar, I said, "Oh. I . . . better hold off, then. My friends are going to be late." I waggled my phone in the air. I'd obviously been texting all my Seattle friends who were definitely real all night.

"You sure? You could wait for them along the back wall," the bartender offered. "I'll make ya a good one."

"I better hold off," I said. "Sorry about that."

And I turned around and left the Wildrose, embarrassed and ashamed.

Back in the rental car, I berated myself, my eyes filling with tears. My first real solo night out at a lesbian bar, on my first trip alone, and *this* was how I was going to act? Like a shy baby? Like a shy, easily cowed baby? *Oh, you couldn't find a seat?* I sneered at myself. *What the fuck, pull yourself together.*

Back at the motel, I journaled in bed like a brokenhearted eighth grader, my pen flying over the pages.

I just really felt like an outsider tonight. And that makes sense, because I am an outsider now—I'm not a regular anymore, I don't live in Seattle anymore—but I never really felt that way at the Wildrose, and it made me feel strange and very young and nervous and ALSO very old and tired, like both, "Oh right, I remember how it felt to be twenty-five and at this bar thinking it really mattered whether anyone here liked me," and also like, "Wow, I do not give a shit about hanging out with people who are too cool to scoot over and let a stranger sit semi-near them, I'd rather be at home." Maybe that's another reason the bars are closing—queers in their thirties are comparing going out to the bars with the question "Would this be more fun than hanging out in my house in my pajamas?" and regularly deciding the answer is no.

Taking a big, shaky breath, I shut my journal and blew my nose. There was still another visit to the Wildrose left. Tomorrow would be different, maybe.

ZOOMING IN MY RENTED CHEVY Spark along I-5, which curves gracefully along the Puget Sound waterline, I saw Seattle looking the same as it always had, making me gasp for a second as downtown came into view on my right. I'd always thought of Seattle as the most beautiful big city in America, the Space Needle levitating, alien-like, above shining water, the houses across the sound rising up in soft hills, downtown's lights winking on in the twilight, Mount Rainier looming in the distance.

But something was off. Now there were jarring, shittily modern condos marring the views I was used to, and every other car on the highway was a Tesla—I'd never seen so many. At the same time, there were more tents lining the highways and streets than I'd seen anywhere else in the country, even in San Francisco. Remarkable amounts of trash piled up along the edges of roads and gusted in the wind, blowing into bushes and trees. This was new, wasn't it? This was beyond crust punks; this was a huge disparity of wealth I was noticing. Was all this happening when I was younger and I just didn't see it? Had the disparity always been there, and now it was just more out in the open? Or had Seattle changed dramatically?

It was Saturday morning, and I was driving to Pike Place Market, because I'd missed it. Most people think of Pike Place as just a tourist thing, but it really is terrific—entirely worth going to. Downtown was a surprise. It was almost empty of people, but full of tents and quiet buildings. It used to be so vibrant. I walked past the old Lusty Lady peep show building, remembering its tacky-feeling floors and quarter slots and impassively erotic peep show dancers crawling around onstage with their fishnets and heavy eye makeup under the dark red lights. A handful of people passed me on the streets, some muttering to themselves and gesturing to the air with frantic, jerky movements. This was not the city I remembered.

"Opioids, Amazon, Microsoft, the protests in Capitol Hill after George Floyd, gentrification, the pandemic," my seatmate at the Saffron Grill had said to me the evening before, ticking the items off her fingers. Late night, I had been wolfing down tikka masala at the Saffron Grill's bar, after I'd finished crying and journaling at my nearby motel. My seatmate had seemed friendly, so I'd asked her if she lived in Seattle. She did, and she clucked when I asked her what had happened to the city. "All of those things kind of smacked Seattle at once, and we got hit hard. I'm thinking of moving, but I've been here my whole life." Her dining companion nodded, chiming in. "No one can afford a house here," she said. "Really: nobody."

It was jarring. This trip felt like meeting up with an old friend and finding out you don't have anything in common anymore. I'd been very happy when I lived in Seattle, and you know how you freeze places in your mind? I'd put Seattle on mental ice as this beautiful green city on the water, with casually amazing views and steep hills and wonderful houses I couldn't imagine being lucky enough to live in. It had an abundance of queers and great coffee and huge Asian supermarkets and liberal politics and Korean spas and so many outdoorsy people wearing entire outfits—down to the shoes and socks—bought at REI. And it still does; Seattle still has all those things. It's just that the gulf between rich people and not-rich people seems very, very wide now. As if half the city makes a base salary of $250,000 a year before bonuses and the other half is worrying about making rent this month, and every month. Parking the car far away from the market, where I could afford the hourly rate, I idly wondered if Jeff Bezos could put up and feed every unhoused person in Seattle without noticing the difference in his bank account.

The Wildrose

They were still throwing fish at Pike Place Market. The boisterous, bearded workers in rubber overalls were still pulling pranks on tourists, sneaking crabs into a lady's purse, dramatically pretending a salmon was too slippery to hold, to the delight of two little kids who were watching. The employees at Tenzing Momo, the market's heavily incensed witchy store, still smiled mistily at you and answered slowly when you asked them questions, as if their bodies were present but their minds were sailing free on another astrophysical plane. At Pike Place Chowder, whose soups I crave with a gnawing, ceaseless hunger, they forgot to give me a spoon for my clam chowder. I was so excited to eat it that I just *drank* it, shaking the chunky, creamy liquid from the paper bowl into my open mouth, making appalling gobbling noises, my eyes fixed on the seagulls whirling in the sky above me. Two teenage girls watched me with obvious disgust. It was delicious.

Full of chowder, buoyed by occasional shots of espresso, watching four people in a row stop in front of the market's flower stalls to take an identical "artistic" photo of the arrayed dahlias, I felt myself cheering up. I'd decided to go to the Wildrose early that day. Maybe I'd be able to find a seat!

I'd planned my entire day in Seattle around the Wildrose's opening hours, and so when I pulled on the door handle and found it locked, I was more than irritated. The bar was closed. The lights were off, even though Google said the Wildrose opened at three p.m. What the fuck! Come *on*, lesbian bars. I checked my phone. Yep, it still said they opened at three p.m. on Saturdays. Then I checked the Wildrose's website, where the hours were . . . completely different.

I sighed, giving the door handle one last half-hearted tug. I couldn't win *this* battle, but lesbian bars, you might lose the whole damn war if you don't start updating your hours on search engines.

A FEW HOURS LATER, I was back, and ready for the bouncer. I put my mask on a block before approaching the Wildrose, and this time was received without a rundown of the rules. Inside, it was almost empty. A blond woman was wiping the bar. She had a proprietary air to her—was she one of the owners?

She was. Martha Manning owns the Wildrose, along with Shelley Brothers, and she told me the bar had just celebrated its thirty-seventh birthday. The Wildrose opened in 1984, so it was one year younger than me. I bought a moscow mule and a sweatshirt to celebrate, and explained my project. Could I talk to her about the bar? And I'd be sitting by the window taking notes all night, was that OK?

Martha lit up. "I'd be happy to talk to you about the bar," she said. "I've worked here for years, so I've seen a lot. Did you know this is one of the longest-running, continually operated lesbian bars on the West Coast?"

"I didn't!" I felt like it would be rude to mention there isn't a lot of competition.

Martha explained that she'd already been a bartender at the Wildrose for three years when she and another person (who sold it to Shelley) bought the business from its previous owner, Joann Panayiotou. I nodded gamely, confused. I cannot follow it when someone explains an even slightly complicated relationship to me. Even something like "he's my stepsister's uncle" is going to make me squint hard, so I knew I'd have to try to look this up later. And, yep, after doing some digging, I later found an article on the Seattle website *The Evergrey* that stated that "in 2000, Martha bought the bar with two of her co-workers. A couple of years later, one of them sold her stake to Shelley. And eventually, in 2005, Shelley and Martha bought out the last person's share of the bar."

Got it.

"Did you see the other room?" Martha asked, looking proud. "We hired mural artists for the wall."

"It looks fantastic," I said truthfully. Then: "I used to live in Seattle and I came here all the time."

Martha smiled. "Did you have fun?"

"I had a wonderful time."

People started coming through the door. Martha would get them drinks, and then turn back to me. We talked about how, in general, gay men's bars still seemed to be doing just fine, and she said, "That's because they go out!"

"Lesbians don't go out?"

"No, they do, but sometimes I'll see older dykes come in here and they'll mention offhandedly that they haven't been here in ten years."

"I literally just did that."

"People who live here."

"Ah."

"It's hard, too, to be a genuinely inclusive space," Martha said. "Sometimes those same people will look around and want to know why there's 'so many men here,' and"—she threw up her hands—"I don't know what to tell you! How am I supposed to have a woman-centric space that's a lesbian bar but *also* be fully inclusive? *How*?"

I nodded.

"Lesbians can also go anywhere now," she continued, "and especially with dating apps, they don't need to come here anymore to verify that someone is queer. And so the bar business suffers. But there's lots of other reasons the bars are struggling. Not just one! And also, people *do* still come, and I'm just happy they do."

She turned to deliver beers to the three people who'd just walked in. In the dance floor room, I could hear someone shrieking with horror and glee, the way you do when you hear really, really good gossip. "*No*," they said. "*NO*. Oh my god, *NO!* THAT'S GROSS!" I pricked my ears up, wanting to hear what was obviously a disgusting sex story, but I couldn't catch it.

Near me, two trendy-looking queers were talking about how you can take "amazing" pictures if you spit on your phone camera. One of them said, "OK, but you know how I feel about bodily fluids," and the other cackled. Were they onto something? After making sure they weren't looking, my mask off because I was sitting, I tried it immediately, spitting on my finger and surreptitiously dribbling it onto my phone's camera before taking a picture of the bar with it. Huh. Nothing looked different. Maybe you need more spit to make it work, like you have to really hock a loogie onto your phone. But during *this* pandemic? I think not.

It was only six thirty, and the Wildrose was so busy! Thank god I'd come early; now there were no tables left in the front room. Leaving my notebook and jacket on my table, I got up to pee, noting an older-looking queer, very dressed up in a vampy femme dress, sitting alone at a table near the bathroom. They smiled at me, and I smiled back. This person looked friendly and hopeful, and was fiddling with their purse as if they were nervous. I knew that feeling. I made a mental note to go see if they would talk to me later.

The bathroom at the Wildrose is, of course, painted red. Sitting on the toilet, I read with interest a poster for an event called Dungeons & Drag Queens ("Watch drag queens play the tabletop sensation Dungeons & Dragons LIVE!") and thought, *This is why you live in a city, even when you can barely afford to. So there's so much of everything that you get spoiled, so that you've seen so much that events have to get nicher and nicher, until you get to this level.*

I'd just settled back at my table when a big group of noisy older lesbians barged through the doors. They dispersed rapidly; several went to pull a bunch of tables together in the back room, and a handful bellied up to the bar, one of them yelling, "Oh my god, I'm in the Wildrose!"

Another, who'd started buying people drinks while announcing she was "in real estate and could afford it," laughed and said, "It hasn't changed, honey, it's exactly the same."

The Wildrose

"Actually, we completely redid the back room a few weeks ago," Martha said cheerfully, and the real estate lesbian looked embarrassed.

The older lesbians were causing a ruckus. One of them started walking through the bar, trumpeting, "All the lesbians are on the couch in the back room. Attention, all lesbians are on the couch." Every minute or so, the whole group would start whooping back there for no apparent reason. One of them yelled, "We're old as hell!" and the back room erupted in cheers.

I was getting tipsy, and they were hilarious to listen to. Like the night before, I wished suddenly that I had a friend with me, that I had any person at all to share this with. It was fun to eavesdrop, but it would have been more fun to be part of things.

And then a woman approached my table. She was a little older than me, wearing a flower-printed dress.

"Hey, are you sitting alone?" she said. "Do you want to come sit with us?"

My mouth fell open.

Never, in my entire history of going to lesbian bars, has anyone ever approached me and asked if I'd like to join them. Never. I don't know if it happens to anyone else, but it sure as hell hasn't happened to me. Not even once. We've talked about this, but again, if I may make a huge, dangerous generalization, queers *simply do not* directly approach. They observe; they stare; they feel you out . . . sure. But they don't ask you to join them. This is not how we do.

The woman was looking at me. "Come sit with us!" she said. "Come on."

"Really?"

"Yes!"

"You're sure?"

"Get your stuff! Come join us!"

I couldn't believe this was happening. I gathered my notebook, picked up my purse and drink, and followed the woman, whose name was Christina, to the back room.

"Everyone move over," Christina commanded. "Make space."

People sitting in a big circle in the back room moved over. They made space. The woman next to me introduced herself. "I'm Melinda," she said. "Where are you from?"

"I'm from Minnesota," I said, and they all laughed. "We're a Facebook group," Christina explained. "The Pacific Northwest Lesbians. Tonight's one of our little get-togethers."

"You are *not*." I couldn't believe my luck. Not only was I being randomly included in a Pacific Northwest Lesbians Facebook group outing, but I was pretty sure I was the youngest person in the room. This never happens times *two*.

I explained my book project, and that's all it took: the PNW lesbians took turns coming over to my chair to talk to me for the rest of the night. They were so friendly and instantly welcoming; it was as if there were no such thing as the Seattle Freeze, a social phenomenon that gets joked about a lot in the city—the belief that it's excessively hard to make friends in Seattle. Which: jesus, it is. I remembered that from living there. I only had a few real friends in Seattle the entire time I lived there, and the only new people I met were people I worked with or went on dates from the internet with. Lots of friends? As a newcomer to Seattle? Not happening. But the PNW lesbians were laughing with me and buying me drinks and chattin' away. It was the eighth—I take it back, I mean it was the *gayth*—wonder of the world!

One of them, I kept noticing out of the corner of my eye, was cute to me. Very cute. Her name was Cherlyn, and she was shy and quiet, an ultrapolite butch, handsome, older than me, with kind eyes. When she came over, she asked me questions, and she was a great listener. As we talked, she maintained eye contact with me for slightly longer than normal. I felt my stomach swoop. Ugh. So cute.

My phone's alarm went off. Shit! I'd set it to remind myself of when my parking meter would expire.

I stood up. "I have to get going," I said. I didn't want to leave. "Thank you so much for letting me sit with you all."

"Aw, stay!"

"No, I'm parked really far away, I'll get a ticket."

Christina waved. "Do you want me to walk you to your car?" she called from across the room.

"Nope. Thanks, though, don't worry about it!"

Cherlyn looked at me. "Would you like me to walk you?" she asked quietly.

They were all so nice. My god. "No, thanks, I should be fine!" I chirped.

"Are you sure?"

"Yep, I'll be safe!"

I speed-walked to my car, many blocks away. It wasn't until I was sitting inside it, holding the wheel, that it hit me. Maybe Cherlyn wasn't offering to walk me to my car to be chivalrous. Maybe she wanted to make out.

Fuck.

I would TOTALLY have made out with Cherlyn! Shit! Davin and I are not poly, but we are nonmonogamous—we both sometimes fool around with other people casually. My god. It had been so long, so Covidy, since any of this stuff was even a glimmer of a possibility that I'd forgotten the rules of the game! I no longer knew how things worked!

"*Idiot*," I moaned, starting the car. "Frickin' *idiot*."

Cherlyn, if you're somehow reading this: I would love to have you walk me to my car next time I'm in town.

Driving back to the motel, I thought about the Wildrose. I'd had such a sad time there on Friday. And such a fantastic night on Saturday, which had turned around my entire experience of the bar, and of Seattle.

Moby Dyke

All that had been different on Saturday was that someone had included me. Christina and the PNW Lesbians, I realized, had given me two gifts:

1. a badly needed night of feeling like a part of things; and
2. a reminder of how easy it is, and how loving it is, to include people.

I'll do better, I vowed, pulling up to the motel.

That's when I remembered the smiling, nervous femme sitting alone at the table by the bathrooms. I'd meant to go back and talk to them, but I never did.

Houston

Pearl Bar

◆ ◆ ◆

The flight to Houston took a long time to deplane. I was sitting all the way in the back, and by the time it was my turn to grab my carry-on and go, I knew I was in trouble. Pressing my thighs together as tightly as possible, I waddled briskly up the aisle, feeling generous surges of warm blood gush out of me and onto my tights. We're talking unrestrained amounts. Lavish. Effusive. *Oh no oh no oh no*, I could feel it dripping down one of my legs, *just gotta make it up this ramp, OK, we're in the airport*, holy shit, it was in my *boot*, my toes suddenly sliding, *oh my god THERE'S A BATHROOM.*

DivaCups can only hold so much, and when the fasten-seat-belt light had come on early into the turbulent flight, I understood that my cup was about to undergo the challenge of its life. It was Day Two of my period, and if you don't understand what that means, picture the scene in *The Shining* where the elevator doors open and a sea of blood pours out. Day Two, for me, is elevator day.

I ran into a stall, slammed the door, yanked down my tights (shit, they were *soaked*), and reached up and in for the DivaCup.

That's when the stall door opened. I looked up. A little girl—maybe four or so—stood there, staring. I must not have locked the door all the way.

"No," I said. I had just pulled out the cup, my hand bloodstained to the wrist, and dumped it, darkly maroon, into the toilet bowl, where it bloomed in the water. There was blood on the floor, blackish blood shining glossily on the outside of the cup, blood dripping down the front of the toilet seat.

The little girl's eyes were huge. She backed away, silent. Carefully, and with the utmost respect, she pushed the door shut with chubby fingers.

It's been months, and I still think about her. I hope she's OK.

Houston was freezing (it was 36 degrees!) and cloudy, and I was unprepared, clothingwise. This was nothing new. One of my many irritating traits is that it never occurs to me to look up the weather before I pack for a trip. I always feel certain that the weather, wherever I'm going, is either

- exactly the same as the current weather in Northfield, Minnesota; or
- the most stereotypical version of what I believe the weather in a certain state will be. For instance, Texas = hot, no other possibilities.

It was late February, and I'd packed sundresses. It was too bad Davin wasn't with me for this trip—this situation would never have happened if he was. He would have demanded I bring a coat, holding one out and shaking it with increasing intensity until I finally accepted it, muttering.

Shivering outside my hotel, I watched the icon of my Uber slowly circle the block, idle, and then circle the block again. I was going to a drag show at Pearl Bar, Houston's only lesbian bar, and I was looking forward to it. Multiple people had told me they loved Pearl Bar, and it seemed like a polished place, with an active Instagram page, listed hours that *almost* matched in all places online, and lots of scheduled events. They had crawfish boils! And gay craft sales! Also, this was my first bar in the Deep South!

The Uber pulled up. It was a white, jacked-up pickup truck. A cherry-cheeked older man rolled the window down.

"Hah," he said. "Yew Krista?"

I nodded.

"Come on in."

I clambered up the tiny stair attached to the bottom of the truck, clinging to the side of the door's armrest far above me for support. *Can you even* have *a truck be an Uber?* I wondered, settling in. A *lifted* truck? Over the radio, a contemporary Christian singer orgasmed for Jesus. What kind of a place was Texas? Was everything I'd ever heard about it true?

No. I won't make any easy, snap, stereotypical judgments about Texas, I told myself, watching Houston flash past the windows. *I'll keep an open mind.*

We passed a margarita stand encircled by cars.

"A drive-through?" I blurted from the back seat. "You can get margaritas from a *drive-through* here?"

"Shore," the driver said. "We got daiquiri ones, too."

"Are you *kidding* me?"

"Nope."

After a few minutes, we pulled up next to a building with a large, colorful neon sign outside. FAT BOOTS TRAILER PARK BAR, it said.

"OK, this is it," said the driver.

"Oh. Umm . . . I don't think it can be," I said, confused.

"Shore is," said the driver. "This is the address. But ah think yew might be next door." He pointed at a building connected to Fat Boots, one with no sign I could see, but with people milling around outside it. It was dark, but I saw several short haircuts and a fanny pack. Definitely the right place.

"Yew have a nice night, now," the driver said.

"You too," I said, surprised. I was used to Uber drivers hardly speaking at all, barely glancing up from their phones to make sure you were in before driving off. But everyone I'd come into contact with so far that day in Texas had been *so* polite. That included the two frightening dudes in the airport wearing cowboy boots and matching NRA T-shirts who'd accidentally run into me ("OH my goodness, so sorry, ma'am") and the hotel employee who'd checked me in, calling me "sweetie" and asking me about where I was from in a way that had felt genuinely curious. Now this Christian-radio-listening Uber driver in a lifted truck, wishing me well. He pulled off, and I walked into Pearl Bar.

There was a five-dollar cover for the drag show. That was fine; most lesbian bars don't usually have a cover, unless some kind of special event is happening. Inside, Pearl Bar was impressive. The first thing I saw, besides a lot of queermosexuals, was a large, mirror-backed bar, illuminated with pink neon signs that said GIRLS GIRLS GIRLS and EAT ME DRINK ME. To the left was a red felt pool table, where four queers, two in plaid shirts, were circling a game, holding wooden cue sticks. They looked as grave as the American Cornhole League players had looked on TV in Denver, like everything was riding on the next shot.

I guess we'd call Pearl Bar's style "industrial chic"? It's bigger than it looks from the outside, with a cement floor, black walls, metal stools, and high-top tables whose bases look like welded-together pipes. Big, cushy, tufted leather couches are set up all around the main floor, with white, cube-like ottomans breaking up the dark color scheme. There's a fairly big stage at the back of the bar, lit up by a pink neon sign in the center that reads PROUD.

Most of the couches and tables facing the stage were filled, and there was an anticipatory buzz in the air. The drag show hadn't started yet, even though I was a little late, and I headed to the ATM, congratulating myself on successfully gaming Gay Time. I'd guessed the correct time to arrive for once.

The ATM was broken. Uh-oh. I didn't have any cash. How would I tip during the show?

Pearl Bar

I went to the bar to ask if I could get cash back from a drink order, already knowing there was no way they would let me do this. The bartender, Kayla, apologized and said that wasn't allowed.

"But you can Venmo me and I'll give it to the people in the show!" Kayla added brightly, as if that would help me when a drag performer sailed expectantly past my table, dressed in a sequined outfit that cost hundreds of dollars, scanning my fingers for dollar bills. I grimaced, took a picture of Kayla's Venmo, and found a seat near the back of the bar.

The lights went down, and the drag host welcomed us all to the show. Then they launched into a great li'l chat about consent, which I loved, reminding us all that we couldn't touch the performers unless we were invited to.

"Consent is sexy!" the host purred into the mic. "And it's—WHAT?" They held the mic out in the direction of the audience.

"MANDATORY!" the crowd yelled back.

"*Good!* You ready to start the show?"

"YEAH!"

The theme of the show was the eighties versus the nineties. A drag king did a flashy "Livin' la Vida Loca" in a skintight black sequined matador outfit; someone in leather pants with black electrical tape covering their nipples air-played a saxophone solo. A performer with cool, feline-looking makeup and green hair told a funny story about how, if they'd met their best friend, who was also in the show, under different circumstances, they'd definitely be dating today, which: ha-ha, but also this is such a *classique* queer plight, and why not remedy this by . . . dating one another? *You could start today*, I thought.

Performers in elaborate costumes would pass through the bar during their songs, walking slowly around tables, but very few people were tipping. No one had cash! Most of us were in the same boat. Did the performers know about the broken ATM? Eesh. I sat on my stool, embarrassed and waving the bartender's Venmo info on my phone, smiling guiltily at each drag artist who passed me in a way that I hoped conveyed, *I appreciate your hard work and this song and your outfit and I usually tip but today I have no cash and I am really sorry, I definitely know that backbend deserved at least two crumpled dollar bills.*

After the show ended, I sat at my little table and made notes about the crowd, but I'd had two drinks, and my notes looked like this:

This bar fun. Good vibes.

 Multiple ppl wearing sweatpants. To go out in! Am over-dressed, WHAT ELSE IS NEW

 Very racially diverse here, nice to see, and ppl are all hanging out together. Also older queers here!!!

When my Uber pulled up, it was not a lifted pickup, and I was disappointed. I was already getting used to Texas.

YOU KNOW WHAT'S HARD IN Houston? Crossing the street on foot. Maybe it was just the businessy district where I was staying, but I was surrounded by places to eat and I could not get to any of them without taking my life into my own hands and skittering across the road like a panicked armadillo. Big driving culture, Houston. Whenever I tried to walk anywhere, I'd notice that the city planners had whimsically decided not to place sidewalks along busy streets, the scamps. I also noticed that I was always the only person on foot. Speeding SUVs slowed down just to have a look at the alien creature scrambling up grassy knolls on two legs, trying to access a Panera. Children pressed their hands against back seat windows, peering at me in astonishment as they whizzed by at sixty miles an hour. I waved, a celebrity. I might have been the first pedestrian they'd ever seen.

Back at Pearl Bar that night, I approached the bouncer.

"Hi! Do you know, is the ATM working tonight?"

"Oh! Uh, I don't know," they said. "Let me ask." They turned to a nearby queer who looked about my age. "Hey! Is the ATM working to-night?"

"Why?" the person asked, coming over. They looked me up and down, their mouth a flat line. "Don't you want your husband to know where you were tonight?"

I was stunned.

"What?" I looked at their face. I absolutely could not tell if they were kidding, but it also absolutely did not feel like they were kidding. "*No.* It wasn't working last night, and I couldn't tip the performers. So I was checking to see if it was working tonight."

"We don't have performers tonight." They turned away from me.

"...OK?"

I went into the bar, heat creeping into my cheeks. I felt myself getting angrier and angrier. *This.* This is what femmes like me mean when we talk about femme erasure. Here I was, a lesbian *writing a book about lesbian bars*, someone who'd publicly identified as a dyke for nineteen! fucking! years!, currently in a space that proclaims it's *specifically designed for me*, as well as *everyone else*, and someone had decided at the door that I was straight and did not belong there. Because I didn't "look" like a lesbian.

And so what? What the fuck does a lesbian look like? What does a queer person look like? Why are there only a few ways we can look? What if I *was* a newly curious person, showing up for the first time to a lesbian bar, nervous as all hell to take a step toward trying something new? I would have been humiliated and maybe never come back. I *was* humiliated. Listen, this might be hard to believe, but more than anyone else, I am aware of how I look. I do not get read as gay, ever, unless I am currently making out with a person who *does* "look gay," and even then, I am publicly suspect. I could be dressed head-to-toe in rainbows, wearing a shirt that says LET'S EAT OUT, and everyone in a dyke bar would think, *Aw, that's cute, an ally!* And I'm fucking exhausted, man. In the grand scheme of things, femmephobia is such a small problem, such a petty thing to bitch about, but also: Is it? Is being made to feel, day after day, for decades, that you don't belong in your chosen community—after your given family and society have already made it abundantly clear that you don't belong—*is* that a small thing? Or is it a huge thing, touching every aspect of how people move through their lives? Isn't it all really about acceptance? About feeling like you belong literally anywhere? Isn't femmephobia just another way for more people to say, "We do not claim you"?

I'd just—I'd just like to be claimed sometimes. To be seen. I am pretty sure that that's all anybody wants, on a basic level. It always amazes me that queers—the vast majority of whom know the nuances of what real rejection tastes like—don't offer each other the gift of belonging easily.

Tears welled in my eyes. I took a deep breath. I let it out. It was just one idiot. There were millions of people who were not like them. I was fine. I was fine.

I was more than fine. I was at Pearl Bar for dildo races! And I'd been looking forward to this for weeks!

If you're not super acquainted with lesbian culture, let me actually explain about dildo races and dildo bingo, before we go any further. OK: In general, I'm gonna go ahead and say that on some level, most queers think dildos are funny. Sure, lots of us use them. They're great! Great for sexy stuff! It's just—they're also funny to a lot of us. They're sproingy. You can get hyperrealistic dicks and huge, veiny dongs and rainbow-striped cocks and glittery schlongs. They make dildos shaped like animals, like handguns, like forearms with fists. They make dildos shaped like octopus tentacles. Like the Virgin Mary, for godsakes! Dildos can be battery powered; they can vibrate like a jackhammer; they can be fit into a harness and wobbled about the room while being worn; they can be used underwater; they can be glass, metal, latex, silicone, or made of smooth rose quartz and charged with the rest of your crystals under a blood moon. Dildos make us laugh. They make us come.

And if a lesbian bar *can* make a themed night about dildos, it will. At some point.

People were ready for Dildo Races at Pearl Bar. It was busier than the night before, and there was a sign-up sheet at the bar—all you had to do to be entered in a race was write your name. I waited for three young, giggling queers to sign up, then scrawled my name and grabbed a drink. The bartender was especially friendly, and when I told them about the book project, they told me that weekends at Pearl Bar were a party.

"What do you mean, you won't be here Saturday?" they asked, aghast. "Saturdays are big! So are Fridays! We get DJs from all over! This place gets so full! Like, you can't see across the room!"

It was too busy (and too boring for them) to explain about my work schedule, my struggle to build up PTO, how I had to visit the bars in a particular order and on particular nights, so I just nodded, feeling regret. There would never be enough time to be at all the good nights at all the lesbian bars. I was missing so much, all the time.

Curled up on a tufted leather couch, I wrote in my notebook, filling page after page with notes. The bar was getting busier. They were playing Lil Jon's "Get Low." There was some kind of dispute about whose turn it was to use the pool table, which had been in constant rotation, with no breaks, both nights I'd been at Pearl Bar.

"I really like your handwriting."

I glanced up. A sweet-faced cherub was leaning over my little notebook, looking admiringly at the cramped cursive I was scribbling.

"Oh, thank you!" I said, flattered. *A babyqueer was talking to me! They thought I had cool handwriting!*

"It's so pretty," they continued. "It looks just like my grandma's."
Ah.

The cherub's name was Gema, and she had come to see the dildo races with a friend. The friend was clearly in some kind of emotional distress and trying to pretend everything was fine. Gema whispered that they were supposed to meet someone from a dating app at Pearl Bar, but the date hadn't shown. Distracted, the friend kept vanishing into corners of the room, texting furiously.

Gema smiled sunnily at me. She had an ease with talking to strangers that I envied. When I told her that, she said, "This is such a friendly bar, though. It's so easy to talk to people here."

"Maybe it's just you. Not everyone likes newcomers in lesbian bars," I said.

"Well, an unfortunate part of the queer community is how we have so few bars, and we so we all judge everyone in them," she said thoughtfully. "Territorial, you know? It's about sharing space when we don't have enough, I guess."

I stared at her. "Scarcity mentality."

She nodded.

"How old are you?"

Gema was twenty-one, and she worked at a crystal and pagan store at the mall. When I explained what I was writing about, she offered to show me Pearl Bar's patio. "It's the best part. You haven't been out there yet?"

I had not, and holy cow, *yes*, Pearl Bar's patio is the best part. So many of these bars have such great patios, and I know I consistently report that the patios are great, but *oh my god*. Pearl Bar's patio is wooden, enormous, fenced-in, and *made* for Instagramming. We're talking neon palm trees. Giant yard games. Rainbow-painted patio furniture. Neon signs everywhere, including a hot pink one that said I LICKED IT SO IT'S MINE. Inflatable pool toys shaped like doughnuts leaning against beach chairs. Garden globe lights strung from tall trees leaning over the patio. I followed Gema around, my mouth agape. I was extremely—*extremely*—jealous of the queers who had access to this patio on a regular basis. I mean, they had a whole, separate bar out there!

It was freezing outside, so no one was around, but the empty outdoor bar still played a looped compilation of cute cat and goat videos on a screen. Everywhere you looked, it was obvious that the owner, Julie

Mabry, knew exactly what would get people to talk to other people. This patio had been decorated by a party *master*.

Inside, the dildo races were starting. An unreasonably attractive, gym rat–looking queer with visibly cut biceps and a microphone—the emcee of the races—stood next to a large panel of corrugated steel roofing. This had been leaned at a sharp angle against the stage. People were grouped around the emcee, watching the dildos being placed at the starting line, which was a painted line at the top of the roofing panel. All the dildos were the same shape; they were smooth, plastic, torpedo-shaped, battery-operated vibes with one speed, the kind you can get for like sixteen dollars near the register at sex toy stores. While they were all the same model, they were each a different color and featured varying prints. They all had names. Big Blue, Coffee & Donuts, Pussy Pop . . . these dildos were familiar favorites to the crowd, the known racehorses of the underground homosexual sports betting scene. If your name was called from the list, you were assigned a dildo, and you went up front to watch the race. Each race was one heat. A pretty assistant twisted the knob at the base of each dildo, and they rattled the corrugated steel, trapped behind a ruler held by the assistant until set free, buzzing like tiny race cars at the queer Indy 500.

"Three, two, one, and VIBE," the emcee called into the microphone, and the dildos were off! Some dildos were immediately and obviously faster than others; a person in the crowd explained to me that they didn't all get their batteries changed at the same time.

"Cheer for your dildos, guys," the emcee commanded. "That's how they're powered." Big Blue, owned by a shouting queer named Aliyah, suddenly surged ahead of the other vibes, so fast it looked like the race was fixed.

"Did you bring lube with you? Aliyah, did you bring lube in your purse? Did you lube this up?" the emcee demanded.

Big Blue won. I was in the next heat, assigned to Coffee & Donuts, which, despite my shrieks and commands to "*MOVE!!!*" finished dead last.

Disqualified in the first round, and now completely hoarse, I watched the dildos compete, over and over, for the ultimate winning title. An adorable high femme won the championship race and, radiating pride, received the prize, fifty dollars in cash. This person—someone by the name of Suzy—was a treasure. Dressed in a blindingly white, fashionable sweatsuit outfit, they had been dancing to every song, all night, and, after winning the money, began throwing *down* on the dance floor to Biggie's "Big Poppa," looking smug. Their partner, a masc-presenting queer, looked thrilled to be at the bar with such a gorgeous, fun femme; they were so obviously delighted every time Suzy swooped over to kiss them or pull them up from a chair to make them dance.

It was time to go home. I'd been at Pearl Bar a long time, and it was late. I'd made a friend. I'd seen an incredible patio. And Gema's friend's date had finally showed up, bringing peace to the rainbow kingdom. People at Pearl Bar had been really friendly, aside from that first queer I talked to, who I never saw again.

It was interesting, thinking about it all. In the same way one person in Seattle turned my night around by including me, one person here had almost thrown my whole night off by excluding me. How we treat other people matters. More than we think. Imagine me having a bad night at Pearl Bar because of that small interaction. And it wasn't representative of the bar at all! I had stayed, and I had loved Pearl Bar. I hadn't won the dildo races, sure, but I didn't need to. I was happy just to have been swallowed up by the crowd, another face accepted among the others, a femme who maybe looked straight, but also knew she had every right to be there.

Dallas

Sue Ellen's

◆ ◆ ◆

The baby cheerleader was bawling. Standing in the middle of the hotel lobby, she was maybe three years old, dressed in a tiny pleated miniskirt and wearing a full face of makeup, topped by a clip-on, curly blond ponytail. The ponytail thrashed as she open-mouth sobbed. She wanted to eat at the Waffle House, which was visible across the highway through the lobby's glass front doors, and she pointed at it, red-faced and screaming, two clear lines of snot running straight from her nose and into her mouth.

The 2022 National Cheerleaders Association All-Star Nationals competition was in Dallas, and so was I. Downtown had been mobbed by thousands of mini, uniformed members of pom-pom squads, their fathers trying to parallel park enormous SUVs in spots that were too small, their mothers doing frantic head counts as kids poured out of back seats and onto street corners. Everywhere you looked: a sea of chattering, microskirted children, glitter silver eyeshadow smearing, bows on their heads. Just getting an Uber to *agree* to take me to my hotel from the downtown bus stop took over an hour. And I know I said I wasn't going to make any easy, snap, stereotypical judgments about Texas while I was there, but wow. *Wow.*

En route to Dallas from Houston, my bus had stopped at a gas station that had Bible verses painted in a border around the top of the women's restroom. I'd seen *cops* driving *police pickup trucks*. My hotel, a run-down establishment in a not-great area outside Dallas, had a person-size slab of granite flanking its doors. A selection of the Ten Commandments was chiseled on it.

The baby cheerleader's father slowly followed her around the room, periodically grabbing the giant white bow on top of her head to keep her from running into chairs as she shrieked. It was six p.m. The line to check in stretched out through the lobby doors. Children wearing neon red lipstick and rhinestoned outfits swarmed, taking practiced-looking selfies with one another and then immediately gathering around their phones to examine the selfies. Exhausted-looking mothers with a certain identical hardness to their mouths shifted from foot to foot in line, each holding a bulky canvas tote spelling out MAKAYLA or ISABELLA in rhinestones, every so often turning to their empty-handed husbands to say, "What is the *holdup*?"

The holdup was a sweating, pink-cheeked man behind the front desk. He was the only person working, and he was doing his best, typing quickly, repeating where the elevators were to people who hadn't been listening the first time, and explaining why the bar wasn't open tonight (too many employees had called out). His glasses kept slipping down his nose.

A woman in pastel coral cargo capris marched to the front of the line. "This is unacceptable," she snapped. "We've got *kids*. They need to *eat*."

"I'm so sorry," the desk manager said. "I'll be with you in just a moment."

I was in hell. We were all in hell, and I was the only one wearing a mask. Just ahead of me, a bucktoothed woodchuck of a kid farted audibly. It smelled like milk left in the sun, and his sister clawed at their father, moaning, "Daaaaaad" and pinching her nose. The woodchuck grinned.

"Are you OK?" I asked the desk manager in a low voice when it was my turn. He glanced up, pushing his glasses back up his nose. He sighed.

"I'm OK," he said. "It's been like this all night."

"I'm so sorry."

"Couple more hours. I'll be fine."

He slid my room key toward me. "One of our elevators is broken." He looked at the line of angry people waiting, their hands on their hips, for the single working elevator in the lobby and offered the ghost of a smile. "I'd suggest taking the stairs."

Up in the room, I showered fart germs off me, napped, and then opened my suitcase, rooting around for the most casual outfit I owned. That's right. The most casual outfit I owned. This was it: I was about to start an experiment.

I was about halfway through my journey to all the lesbian bars at this point. Before I got to Dallas, I'd always dressed up for the bars. I'd curled my hair, worn high-heeled boots, sometimes worn red lipstick. But after my experience at Pearl Bar, and thinking back to how queers had looked at me and responded to me in all the other dyke bars before that, I'd gotten . . . curious. And then I'd decided to try something.

For the rest of the bars, I was going to dress in a generic, all-black, "queer-looking" outfit, and see if people treated me differently. I was going to project a base level of "belonging" by dressing within the recognized queer fashion canon. Meaning: I'd wear an outfit that allowed other queers to mark me as a homo, an outfit that also allowed me to vanish completely.

My hypothesis was this: People thought, from the way I looked, that I was straight, and were therefore suspicious of me in the bars. If I removed the barriers to belonging—if I looked "gayer" by dressing in established queer items and styles, signaling to people that I knew how to move in their circles and speak their language—they'd treat me differently.

A depressing hypothesis. But one I wanted to test.

And so, out from the suitcase came a black, faded, zip-up sweatshirt dress with a visible hole torn on one side. Underneath, black leggings. I put on black Blundstones, which are shoes that look like baked potatoes and are basically queer bat signals for your feet, and I slicked my hair back into a ponytail. Big gold earrings (I needed flair *somewhere*), mean liquid black eyeliner sharp enough to stab someone with, and the final touch: two spritzes of a gorgeous, expensive perfume I'd saved up for. If anyone complimented me on it, I'd say it was "essential oils."

I was done. I stepped back from the full-length mirror in my room, admiring myself. Gay. I looked gay. This was muted queer cosplay. Switching out my regular purse for my new Walker's Pint fanny pack, I headed out the door.

I was eager to get my first look at Sue Ellen's, the only lesbian bar in Dallas *and* the oldest lesbian bar in Texas. I mean, there's only two, but still—it had been around since 1989! A couple of friends had told me Sue Ellen's was a great bar, big and fun and loud. Someone had also told me that it was named after one of the lead characters in the eighties soap opera *Dallas*, and that there was a gay bar nearby called JR's, which was the name of Sue Ellen's husband on the show. I loved that. Hope in my heart, picturing a mechanical bull and hundreds of hollering queers in cowboy hats, I summoned an Uber.

Oh my lord, Sue Ellen's was not a "bar." Sue Ellen's was a *club*. A CLUB-club. A huge, two-story nightclub on "the strip" in Oak Lawn—Dallas's gayborhood—with thumping music, people streaming in and out, and queers draped across the rail on the front patio, vaping. Within five seconds, I saw *three* high femmes, all decked out in very tight, very colorful outfits, complete with makeup and *nails*. They were stunning, and heading inside as a group with masc-presenting queers. Eyes filled with regret, I looked down at my ripped, faded black sweatshirt dress. Guess again, bitch. Texas was full of surprises.

A cutie behind the door in the entryway was checking IDs and collecting cover charges. I handed over my license, and they examined it and handed it back.

"It was just your birthday!" they said. "You get in free."

"Thank you!" I beamed, as pleased as any eight-year-old to have someone notice my special day.

Sue Ellen's

Whoa whoa whoa. Stepping into Sue Ellen's on a weekend night is overwhelming. Especially if, say, you've recently spent a few years not going anywhere or seeing anyone. There's a big—and I do mean *big*—four-sided bar with TV screens above it when you first walk in, and get this: *every screen had a different Guy Fieri show playing on it.* Not *some* screens, you understand. Every screen.

Transfixed, shocked by how busy Sue Ellen's was, I stood still for a moment, my mouth open, feeling clouds of homosexuals brush past me as I watched Guy take an enormous bite of something that squirted liquid cheese all over his facial hair.

Every inch of space around the stainless steel bar was mobbed, people clustered up in packs, queers sitting, queers leaning, queers ordering shots, a masked bartender pouring drinks with the fluid movements of an Olympic athlete and a barback hauling in bottles, sweating profusely. Beyond the bar, I could see a railing, also swathed with queers (my *god* do we love a spot where we can lean while we stare at each other without engaging), and beyond that, a large, open dance floor, where a DJ was bobbing their head, arms up in the air, and lots of people were dancing. And it was *serious* dancing, like *club dancing*, as in, people were "getting low" (help what do we call this now?) and pressed up against the walls and railings. I saw even *more* femmes, and queers in honest-to-god, actual "I Tried" Outfits™! The dance floor's ceiling went all the way up to the second story of the club; it was hung with a disco ball and big moon- and star-shaped balloons. Queers on Sue Ellen's upper floor hung over the railings, looking down on the people dancing. This bar was an incredible place to people-watch.

Astonished to be in a loud, busy lesbian nightclub, basically a lesbian Studio 54, I went for a little exploratory stroll. Here's what I turned up at Sue Ellen's: *Four* separate, named bars, all with different decor and ambiance. A game room with basketball tosses and video games and pool tables. Two different patios. A large room with a stage. Big bathrooms, with enough toilets that multiple stalls could be occupied by people fucking and you'd *still* be able to get in to pee in under a minute. And a goddamn indoor twisty slide!!

I had never seen anything like this. I settled in at a spot along the second-floor railing, looking down at the dancing below. The DJ was working hard, playing mostly songs I didn't know, all with heavy beats. Everyone dancing seemed to know the songs, though, and I assumed that was because almost everyone dancing looked to be under twenty-five years old. If I'm being honest, unrecognizable songs were a nice change from the early-aughts jamz that most lesbian bars specialize in. Like, I adore JLo's "Love Don't Cost a Thing" and Britney's "Oops! . . . I Did It Again" as much as anyone else, but there are *queers alive and dancing in dyke bars today* who *weren't born yet* when those songs were number one on the charts. At Sue Ellen's, if I *did* know a song, it was because a clip of it had been popular lately on TikTok, which I usually only watch via Instagram, days (weeks?) after they've gone viral. Well, I'm sorry! Your mother is trying but she can't keep up!

On the dance floor, a beautiful femme wandered around in an all-red Carmen Sandiego outfit—a tight red suit, the hat, everything. A slender gay *arrived* on the floor in a big leopard coat, no shirt on underneath, carrying a bottle of champagne and two glasses. They peered over the dancers with a royal, expectant manner, as if they were waiting for someone to come up and compliment them. Several people did. Two masc-looking queers leaned against a wood-paneled wall, clearly flirting with one another, trying to outdo each other with how many times they could run their hands through their hair and look down at the ground in a pretend-bashful manner.

At the downstairs bar, as I watched from above, a twentysomething queer made heavy eye contact with the total babe sitting next to them. Then, never breaking eye contact, they s l o w l y licked up the neck of their own beer bottle before taking a drink. Holy fuck, what kind of chaotic Scorpio-levels of confidence would you need to have to try a move like that on a *stranger*?? It worked; they began talking. Next to the bar, some gray-haired older queers in jeans and sweatshirts danced together. Two adorable babydykes swayed, one leaning backward, wrapped in the other's arms, eyes closed. On the fringes of the room, then, I suddenly saw him: Solitary Creepy Unwelcome Man again, another SCUM in khakis and glasses. He was watching the babydykes with a kind of chilling intensity that alarmed me from one hundred feet away. *I would keep an eye on them*, I decided, my lofty perch upstairs allowing me to see so much at once.

Man, as a person who, on weeknights, frequently says, "Jesus, it's *ten o'clock*?" being at an actual nightclub again is really something. I'd kind of forgotten what all this felt like. I headed to one of the bars, a dim, blue-lit one, where the bartender, a friendly gay man, told me this was a *slow* night.

I took my gin and tonic back to the railing. Queers eyed me, noting the fact that I was watching everyone in the bar and taking notes about what I saw like a discount-rate private detective, but no one broke out of their friend group to investigate further. Was my outfit helping me blend in? Did I now look like less of a threat, someone whose presence didn't need to be questioned? I was just thinking that Sue Ellen's was one of the first bars I'd been to where no one, not even anyone on staff, had gotten curious/suspicious enough of my behavior to walk up to me and ask what I was writing, when a voice came from behind me.

"Whatcha writing about?"

I turned around. A young queer with big eyes was looking at me, holding a tray with empty glasses on it.

"Do you work here?" I asked, delighted to see a Sue Ellen's staff member who didn't look like they were trying to do three tasks at the same time.

"I do! I'm a barback," she said, sticking out her hand. "Naomi."

"I have a lot of questions for you, Naomi."

We chatted for a minute. Naomi was very bubbly and told me she loved, *loved* Sue Ellen's.

"It's a special place," she said, putting the tray down on a table. She gripped the railing and leaned backward to stretch. "There's too many people for it tonight, but if you come back on a slower night, you'll form relationships with pretty much everyone in the bar. And as long as you're respectful, everyone's welcome to hang out here. We don't care about who you are—you just have to be nice. We actually had a straight guy in just last night, and he bought rounds for the whole bar." She widened her eyes at me. "I'm not kidding. The *whole* bar. He said it was the only place he'd been in Dallas where he felt like anyone gave a fuck about him."

"I love that!"

"So did everyone here!"

I walked around Sue Ellen's for hours, watching people flirt over games of pool and gossip at tucked-away back tables. The babydykes from the dance floor had vanished, and SCUM was still hanging around, so I took it as a sign they'd made it out safely.

Everyone is welcome in lesbian bars, btw. I want to make that clear. Just don't be SCUM.

At the bar, a gregarious gay man named Jerad was excited about *Moby Dyke*, telling me that he used to work at Sue Ellen's. He explained that the space we were standing in now was not where the original bar was. "A bar that's called TMC now was the original Sue Ellen's," he said. "Hey, did you know there's a bar near here called Woody's that used to be called Moby Dick's?" He tapped the bar top. "You should start your book with *that*."

"Maybe I will," I said.*

"You're welcome in advance."

I asked Jerad why he thought Sue Ellen's was thriving, even though other lesbian bars around the country were closing.

"I'll tell you why," he said, without even pausing. "I've thought about

---

* Sorry, Jerad.

this. It's because Sue Ellen's is a diversified bar. This bar has a dance floor. It has bands. It has DJs and live music. It has amazing happy hours, game nights, theme nights—by the way, are you coming to PriMadonna tomorrow? You *have* to. They're a Madonna cover band, you *don't* want to miss that. Anyway! This bar opened back up the second they could when Covid restrictions were lifted, and most of all, *everyone's welcome*, and that's not just something they say." He stopped to breathe. "Also? Sue Ellen's is run by Kathy Jack, the general manager, and she's the magic ingredient. Did you know she started this bar? Not the owners. The owners didn't think it could be successful. They said, 'We'll give you five years, and if it's not making enough money, that's it.' Well, guess what: Sue Ellen's has been open for thirty-three years."

Jerad looked proud. I smiled. I'd spoken with Kathy Jack, the recently promoted director of operations for all the Dallas bars owned by the corporation that owns Sue Ellen's. It was interesting to me that a corporation owned this bar. A corporation! Formed solely to make money! Of all the bars I visited, this was only one of a few that was not directly owned by queer women. Kathy Jack had opened Sue Ellen's in 1989 at the other location, done a lot of different things, and then come on as the general manager of Sue Ellen's in 2014. At sixty-five, Kathy was disarmingly amiable over the phone, describing Sue Ellen's as a "bar with a nightclub and friendly neighborhood feel at the same time." She'd also explained Sue Ellen's giant bathrooms—the biggest and best bathrooms of my entire journey—with a laugh.

"Everything's bigger in Texas!"

Her theory about why lesbian bars were closing was multifaceted. "I think there are so many reasons," she'd said thoughtfully. "One of which is that women, once they get to a certain age, find new ways to spend their money, and we can go other places besides our bars and feel comfortable now. Women also don't have the kind of income that men do, and when they have the opportunity to buy a house, a trip, a car, they might appreciate that more than having a night out." She also mentioned something I hadn't heard anyone else say: a lack of succession plans could be a factor. "A lot of lesbian bars were long-running, historic, but when the owners passed, they didn't have plans in place for how to continue their bar. If it's one person who owns the place, who will run the bar if the owner passes? What if they pass unexpectedly?"

Kathy's been in the bar business for forty-two years, long enough to become someone who's hard to shock. "Every time I see something really wild, I say, 'Well, I've seen it all,' and then I have to take it back a couple weeks later," she chuckled. "I think that's great. The new generation, they don't realize all the things we did to get to where we are now, and I love talking to them. I'd love to be around for the next fifty years to see where they go and what they do."

Did she have succession plans for Sue Ellen's?

"Sue Ellen's will be there long after I'm gone," Kathy promised before our call ended. "It's in great hands."

"Kathy Jack?" Jerad's husband, Brad, had appeared by his side. "She's a legend. She's in charge of it all. And she's fair—treats everyone the same."

"You guys love this place."

"We do," Jerad said, gazing fondly at the dance floor. "Before Covid, we were regulars. Now we're ramping back up."

Brad smiled and waved his drink. "Supporting!"

"Let me ask you something: Do you think dyke bars need gay men to survive?" I'd been thinking about this question a lot on my bar visits lately.

Jerad looked shocked. "Absolutely not!" he said. "Dyke bars used to be the catchall spots for all the people that men didn't want at *their* bars. But Sue Ellen's is its own thing. It has its own edge. Gay men leave the other bars on the strip to come hang out *here*. But Sue Ellen's doesn't need us. It's made its own way."

I took a final lap around Sue Ellen's, wishing I lived anywhere near it and that I could come hang out whenever I wanted. It really was a great bar. I hadn't seen people dressed up for a night out at a dyke bar in *ages*, and I felt blessedly shabby in my drab queer cosplay outfit. It didn't seem to have had a noticeable effect here, either, but maybe that was because everyone I'd encountered had been friendly and open—exactly what I'd been hoping for when I thought about visiting Texas. I had wanted slow drawls, to see queers wearing cowboy boots, to share a dance floor packed with gays, and I had gotten it all at Sue Ellen's within the first half hour I was there.

As I headed out the door, someone called, "Bye Krista!"

What? I turned around. That couldn't have been for me.

It was Naomi, waving from the bar. "Bye Krista!" she called again, definitely at me. People turned to look. "See you tomorrow!"

I couldn't believe she'd remembered my name. We'd talked three *hours* ago. She'd probably interacted with hundreds of people that night.

"Oh! Bye, Naomi!" I called, feeling suddenly warm all over, stunned at how welcome Naomi had just made me feel. Someone knew me here! "I'll be back!"

I would be back. The next night, I saw PriMadonna perform on the drag stage at Sue Ellen's, surrounded by a lot of very excited gay men. In the middle of "Like a Virgin," I crept away from the show, posting back up in my spot against the second-story railing of the bar. Down below me, masses of styley young queers were dancing to music I didn't recognize.

It was the same scene as the night before, but it also wasn't at all. Different queers were meeting each other; different dramas were unfolding; every person down there was having their own version of tonight. Sue Ellen's was just the place where it could all happen. A backdrop for the queer community—necessary, needed, and loved.

Feeling like a gay shepherd fondly watching over my flock of baby-queers, I smiled down at the dance floor. I was glad Sue Ellen's was in good hands. I hoped it would be there, long after I was gone.

Mobile

Herz

• • •

Tap tap tap. A long, red fingernail was tapping my license. I was standing at the front desk of a rental car kiosk in the Atlanta airport, having just gotten off my flight.

"This is expired," said the nail's owner.

I didn't hear—I had been focusing on the nail. Shiny, wet-looking red acrylic, with a tiny clear gem at the tip, it was beautiful, and made such a nice sound against the plastic of my license. *A rental car ASMR video*, I was thinking. *Has anyone done that yet?* And: *How does she type so fast with those things? How does she do* anything? I have a friend who gets her nails done a lot, really long acrylics, and she'd told me that she'd had to "relearn how to wipe" when she first started going to the salon.

"Ma'am?"

I snapped to attention. "I'm sorry, what?"

"This"—*tap*—"is expired." *Tap tap tap.*

"*What?*" Even as I said it, I knew it was true. *That.* That was the thing I'd been forgetting to do. After glancing at my license at the Wildrose in Seattle, the owner, Martha, had warned me that it was about to expire. Renewing my license had been on my mental to-do list for exactly two days after I'd gotten home from Seattle. Then I'd forgotten all about it.

"Oh no," I said faintly, feeling a cold sweat begin under my boobs. I *needed* a rental car. It was three p.m., and I needed to be in Mobile, Alabama, *that night* to go to Herz, a lesbian bar I'd been looking forward to ever since I'd heard about it, and . . . Mobile, Alabama, was a five-hour drive from Atlanta. I had—oh my god, I had a nonrefundable Airbnb booked in Mobile. It had been shockingly expensive, especially since Davin and I had assumed Mobile would be one of the cheapest places to stay. And—I began breathing shallowly—car rentals are nonrefundable if you don't cancel them twenty-four hours in advance. And *this* one had cost more than I'd ever spent on a car rental. Shit, *and* the travel credit card I'd taken out to fund the book trips—it was almost maxed out. Davin had warned me yesterday we had less than $200 left on there. *And* our checking account was super low—all the money in there was earmarked for bills. The cold sweat migrated to my crotch.

"What do I do?" I bleated helplessly at the woman behind the desk. She looked at me, zero emotion on her face.

"I don't know."

"I need to be in Mobile *tonight*."

She considered me, her face impassive. Was she . . . was she enjoying this? How many panicky idiots freaking out about things that were not her problem did she deal with in a day?

"Well," she said evenly, "you ain't driving there in one of these cars."

What was I going to do? I flopped down on a bench, shaking. I was stranded in Atlanta. I didn't know anyone there. I didn't have a place to sleep. Jesus, I couldn't actually afford one, anyway.

OK. Should I stay in Atlanta tonight, putting it on my last remaining credit card—the one with the *bonkers* interest rate—eating the cost of the car rental and the Airbnb in Mobile? There was a lesbian bar in Atlanta, too; I was scheduled to be back here in two days to go to it. But no, that would mess up the whole trip itinerary, and I'd specially chosen which nights I'd visit each bar based on my schedule and each bar's events. *And* it didn't solve the problem of needing to get to Mobile.

Should I forget Mobile and just stay in Atlanta for four days, doing Mobile another time?

Nope, that'd cost a fortune in hotels, and flying to Mobile from

Minneapolis was wildly expensive, *and* I didn't have enough PTO from work to do Mobile another time.

Wait, I was *at* the airport! Was there a flight to Mobile from Atlanta? Davin and I had looked into me flying right into Mobile when we were booking this trip, but we'd dismissed the idea. It had cost too much, and the flight times were all wrong. But maybe there was a flight to Mobile right now!

... Nope, the last one for the night had just taken off.

Cool, now Davin wasn't answering his phone.

Was there a bus I could take? How about a car service?

Fuck. No buses leaving tonight with any seats left. And hoooooly cow, a car service was $700.

I took a deep, shaky breath. I was out of time and I was out of money. I was stuck. I needed help. I was going to have to ... ask for it.

Goddammit. My personal nightmare. I hate asking for help. I don't mean, like, asking a store employee where the trash bag aisle is, or asking a café seatmate if they can watch my laptop for a sec while I go to the bathroom. I mean I hate asking for real help. Big favors. Something like asking a friend, "Can I stay with you for one night when I'm passing through your city?" Hoo. *Very* hard for me. Unless you offer this, I will likely never ask, because I strongly don't want to bother anyone, even though I am aware this is stupid. Also, I am *never* bothered when my friends ask *me* for help. In fact, I am happy when this happens! I like helping people, and assume they like to help people, too! What is *wrong* with me?

Fuck it. I called Sweetpea and Seven. Pea and Seven are two of my closest friends. I've known Pea since I was in my early twenties and auditioning for a burlesque club in downtown Minneapolis. The audition went well, and the emcee told me to go start getting ready to dance in the show that same night. I went back to the dressing room and sat down in front of a mirror, unable to believe I'd just been asked to be a dancer at Lili's Burlesque Revue. I am a *horrible* dancer, but I had fooled them by memorizing a tightly choreographed routine set to vintage music.

That's when I met Sweetpea. She wandered into the dressing room, a tiny woman in an even tinier shirt, and stopped right in front of me. "Oh," she said. "You're in my seat. That's OK. Who are you?"

Within minutes, Pea and I had figured out that we were both dykes, and she was showing me how to put on my first pair of fake eyelashes. Pretty much overnight, Lili's became my home away from home—the club where I danced most Friday and Saturday nights for years. Pea became my best friend. She was seven years older than me, and so she also became my guide to being a lesbian in Minneapolis in the mid-aughts, handing me gay books I needed to read—"Educate yourself"—and teaching me how to navigate the city's dyke scene as a femme. We'd wander around lesbian events together, Pea keeping up a running murmur in my ear. "That person is trouble, she is going to come up to you and be really charming, do *not* engage, shit, here she comes," and "OK, this li'l butch right here? *Really* nice, also *just* broke up with her girlfriend, go talk to her," literally pushing me forward, forcing me to speak to people.

Much later, through Pea, I met Seven. Seven loves to *hang*, more than anyone I've ever met, and is always down to go get food, scour the shelves of Marshall's with me for discounted perfume deals, or watch trash TV. Seven and I have a yearslong standing weekly date to watch *The Bachelor* (and all other *Bachelor*-related shows, our favorite being the one with the most crying, *Bachelor in Paradise*), and when I am in physical or emotional trouble, Seven swells up to three times their size, ready to defend me with their life. When I had my bad breakup in Chicago in 2016, the *only* people I called were Pea and Seven, who were married at the time, and the first thing they did was offer to let me move in with them that same week. So I did—I moved, and lived with them for almost three years in Minneapolis. They've both changed my life, and they're some of the only people on the planet who I feel comfortable asking for a substantial favor from.

I remembered them once talking about hanging out with someone they knew in Atlanta.

Pea picked up. "Hi. I'm in trouble," I said.

"Tell me."

I explained the situation, and Pea said she'd call back. Then Seven called me. I explained again. Seven said they'd call back.

Five minutes later, I was on the phone with an energetic-sounding man named Titus. He was Seven's friend, and he lived in Atlanta. He was between meetings, he explained, speaking quickly, so here's what we'd do: He would postpone his next meeting. I was to walk downstairs to the MARTA train station in the airport. I would get on it and get off at a stop downtown. From there, I would walk three minutes to meet him at a rental car chain location, and he would rent a car for me under his name.

"But my license is expired."

"That's why we're renting it under my name," Titus said patiently.

"Isn't that illegal? What if I crash it?"

"Don't."

Within the hour, I was at the front desk of a rental car franchise in downtown Atlanta, pretending to be the girlfriend of a very handsome, very muscled cis man who was charming the rental car guy into giving us a car without a reservation.

"It doesn't look like we have any available . . . " the young employee said, clicking his mouse doubtfully.

"I know you have a car for us. You'd be doing us such a favor, my guy!" Titus smiled winningly, relaxed and confident he'd get his way. He for-real looked like a cartoon of a fireman, a child's idea of what a hero looked like. We could not have been less of a pair. My face was shiny with grease; I was in a ratty hoodie; I hadn't even brushed out the knot on the back of my head where my hair had rubbed against the airplane headrest for hours. Titus was groomed and handsome; he looked pulled together, expensive. There was no way anyone would buy it, our being together. For the first time in my life, I realized, I was hoping to be mistaken for straight.

The rental car employee, a skinny, shy-seeming guy, wanted to please this friendly muscle man. "OK . . ." he said slowly. "We do have a Ford Mustang that's just been returned early, but you'd need to wait until it's been cleaned."

"We don't care about it being clean, do we, honey?" Titus boomed. "We'll take it!"

The Mustang smelled strongly of weed. With me sitting shotgun, Titus drove it out of the rental lot, smiling and waving at the employees in the garage. I couldn't stop thanking him. This man, this busy business-man I'd *never met before*, had dropped everything to help me. Just to be nice, to help out a friend of a friend. *Would I have done that?* I wondered. If someone had called me, asking me to interrupt my entire day? To help a friend, sure. But to help someone I'd never met? If my schedule was packed? I didn't know, and not knowing made me feel like a worm.

"You really saved my ass," I kept saying. "I don't know what I would have done."

Titus grinned, pulling into the parking garage where he'd left his truck. "Hey, 'everything is for the best in this best of all possible worlds,' right?"

"What?"

"*Candide*," he said. "Voltaire. Anyway! You're all set, and I hope you make it to the bar in time. Can't wait to read the book."

Titus got out of the Mustang and climbed into his megatruck. Waving, he drove away, windows down, speakers blasting . . . opera music.

Alone in the garage, I pushed the ignition button for the Mustang and held the wheel for a minute, just staring. Opera music? Jacked-up truck? Muscle man? *Voltaire*? What had just happened?

I DROVE THE FIVE HOURS from Atlanta to Mobile without stopping. Even though I was in a hurry to make it to the bar in time, I went EXACTLY the speed limit the entire way, body clenched over the steering wheel, eyes peeled for cops who might not be in the mood for a good story about why I was driving a flashy purple rental Mustang under someone else's name on an expired license. When I pulled in front of Herz, I let out a long breath. I'd made it.

Or had I?

The bar was dark.

It was closed. Once again, I had fallen for the oldest trick in the lesbian-bar-visit book: believing the hours posted online. Sitting in the darkness, hands still on the wheel, hysterically tired, hangry, and covered in dried stress-sweat, I started laughing. *The problem is me. The bars are not the problem. I'm the problem, because I cannot learn.*

Shaking my head, still laughing in disbelief, I drove to my Airbnb. I had done my absolute best, but it couldn't be helped: For the first and only time so far, I had broken a foundational rule for *Moby Dyke*. Herz would only get one visit.

THE NEXT NIGHT, DIRECTLY AFTER ordering a real blue plate special in a real southern diner and subsequently putting away a brick of meatloaf, a mound of mashed potatoes, a metric ton of fried okra, and a square of warm peach cobbler the size of a lesbian's misguided newsboy hat, I pulled up in front of Herz.

It was still light out, and I could see the bar much better now. And this was—this was interesting.

Herz is housed in a tan building topped by a roof that makes it look like it used to be an old-school Pizza Hut. It has a roomy, well-lit parking lot, and can I just say, as a person from the Midwest, how fucking nice it was to be able to park in *front* of a lesbian bar? For free? For the very first time on one of these trips? UNUTTERABLY NICE. I was *in love* with this parking lot; imagine going out to a queer bar, then not having to wait for your Lyft with twenty-six other gays on the same city corner, everyone squinting at the license plates on identical silver Toyota Highlanders.

Herz

Instead, at Herz, you could simply walk three steps to your car, or your sober friend's car, and drive home. Civilized, *non*?

Herz's front windows were completely covered up, just like Wild Side West's were. Completely different feel, though. The sign for the bar was an illuminated white rectangle on a tall post, with a logo featuring two curvaceous femmes with long hair and high heels, drinking martinis in front of a stylized sunset. *Total* strip club vibes. I texted a picture of the outside of the bar to EmJ, who texted back immediately, I love it.

I walked in, and every head in the bar turned. "Hi!" chorused *everyone in the bar at once.*

I was dumbfounded. I must have looked like a deer caught on a motion cam. I have never, in the history of my whole life, walked into a gay bar as a stranger and had everyone in it greet me, and if you have, I'm sorry, but I don't believe you. Queers are usually *fully* aware when anyone's entered a room, sure, but it's customary to then ignore said person, *especially* if you vaguely know *of* the person who's just come in but have never been formally introduced, *or* if you happen to've seen their dating app profile at any time. What I'm saying is: When you enter a dyke bar, queers always know you're there. They are going to pretend like you're not, though, while also subtly checking you out. So for everyone to both crane their necks to see you and then *audibly welcome you in, in unison*? Shut up, it's never happened before.

It was a bit dark in there. Herz was lit with soft purple and pink lights, the glasses at the bar shining under small white spotlights. The bartender, a tall, Black dreamboat, smiled, waggling their fingers exaggeratedly at me, and said, "Heyyy. Welcome in."

"Hi," I said, suddenly feeling a little timid. This was clearly not a bar where I could choose a back table and watch the scene for a while. Here, on a weeknight, all the customers were seated around the bar, and from the joking going on among them, they all knew each other. There was a stool open between two people, and I looked at the person to the left and said, "Would you mind if I sat here?"

"Please do," they said.

Well, it was the owner. Co-owner, actually. I was sitting next to Rachel Smallman, and *she* was sitting next to Sheila Smallman. Together, Rachel and Sheila own Herz, which they opened together in 2019. The only two Black lesbians who own an inclusive lesbian bar in the country were just sitting on stools, teasing the bartender, whose name was Beyoncé, as he shook up a cocktail.

"You're writing about this place? Oh, they already willed this bar to me," Beyoncé said, pushing a drink toward Rachel.

"I don't know if I would drink that," I said to Rachel, pointing at the glass and raising my eyebrows. She laughed.

"Keep drinking," Beyoncé cracked.

He turned to me. "You should have told us you were coming! If you had, they'd have fed you. You don't know what you missed; they'd have stuffed you silly."

Because I was already so full of peach cobbler, this sounded like a threat to me, but I appreciated the sentiment.

Rachel and Sheila were kindness itself. They'd met in the eighties, they told me, but started dating only in 2015.

"Wait, you met in the *eighties*? How *old* are you? Sorry to be rude, but . . ." Neither Sheila nor Rachel had a single wrinkle; neither appeared to even have *pores*.

"I'm sixty-two," Sheila said easily.

"You're not."

"I am! I was the first Black person to go to an integrated high school in my neighborhood," she said. "I'm sixty-two."

"Holy cow. OK. Please. Please. I know there's no way I can age like you, but: *what* are you using on your *face*?"

"Vaseline," said Sheila. "Just straight Vaseline, before bed. It's all I've ever used."

"Gahhhhh."

Sheila smiled the satisfied smile of someone who will never need to buy eye cream. "Anyway, in 2016, we made it official, and we got married in January of 2021," she continued. "I had started talking about wanting to give back to the community. Before this, I was also a social worker, a probation officer, and I was in law enforcement; I worked my way up from a jailer to the chief of police. I wanted to do something I'd truly enjoy and work my own hours. Rachel and I looked at a lot of local spots in the South before moving here."

Sheila and Rachel moved to Mobile in 2017.

"Shelia and I always drove past this place," Rachel said, gesturing to the bar, "and one time we drove past and I said, 'Oh look, it's for sale.'"

How had they been welcomed by the neighborhood? I asked. I knew that Alabama was more than half Black, but I couldn't imagine it had been easy to be Black lesbians trying to open a lesbian bar in a state that had some of the worst, most discriminatory laws against queer people in the country. Trans kids can't use school bathrooms consistent with their gender identities in Alabama. Teachers aren't allowed to discuss LGBTQIA+ topics with students. In much of the state, nonemergency medical professionals can decline to provide care to LGBTQIA+ clients on grounds of religious exemption.

"Well, there's a large LGBTQ population in Mobile," Sheila said. I must have looked surprised, and she nodded. "Yes. And neighbors were already used to gay bars, so this wasn't something to get bothered about. If someone wants to get rowdy, I just escort them out. I want this to be a safe space."

"We only have two rules in here," she added. "Number one: no politics. Number two: no religion, and we mean it!"

Beyoncé set a new drink in front of me. "A lot of people here are close. We keep politics and religion out of here."

"That's why the windows are covered," Sheila said. "When you're in here, you're in your own little world. The *real* world is out *there*."

I looked around Herz. We *were* in our own little world. Pretty soon, I had met every person in the bar. To my right was a friendly queer named

Papi. Near Rachel was a loud young white queer in a cowboy hat named Angel Dust, who was walking around the bar, telling stories about their sexual adventures, which were so detailed and outlandish—one story involved waking up naked and bewildered in Juárez two days after a drinking binge—that they had to be either 100 percent lies or 100 percent true. A genteel older butch nicknamed Freaky Veeky (I could be spelling that wrong) bought shots for the entire bar. Karaoke started, and three new arrivals began singing "The Devil Went Down to Georgia" and playfully spanking each other's butts in time to the music.

Hours slipped by. Sheila and Rachel went home. More and more people kept coming in. Beyoncé leaned over the counter to chat with me, and I asked if he liked working at Herz.

"I love it," he said. "The owners here always care about my well-being. A little while ago, I had a surgery that was pretty scary, and the owners took care of me, praying and calling and helping. I also work in an HIV clinic—I'm a sexual education and outreach coordinator; I have all the condoms, straight up—and we've been able to do community events here surrounding HIV status. The support here is real."

"I like your Crocs," I said, leaning over the bar to point at his shoes. "That's a genius shoe to wear to bartend."

"Honey, I have a *collection*. My best friend bought me the Balenciaga crocs! They make me stand about a foot taller."

"Whoa, I've seen those! You have them?"

"Believe me, I *screamed*."

I loved Beyoncé, and it was obvious everyone coming into the bar did, too. He had that gift of instant warmth, of talking to you like you were old friends. As an innocent-looking Gen Z queer shouted out the (disturbing) lyrics to Kesha's "Cannibal," Beyoncé brought me out back to show me the patio. I asked who, in his opinion, kept Herz in business.

"Honey, the lez comes *out*—every type you can imagine," he laughed.

Herz

"But we do a lot here. Saturdays we have a BOGO [buy one, get one] on hookah, and everyone comes in and is smoking hookah and *dressed*; it's a vibe. We have karaoke; we have good old-fashioned crawfish boils. It's a place for everybody to just come and party without any inhibitions. We have a good time in here."

Back inside, I watched a baby-faced masc queer who could have been anywhere between twenty-three and forty-three sing "For Your Entertainment," that techno-y Adam Lambert song with lyrics like "I'ma hurt ya real good" and "Give it to ya till you're screaming my name." The whole time they sang, they were giving off HUGE, totally unexpected top vibes, and throwing the person they came with significant looks.

Angel Dust, who'd been causing a ruckus all night, was still at Herz, and had not settled down even slightly. It was their turn to sing, and I watched them get up and choose a hip-hop song I didn't know. The lyrics appeared on the karaoke screen, and I saw a starred-out N-word at the end of the third line. *Oh no*, I thought, cringing, bracing myself for the worst.

Angel Dust skipped it. A *very* drunk, white, cowboy-hat-and-boot-wearing queer in the Deep South, they rapped that entire song, barely glancing at the screen, skipping over the word neatly each time it occurred. Allowing my shoulders, which were now at earlobe-touching level, to drop back to their normal position, I resumed breathing normally. No one else seemed stressed, but I had been sure Angel Dust was going to say the word as it flashed across the screen. Here, in this welcoming, Black-owned bar. The worry was not unfounded; I have seen white people in bars across the country not skip that word if it was in a karaoke song. I'd been holding my cup of ice water with white knuckles the entire time Angel Dust had the mic.

It was eleven thirty on a weeknight, thirty minutes till bar close, and I was fading. It was time to go. People were still getting up to sing in an unceasing stream. Beyoncé was still greeting and flirting with each new customer who walked in the door. I paid my tab and said my goodbyes, suddenly feeling sad that it was over, sad that I hadn't had enough time there, sad at the thought that I might not be back to visit Herz for a long time. Mobile had been so hard for me to get to. When would I be able to come back? To what was—I suddenly felt it, standing there—one of my favorite bars on this trip?

The feeling of being immediately welcomed at Herz had been almost overwhelming. And while it had meant a lot to me, I also knew it wasn't specific to me. I had seen everyone in that bar get welcomed like I had been. It was just how Herz was, the gift it was offering.

Getting into the car, I smiled then, filled with joy at the idea of watching a self-righteous white Twitter queer grapple with all the contradictions I'd seen peacefully coexisting here in one evening. Here, in the only dyke bar in Alabama. Which was owned and founded by a Black lesbian ex-cop and her wife. Who didn't allow politics or religion to cross the threshold of this space. Sheila and Rachel really were keeping Herz open for everyone, and there were no neat boxes you could put them, or their bar, into.

The next morning, as I drove for five hours back to Atlanta at exactly the speed limit, I mean *not one mile over,* I spent a lot of time thinking about Herz, why it had felt so special. As queers, we bridle against anyone putting labels on us. Queerness provides gray areas, we say, space between the little binary categories that have held society hostage. But a not-small part of queer culture feels like it's about making those same kinds of binary delineations within our own community. *You're good or you're bad. Your ideas are 100 percent perfect or you're part of the problem. You're saying the right thing or you're canceled. You look queer or you don't. You're one of us or you're not.*

Pulling slowly into the rental car return, I remembered how Titus had looked, driving away in his megatruck, versus how he'd acted. He was someone you couldn't put in a neat little box, either. Everyone is someone you can't put in a neat little box, of course, but it's something that's easy to forget.

Herz was special, I decided, not because of *what* it was, but because it was Sheila and Rachel's bar, a space they had created for all of us, gray areas included, in a place where it's amazing a lesbian bar even exists.

Leaving the rental keys on the front seat, I walked out of the garage into the sunshine, feeling something expand in my chest as I thought about Herz. They were offering us all a little grace.

Atlanta

My Sister's Room

♦ ♦ ♦

I am the worst-dressed person in Atlanta, I thought, scanning the dance floor at My Sister's Room. It was late Friday night, and I was there, alone, for Femme Friday, the event I'd scheduled my Atlanta trip around.

"You're not ready," Pea and Seven had told me, referring to the queer scene in the gayborhood, Midtown Atlanta. "You won't believe it."

I was ready to not believe it. To be honest, I'd been feeling worn out. Now, I love lesbian bars, y'all know I really, really do. But lately, lesbian bars, to me, had been feeling a bit like Lucky Charms. And by that, I mean: I *love* Lucky Charms. I love them with a boundless, insatiable, unreasonable love. I love the bizarre smooth-crunch of the freeze-dried neon marshmallows. I love how the marshmallows get frothy-slimy when they've been sitting in almond milk too long. I love the lightly frosted cereal bits; I love the disgusting purple-gray color the milk turns in the bowl.

The first bowl is an amuse-bouche, really—something to whet Madame's palate. The second bowl is always the best, the entrée. The third bowl is delicious, yet always immediately regretted. That's because, even while being so full of Lucky Charms that I'm actually breathless, I'll *already be sadly eyeing the level of Lucky Charms left in the box*, concerned that I do not have enough charms for next time.

For me, I have finally learned, there is no amount of Lucky Charms that is enough Lucky Charms. There is no such thing as keeping a box in the house and having a nice bowl every now and again. And so the only cure I've ever found for the helpless, unending longing I feel for Lucky Charms—the only way I can lead a regular life, free of compulsive thrice-daily urges for corn syrup and red dye 40—is this: About twice a year, I buy a family-size box of Lucky Charms. Then I consume as much as I can in one sitting. Hunched on a stool over my kitchen counter, I eat it until I'm physically ill. Until even the *idea* of another bowl makes me feel like I'm going to puke. Then I don't want Lucky Charms again for months.

Please understand: it's the only way.

By Atlanta, I was on my fourteenth consecutive lesbian bar, and I . . . I didn't want to go to another lesbian bar. I just wanted to go home. I felt like I had just eaten a whole family-size box of lesbian bars.

March had been a lot. Because of Omicron, I'd canceled all the January trips, and all the February trips but one—Seattle, and that was because my real, full-time job had sent me there. Canceling all those trips meant cramming them all into the spring instead. Every weekend in March, then, had been a lesbian bar trip, and April would be the same. I had used up all my PTO, and my regular job was suddenly demanding more of my time than ever before. I was stressed out. I was also *maxed* out—the travel credit card was officially full, and we'd be funding the rest of the trips out of pocket. Since we could not afford to do this, Davin and I had been having a lot of tense money conversations about how we could shift things around to make it happen. I was tired of taking rapid tests all the time, tired of following the rise and fall of Covid rates like a stock trader, tired of glaring at people in airports who weren't even *trying* to keep their masks over their noses. The details of the trips themselves were blurring—the hotel rooms were the same, the protein bars hastily eaten at eccentric times were the same, my ragged lesbian cosplay outfit was identical for every bar. And, if we're being honest, by March, sitting alone at a dyke bar in a strange city trying to get homos to talk to me just didn't feel as shiny and exciting as it once had. Tiny violin for me achieving my lifelong dream of writing a queer travel book,

I know, but I'd become a run-down version of myself, and I very much wanted to feel excited about the trips again.

So standing on the dance floor in My Sister's Room on Femme Friday, surrounded by the most beautiful femmes I'd ever seen, was like having a crack of thunder wake you up from a dead sleep in the middle of the night. Instant heart attack, but you're safe in bed, and fuck, *you love storms*, ya know? I thought I'd lost the will to go on, but here it was: *my will to go on*, in the form of a stunning femme striding across the floor in sky-high rhinestone heels and a hot-pink dress so short and tight it would have made a cute tube top for a guinea pig.

I smoothed my faded black sweatshirt dress, now extremely aware that I looked like your dad's oldest pair of dress socks. Pea, specifically, had tried to warn me about Atlanta.

"You need to look *good*," she'd said. She knew about my queer cosplay outfit. "Do it up."

I had ignored her, and I was so, so sorry.

There were femmes everywhere. Everywhere! I saw femmes come in My Sister's Room together holding hands; I saw *two* (!!) different femme couples make out. I saw femmes in tight jumpsuits; femmes in those short-onesie-things that websites call "rompers" or "playsuits" (suuuuuch shuddery, childlike names for clothing for adult humans). Almost everyone on the dance floor was Black—the first time I'd been in a lesbian bar where that was the case. And the *lashes*! The bodycon dresses! The heels! *No one* in plaid, or sloppy sweatpants, or washed-out hoodies with sports logos on them. I could barely take the scene in; I spun in circles trying to see it all. I was in a dark-paneled room with a wooden floor, gay flags hanging over my head, music thumping, a constant crush of queers hustling past me. The air smelled like a luscious thick fog of powerful vanilla body spray, sweat, blue raspberry vape smoke, and men's cologne, and I stood with my mouth open, able to *taste* Femme Friday.

My Sister's Room

As at Sue Ellen's, I was standing in a CLUB-club. I was also absolutely in the way. People were trying to dance. I scooted against the back wall, flattening myself into invisibility. (I dance like your least-favorite drunk aunt three hours into a wedding reception with a live Prince cover band, so don't ask me if I was dancing.) A stud carrying an oversize pastry box walked by, flanked by an excited-looking femme, and I peeked through the box's clear lid as they passed, catching a glimpse of a generous birthday cake bedecked with elaborate frosting roses. They were heading downstairs, and after a not-creepy thirty seconds of waiting, I followed, just to see what was down there.

The basement at My Sister's Room is called the Red Light District, and I know that because the walls and stairs to the basement are painted in fluorescent black-light paints that spell it out. At the bottom of the stairs, you turn a corner, and . . . there's whole separate bar down there! People were sitting at little tables, and the bartender was just as busy as the ones upstairs, and it looked like the birthday party was already getting going. And instead of thinking, *Wow, that's so cool they have a whole other bar in the basement,* my first actual thought, climbing back up the steps and onto the main floor, was, *I bet if I knew the rent for this building I'd pass out.* Annnnnd that's how you know when you really are middle-aged. But I mean, we were in Midtown Atlanta, a super busy, skyscrapery area, and MSR was huge. How many drinks would you have to sell each night to keep a place like this going?

I stood for a while longer on the edge of the dance floor, watching three femmes *(who could have been models! fuck!)* take a shot and then burst out laughing, like an ad for a girls' night at a casino. Then I headed to the front room, a kind of large, covered four-season porch, filled with pool tables and TV screens and seating in front of big windows. My Sister's Room is a curious place. It's been around since 1996, and I was standing in its third venue, where the club has been since 2015. From the outside, with its farm-red paint job and corrugated metal roof,

MSR looks a little bit like a barn that's been plopped into the middle of Atlanta. It's unexpectedly cute, with carriage lights outside the entrance. Its cuteness is highlighted by the fact that it's a short walk from many, many other bars, yet doesn't appear to have the same problems the other bars have at *their* entrances (e.g., boys in khakis fighting while twenty-one-year-old girls wearing blush pink bandage dresses cry and scream "MIKE! Just leave him *alone!*" out front).

My Sister's Room looked and felt like it was doing really well. Actually, almost all the lesbian bars I'd been visiting had seemed to be doing brisk business. Most of them had been *busy*, and My Sister's Room was one of the busiest I'd been to yet. Why was that? Was this a post-height-of-pandemic crush of bargoers? Were the bars crowded because of scarcity—because they were the only dyke bars for hundreds of miles in any direction? Or was it simpler than that—just an "everybody's queer now, let's fucking go *out*" mentality, and lesbian bars were the obvious choice for anyone queer who wasn't a cis gay man? Someone shoved me accidentally, but I hardly moved, rooted to the spot by a sudden, electric thought: Was I possibly experiencing the dawn of a new era of lesbian bars needing to *open* instead of close?

Whatever the reasons were for being jostled by this many homosexuals, Pea and Seven had been right. I was not ready for the scene in Atlanta. Everyone was so *polished*. I had not seen this many queers absolutely killing it in . . . years. I was also acutely aware of being white, which—while a good thing for me to have to feel for a change—made me wonder if I was taking up space that wasn't meant for me.

One of the TVs in the front room was playing the Pussycat Dolls' "Beep" video. I watched for a minute, marveling at how many accessories (crocheted minishrugs? crazy-quilted cabbie hats?!) you needed to have in 2005 to be fashionable. Then I realized I was standing stockstill, watching a music video from 2005, while hundreds of good-looking queers partied around me. *Go home, dummy*, I told myself. *You're just tired. And badly dressed. We'll try again tomorrow night.*

My Sister's Room

Tomorrow was sure to be even busier—if Femme Friday was any indication, Saturday night might be hard to get into.

I SPENT THE NEXT MORNING walking around downtown, trying to do free things. It turned out I was staying about two blocks from the 185-acre Piedmont Park, which was home, on a Saturday morning, to every person in Atlanta with a dog, a pair of leggings, and a stroller. Later, I went to the Atlanta Botanical Garden, which was *not* free. It was actually confusingly expensive (twenty-eight dollars!), something I did not find out until I'd reached the head of the twenty-minute line to get in. At the gardens, I saw a young queer couple in complementing athleisure outfits sitting under a flower-draped arbor, flirting. I was on the bench closest to them, and when I swiveled my eavesdropping ears in their direction, I deduced that what had looked like murmurs of love and adoration were actually earnest discussions about finance and investing, albeit with heavy eye contact. They *were* flirting, but with, "You really think I should open a Roth IRA?" replacing the more traditional, "Hey, my roommate's gone all weekend, if you want to meet my dog."

I got to My Sister's Room by late afternoon, and I was ravenous. Sitting on the bar's front porch, I scanned the menu. MSR was known for its wings, but I have a debilitating medical condition called "if I can get food poisoning while traveling, I will get food poisoning while traveling." It's quite an affliction. I once threw up so hard after eating a suspicious fish taco that I popped a rib out of joint while puking and shitting myself at the same time, and the rib hurt so bad I thought I was having a heart attack, but I refused to call 911 because I was covered in my own liquid feces. Over the years, I've learned that the best way to prevent this serious, unstudied malady is to eat vegetarian on trips. Fortunately, for these bar trips, finding vegetarian food simply wasn't an issue. If a lesbian bar offers food, I was learning that you can be sure that they have at least one vegan or vegetarian option, and My Sister's Room did *not* disappoint. I had the best goddamn Beyond beef tacos I have ever had on that front porch, and I leaned back in my chair, happy and covered in grease.

It was dusk, and people were starting to trickle in. The pool table across from me on the porch was occupied by two sporty-looking queers, and their friend, a gay man, arrived and came over to join them. He'd just been through a major breakup, it seemed. When they asked him if he wanted to play pool, he said "Noooooo," drawing it out in a flat moan, like Eeyore. He slumped into a chair near them, saying, "I just wanted to be here, where it's friendly, tonight," and brought a beer up to his lips, his eyes closed in agony. His friends kept trying to talk with him and cheer him up, but he would just sigh dramatically, accepting the back pats and free drinks they proffered as if they caused him physical pain. *I'd have broken up with you, too*, I thought.

The night before, I'd seen some outdoor steps leading down to a back patio, but there had been so many other things to look at that I'd forgotten to check it out. I decided to go see it now.

Well—and you probably knew I would say this—do not miss the back patio at My Sister's Room. To get to it, you walk down the bar's side steps and enter a dark, private-feeling, stone-walled alley trimmed with Christmas lights. This alley seems to have been custom-designed for making out with hot strangers, and I'm sure *some things* have happened down there. As in, I'd be willing to bet that alley could have its own storyline on *If These Walls Could Talk 2*.

Walk through the alley and there, at the end of it, is . . . all of Atlanta. You won't believe the view. My Sister's Room has a big wooden deck overlooking an expansive artificial grass lawn, set with tables and strung with garden globe lights. It's lovely, but it's the city, all lit up, in the background, that you can't take your eyes off of. It's *such* a romantic setting. And so unexpected! I'd had no idea a whole *skyline* was back there! Phew, I already knew that this patio was the place to be. I sighed, wishing I could teleport my friends to this spot. I'd *love* to sit at a table on the back patio at My Sister's Room on a hot Atlanta night, the city behind me, making too much noise and gossiping about who was being a little less than an ethical slut in their polycule.

But I was by myself, so I went back inside. I sat down in the front room to take some more notes. It was getting busy; a line was forming inside the front room to show IDs.

The blond sporty who I'd seen working security at the front entrance wandered over. Uh-oh. Had someone reported me as a suspicious character? Was I a security threat at MSR?

"What are you writing about?"

I smiled. Another gay fly had wandered into my web. Anyone who asks me that question is invariably willing to chat.

"I'm writing a book about the last lesbian bars in America," I said. "This is one of them, and I'm here to check it out."

"Oh, OK. That's cool. I'm Jill," she said. "I've worked here for more than ten years, if that helps."

Jill is the head of security at My Sister's Room. "I love it; it's such a fun place to work," she said, nodding to two people who were heading outside. "I also teach gym. And play on four softball teams. I guess you could say I'm like a lesbian's lesbian."

"I'm sorry, a *gym teacher*? And *four*??? softball teams? That is . . . so gay."

Jill grinned. "Yep." She told me she was headed to "the Lesbian World Series" in August. She explained that the event, which would be held in Washington, DC, in 2022, was actually the Amateur Sports Alliance of North America (ASANA) World Series, ASANA being an LGBTQ+ sports league, but—she said, looking mischievous—uhhhh, it was definitely the Lesbian World Series.

"We all stay in the same hotel. You should write about *that*," she suggested.

"I would love to," I said. I was telling the truth. I could not imagine the drama I would witness, staying for a week in the same hotel with hundreds and hundreds of softball players, all of them sporty queers, many of whom were teammates, some of whom were likely *also* sleeping together. A gay softball world series? The official sport of lesbians?! *Fuck, should I actually go to that?* I wondered, carefully writing down the name and dates of the event.

The line was now snaking through the front room and back out the door. Jill got up, beckoning me to follow, and reassumed her position at the front entrance outside. I stood across from her, watching her work security. There were so many queers waiting to come into My Sister's Room. Jill would pat each one of them down, and almost everyone would look more than a little delighted to be patted down by Jill. One person got patted down and then jokingly went to the back of the line, calling, "Let's do it again!"

"I'm looking for guns," Jill explained, running her hands lightly over the outline of a babydyke's baggy pants, pressing her hands against any loose fabric. "Guns and water bottles. No water bottles, because this time of night, they're usually not filled with water."

"Have you found guns?"

"Oh, definitely," she said, straightening up from patting down the bebe's leg. "But people are usually really cool about it. I can't let them in here, and they're almost always fine with it."

"You missed a spot," the next person to get patted down pointed out helpfully. Jill laughed, then turned to me. "Hey, you want to hear an inappropriate joke?"

"Always."

"What did one lesbian frog say to the other?"

"I dunno."

"Damn, we really do taste like chicken!"

Was I in love with Jill? I wondered. Half the line seemed to be. I couldn't trust myself, though—I'd watched the bartender pour my second drink. It was as if a tumbler of Bombay Sapphire had had a tonic prayer said over it. This bar knew how to have a good time.

Heading back inside, I saw that My Sister's Room was full of people now—a more racially and age-mixed crowd than Femme Friday had been. There were a lot of gay men hanging around the bar that night, too. As I watched, a man in an orange T-shirt so tight it looked like it had been painted onto him competed with a butch friend to see who could flex their pec muscles more accurately in time to Lil Nas X's "Call Me by Your Name."

"My titties are winning! MY TITTIES ARE WINNING, BITCH!" he cried, both his pecs twitching frenetically.

"BITCH, MINE ARE!" the butch called back, their left pec jerkily jumping.

"Nonono, I got *both* mine going!" He turned to their friends, demanding, "Who's winning? Who's winning this?"

I'm having a great time, I realized. Here I was, again, alone in a dyke bar in a strange city, having spent my evening trying to talk to queers I'd never met before, and it was not tiring, or too much, or blurrily the same as it had been at another bar. *This* was the Saturday night I was having at My Sister's Room, and I would never have it again. I was completely lit on 1.5 drinks, and—someone wearing a black mesh bodysuit and Lucite heels sauntered by—there was too much to look at, and I was having the time of my life. *Again.*

And I still had six more bars!! *Oh my god, and the next one is PHOE-NIX*, I remembered. *What* was *that* going to be like? Phoenix would come with so much baggage; I didn't know how to even begin to unpack it. I'd been half dreading and half looking forward to Phoenix for months. This time next weekend, I'd be there.

The man in the orange shirt was declared the pec-twitching winner, and he was crowing about it, hopping around and pulling his friends' heads down onto his chest so he could motorboat their faces, shimmying like a perverted Energizer bunny. I left my half-finished drink on the bar and wobbled out the front entrance, making sure to say goodbye to Jill. I was already thinking about the next bar on my itinerary, and I walked the two blocks back to my hotel in a daze, lost in my upcoming travel plans, suddenly as excited as a kid. My Sister's Room had been a joy, and it had also been exactly what I needed: a reminder of why I was doing this in the first place.

Because I *love* lesbian bars. They are important. They are needed spaces; rare places where queers can come and be themselves, together. Lately, I'd been taking my book mission *so seriously*, and in the process, I'd forgotten how fucking fun this actually all was. What an absolute privilege it was. I was going to see every last dyke bar in America. And I could not wait for the next one.

I was ready for another bowl of Lucky Charms. Pass the almond milk.

Phoenix

Boycott Bar

♦ ♦ ♦

'm so glad you're here."

We were sitting on a metal bench outside Sky Harbor Airport, me and my sister, Shelley, waiting for a hotel shuttle. She smiled lazily, sunglasses on, and turned her face upward to the sun. It was late March, and we were both coming from Minnesota, where it had been freezing and gray and sleeting for weeks. I copied her, closing my eyes, letting the warmth seep across my eyelids. It always feels good and novel to step out of the airport terminal and into the dry Arizona heat for the first five minutes of your visit to Phoenix. Then the shimmering air presses you down, flattening you out, and you realize, *Hey, this is an oven*, and retreat into icy air-conditioned cars and houses as fast as you can. Everyone moves to Phoenix for the weather; nobody ever goes outside.

All right, all right. I'm sure there are people who genuinely spend a lot of their time outdoors in Phoenix, or really do love hiking up craggy red sandstone bluffs, but I've been coming to Phoenix once or twice a year since I was born, and I've never met any of those people. The Phoenix I know is mostly Mesa, where my Nana, my mother's mother, used to live in a pink-painted brick triplex when I was little, and Gilbert, where she lived in a beige stucco house after that. We're not Scottsdale people.

My parents moved to Mesa after the 2008 recession. My dad's business, a company that tested soil for environmental hazards, had gone under right about the time I left for college, in 2001. He and my Mom had sold the house in Green Bay where Shelley and I grew up, and they'd been hopping from job to job, and state to state, ever since. A job in New York, a job in Texas . . . nothing had worked out. Nana owned the pink triplex in Mesa; she'd been renting it out. One of the units was empty, and so, knowing my parents were having financial problems, she offered to let them live in it. This was good timing, because Nana, while mostly physically and mentally sharp, was also beginning to make eclectic choices when driving. "It's a temporary solution," Mom had said over the phone, a little too brightly, explaining her and Dad's upcoming move to Mesa. "We probably won't stay at the triplex for long. Dad'll find a new job, and we'll move into something of our own. Your Nana just needs some help, and we're happy we can do it."

Mom grew up in Mesa. She never had plans to come back. She loved the green of Wisconsin, the shady forests trying to grow over the highways. On summer drives to anywhere, she'd sometimes murmur, "Isn't it *beautiful*," to herself, and then try to get Shelley and me to also look. We'd grown up in Wisconsin, though, so when we glanced at what she was pointing at, the scenery just looked normal to us, totally unremarkable. We couldn't see the riots of grass whipping in the wind, the lakes, the dark line of the trees the way she could, with her parched, desert-raised eyes.

The move to Phoenix was not temporary. Mom and Dad lived together in Nana's pink triplex for ten years, driving across town to Gilbert every day to take care of Nana until she needed to move to an assisted living facility. They visited her there every day, too. Then Mom died, unexpectedly, in 2017. Her sister, my aunt Carol, brought Nana home with her to Canada in 2020, where Nana lived for the rest of her life. Now it's just my dad in the pink triplex, which he owns now, the decor inside basically unchanged from how two generations of women liked it arranged. When you walk in the door, it's a time capsule. No furniture in the living room has been moved; my mom's collection of tiny wooden boxes from around the world sits on a side table, dusted, waiting for one of us to add to it. A candle in a glass jar Shelley gave our parents in 2015 sits, half-burned, on top of one of the bookshelves. "It smells too good to burn just any old time," Mom had said. That same bookshelf holds her cookbooks, which I saw so many times during my childhood—out, open, propped against bowls, spattered with stains, used every day— that seeing them all lined up, closed and quiet, makes me look anywhere else, like when you close your eyes during a violent scene on TV.

The now-abandoned hospital where my grandfather died of an early heart attack is within view of the triplex's front "lawn" (it's pink gravel). The white spire of the Mormon church, which my dad still belongs to, is also visible from his front gravel.

Phoenix is haunted.

Shelley had come along with me to go to Arizona's only lesbian bar, Boycott Bar. I was so grateful. I couldn't face going on this one alone. It wasn't the bar—it was Phoenix.

Shelley understands Phoenix. She was almost always there, with me, in Phoenix, when we visited our parents together as adults. We timed our visits to coincide, so we'd be a team. Shelley, who's two and a half years older than me, left the Mormon church when she was twenty-five, but she perpetually took my side during the years after I came out, the years when my mom either wasn't speaking to me at all, or she was, and was ending every phone call by weeping and bearing her testimony of Jesus Christ at me. When my parents finally announced, after I had been out for ages, that I was allowed to come visit Phoenix *with* my partner (as long as we slept in separate rooms), Shelley announced that she and her husband would be getting a hotel for the duration of the visit. With a pool. And helped pay for our room, too. Shelley's like that.

By age twenty-eight or so, after going through years of fights, painful handwritten letters arriving in my mailbox, Mormon missionaries being sent to my door no matter *where* I moved—after sitting quietly as my parents talked to me about "the gay lifestyle," which they knew nothing about—I had taken a deep breath one morning, and let it go.

It was OK, I decided. You couldn't change people. They couldn't change me into who they wanted me to be, and I couldn't change them into people who loved me for who I actually was, in my entirety. I had struggled with wanting their acceptance for a long time, and I was tired, and everything hurt, and I was done. Just . . . done. I felt too happy with all other areas of my life to let this shit continually bring me down.

After thinking about it a lot and discussing the idea with Shelley, I decided to stop allowing our parents to hurt me. I tapered off on dutifully calling them, from calling once a week to once every two weeks to monthly to never. I didn't email back. I didn't pick up the phone when Mom called. I stopped visiting Phoenix. It was easy. Quietly and efficiently, I cut the two people on the planet capable of doing the most emotional harm to me out of my life.

And at first, it was wonderful. I felt assloads better. It was like when you finally dump a toxic friend, except *250 times* that feeling. I was invincible! Nothing could touch me! My heart was stronger and brighter than one of those ornate gold-plated septum piercings!

But then, as time passed, I started to feel less great about my decision. As a kid, I never used to understand how the scary old guy in *Home Alone* (remember Old Man Marley?) could have not talked to his son for *years* when he obviously loved him so much. As an adult, though, I finally understood. This—what I was doing—was how estrangement occurred, how lifelong family grudges were formed. I was actively making it happen.

Months went by with almost no contact. Then a year.

And I wrestled with it. What was I doing? This was my family. It was so small. Just me, my sister, and my two parents. And those two parents were the people who had raised me and reminded me to double-knot my shoelaces thousands upon thousands of times. They'd put up with me at fifteen, which is the age I discovered the exact, heady power of saying, "I hate you" to the people who'd clapped and hollered at my swim meets and photographed me in homemade Halloween costumes every year. These were the people who had forced me—fought an exhausting battle with me *every single night*, for *two years*, against *all odds*—to wear headgear to bed, knowing they were saving me from a life-altering over-bite and also would never be thanked for it.

After I came out, all I had been able to see is what my mom and dad *weren't*. Eventually, with time and space giving me perspective, I realized: I would only get two parents in my lifetime. These were mine. And they weren't the only ones who were having a hard time with acceptance. I couldn't accept *them*. I didn't love them as they were, just as they couldn't love me as I was. We didn't know each other anymore.

Over the many months I didn't speak to them, I learned that, for me, shutting my parents out completely wasn't the answer. Shutting them out for a long while gave me time to think, however, and it had given me an idea. I wanted to be a real person to my parents again—to not allow their ideas about my "lifestyle" to be formed by Fox News.

So I started a project. A project where, after a year of near radio silence, I started sending my mom and dad a postcard every day for one hundred days.

I didn't tell them why. I just started. I bought a boxed set of one hundred Pantone-color postcards, and began writing to my parents.

I talked about what I was doing each day (obviously, worshipping the devil and snorting drugs and attending winter solstice gay orgies in sex dungeons) and talked about my relationship and what was annoying me and what I ate for dinner and who I was hanging out with that weekend. I didn't do much editing. For the first time ever with my parents, I wrote to them in the way I actually talk—that is, with a liberal sprinkling of the word "fuck" every few sentences. I told them about going to gay events and talked about my friends; I told them about essays I was writing and all the shit I was worrying about. I figured they could read the postcards and see for themselves what "the gay lifestyle" was all about. I really just wanted them to see it was similar to their life, only with *Queer Eye* swapped in for *Two and a Half Men*.

Moby Dyke

One day, my mom wrote back. A little blue card in my mailbox. Then an orange one. Then a red one. They weren't even real postcards—they were just colored three-by-five index cards with stamps on them, but they arrived regularly. Pretty soon, we had a daily postcard exchange going. Slowly—*really* slowly, because my mom's handwriting looks like spiders—we got to know each other again. The horrible awkward small talk between us dissolved, as the weeks went by, into descriptions of windstorms in Phoenix and point-by-point breakdown reviews of which dishes she and my dad had ordered at the Thai restaurant they loved, and my questions about how to get my indoor rosemary plant to get as big as their outdoor one. Eventually, I reached the last postcard in my set. It was black. We'd gotten through the entire rainbow.

And as I mailed it, I felt happy with what we'd done. The whole thing had gone better than I had even hoped. I also thought that was the end of it. You know: Successful project! Relearning to love people you are incredibly angry with! Letting go of bitterness and the past and working on the beginnings of forgiveness!

But it turned out that wasn't the end. Months after the postcard project, Shelley and I went to visit our parents in Phoenix together, for the first time in more than a year. I was nervous to go, but ready to try again with them in person.

Immediately, I felt a difference. During the visit, my parents seemed to have changed. They were casual and relaxed; our conversations as a family happened naturally. I assumed my parents felt more comfortable with me because we'd been in constant daily contact, but it was kind of strange, actually—we were easily bantering with each other in a way we hadn't talked since I was twenty. I mean, I'd been there four days, and *no one had cried yet*. Mom made a *lesbian joke* over dinner one night, for chrissakes. This! This was progress!

On our fifth morning at the triplex, Shelley and I were standing in the kitchen, quietly discussing our plans for escaping the house that night to go to Cash Inn Country, an incredible (and gone, and sorely missed) gay line-dancing bar in Tempe.

Mom came into the kitchen.

"What are you two whispering about?" she asked.

"Oh, Dad said we could use the car, so we're gonna go to a dive bar later tonight," I said. "It's called Cash Inn Country."

"It's this really fun western bar," Shelley explained. "I think tonight is lesbian night."

From across the kitchen, I stared daggers at Shelley. They'd never let us take the car if they knew we were going to a gay bar!

"It's a lesbian bar?" Mom asked.

"It's a gay bar, yep," I said carefully.

"Oh," Mom said. She paused. "Can I come?"

And that, folks, is one of the biggest things that has ever happened to me. Right there.

Shelley and I locked eyes for the briefest millisecond.

"Of course you can come," I said. I was trying to sound normal. "We'd love that."

WHAT THE FUCKING FUCK, HOLY SHIT *YES* YOU CAN COME WITH US TO A *GAY* BAR WHAT THE HELL IS GOING ON ARE YOU *SERIOUS*?

My mom asked to go to a gay bar. *My* mom. A devout Mormon. A person who, with my father, had donated a large portion of her savings toward the cause of banning same-sex marriage. A person who hadn't been inside *any* bar in thirty years. She'd never even seen me take so much as a *sip* of alcohol.

She put on makeup with me and my sister. She asked us what she should wear. (*Anything omg Mom you wear anything you want.*)

She drove us to the bar, parked the car, triple-checked the locks, and . . . nervously walked into Cash Inn Country with us. I took her arm. I couldn't believe this was happening.

Inside, it was noisy and loud. Mom stood in line with us at the bar and watched me order gin from a blond, butch, muscled bartender who called me "honey."

We were all a little on edge. All three of us walked slowly around the packed bar. As we walked, I told Mom that this was called doing a "fruit loop," and she . . . she *laughed*. And then it was like the tension broke, and suddenly she was asking about the gender-neutral bathrooms, asking about who leads when it's two women dancing, asking why the bar didn't smell like smoke. (Answers: so everyone feels welcome to pee wherever; whichever person wants to; because smoking in bars was banned *eons*, ago, Mom.)

We set our drinks down on a table and watched all the homos line-dancing and two-steppin' and generally having a great time.

I kept glancing at Mom. It was rowdy. Two minutes in, a young queer couple standing directly in front of us started making out. The taller of the two had their hand underneath their partner's shirt. I saw my mom watching them.

They slid their hand down their partner's pants.

I vaporized them both on the spot with the white-hot laser beam of my telepathic thoughts, which were something like "YOU ALL BET-TER BE ON YOUR BEST BEHAVIOR, I AM HERE WITH MY MOTHER AND IT'S HER FIRST TIME IN A GAY BAR SO YOU JUST STOP THAT HANKY-PANKY RIGHT THIS SECOND."

The couple left a smoldering hole where I vaporized them. Two other queers wandered over and started making out. I began to hyper-ventilate. *GAYS WHAT ARE YOU DOING TO ME?! BABY STEPS!!*

Shelley caught my eye. We moved to a different spot.

Mom seemed to be having a good time. She was swaying to the beat, watching everyone. Shelley grabbed her hand and pulled her out on the dance floor. And then: My mom danced to Kesha. And then a Lady Gaga song. And then Beyoncé. Then they played country music. And Shelley and my mom clumsily two-stepped around the bar in a sea of queers, bumping into people and giggling their heads off together.

I couldn't believe it. I stood against the rail of the dance floor taking pictures of them, my eyes spilling over with tears, swimming in them. It was one of the greatest nights of my life. It wasn't even my life; it was like watching something out of someone else's life.

My tiny mom in her coral-colored sweater and turquoise pendant.

Dancing with my sister.

At a gay bar.

All right. Just to be clear, I still think it's true that we can't change people. And sometimes the people who love us most hurt us so badly that we can't recover, to the point where it's necessary, even healthy, to ban them from our life of fabulousness and *Tampa Baes* marathons.

But sometimes, just continuing to try is enough. Sometimes even just a little bit of progress takes a lot of time—way more time than we maybe think we have to spare. Sometimes just the fact that you're trying, reaching out, again, to say *I'm here when you're ready, I've been here the whole time*, is what finally makes a difference, even if the message has been rejected over and over again in the past.

Now, one night dancing at a gay bar in Phoenix did not fix my relationship with my parents. It wasn't magic from there on out. But before that visit, my mom would have choked just *saying* the word "lesbian." For her, one night at a country-western gay bar with her daughters was *light-years* of progress. And I couldn't ask for anything more than someone trying.

So Shelley's Phoenix is my Phoenix. She knows what it means to book that Sun Country flight. She doesn't need the whole backstory; she's just lived it with me, because we've always gone together. Shelley knows the kissy sounds the hummingbirds make at the feeder out on the cement deck of the pink triplex. She knew the struggle of trying to get our parents to open any of their window blinds, even an inch, to let the sun—*which they said they moved to Phoenix for*—into their darkened house. And in 2017, years after our night at Cash Inn Country, Shelley was also with me in Phoenix, staying at the triplex with our dad while we waited for Mom to wake up from the coma she didn't wake up from. She'd had a benign brain tumor. It was the size of a duck egg, and it was "squeezing her brain like a sponge," the neurologist had said. After they removed it, Mom never regained full consciousness. We took her off life support after thirty-three days.

The hotel shuttle moved slowly away from the airport. I took a deep breath, turning my face to the window, where giant cacti flashed by, each looking exactly like what you would draw if someone asked you to draw a cactus. The sky was white with heat. The noise-buffering walls of the highway crawled with stylized renderings of salamanders, turtles, snakes, all done in shades of terra-cotta.

We exited the highway, the sun glittering the pavement, used car flags flapping over dusty lots. At the corner, a pale girl in black lipstick, a black belly shirt, and tight black pants with a lot of bondagey-looking red straps stood, tapping on her phone and frowning. There's an amazingly large population of goth kids in Phoenix, which I love, because it's ridiculous to be goth in the desert. You'll die of heatstroke fully covered in black—any makeup will run down your face in chalky rivers—yet the whole goth aesthetic loses something if you have to wear shorts. But I do understand it. There's an unshakable creepiness to Phoenix. You drive by marble fountains trickling merrily atop emerald lawns in expensive neighborhoods, but the city has no water source of its own, and much of the grass, on closer inspection, is really good fake grass, the softest, most realistic fake grass you've ever felt. There are palm trees everywhere, giving you a tropical oasis vibe, but they're not native to the area. Every single tall palm in Phoenix—like every drop of water—has been imported. If I were sixteen, living there, I'd be wearing black and scratching EVERYTHING YOU KNOW IS A LIE into the top of my desk with a ballpoint pen, too.

Boycott Bar

"This is going to be fun," Shelley said, pulling her suitcase behind her in the hotel hallway. "I love these glass elevators, where you can see everyone in the lobby!"

Shelley's an ideal person to bring on trips. She's ready to see the positive side of things, ready to try something she's never tried before, ready with a reason why something isn't *that* bad ("See, look, only the middle is raw, I can eat around it!"). She's also always up for thrifting, napping, and pastries that cost more than they should, so we do well together. Tonight would be her first night at a real lesbian bar in more than a decade. This was monumental because, since her recent divorce, one of the new things Shelley had been trying was dating women.

I was thrilled about it. I was also jubilant; I'd totally called it. Shelley had had an obvious obsessive crush on one of her close friends in her midtwenties—I mean, she *never* shut up about this woman—and I'd noted this down in my little mental black book of Likely Queers, which I keep constantly updated. Always the first homosexual trying to recruit innocents into my godless coven, I'd insisted we make Shelley a Tinder profile the *second* she told me she was interested in dating women, and then spent hours with her, teaching her how to spot red flags.

"What about her?" she'd ask, waving her phone.

"Absolutely not, did you read her profile?" I'd say, snatching it away. "The first thing she does is issue a direct order. 'Message me something to make me smile. Be creative': Are you fucking kidding me? Like an emperor, sitting back and ordering you? Not even a 'please'?"

"Oh, OK. What about this one?"

"Their main profile picture is a cat? Please tell me you're joking."

"This one?"

I scrolled. "Dude, this is a couple."

"No it isn't."

"You have to scroll to the last picture. That's where 'Hubby' is always hiding."

"Oh my god. Wait, what about this one? *She's* cute."

"'Looking for my partner in crime': Are you *kidding* me?"

No one was good enough for my sister. In the end, she'd just quietly started dating women on her own, figuring it out herself, like we all do.

Our flight had gotten into Phoenix early in the day, and so Shelley and I had cruised around town in a rental car, looking for vintage shops. Now it was time to go out. After the femme majesty I'd seen in Atlanta, I was not going to leave my makeup for Boycott Bar to chance. Shelley and I stood side by side in the hotel bathroom mirror, carefully doing our makeup and—I scowled—using almost exactly the same products to create the same basic look. The same concealer, the same undereye highlighter, the same frickin' shade of cream blush? Ugh. This is what came of recommending products to someone with your exact genetic composition. Side-eyeing her resentfully, I wiped off the shimmery copper eyeshadow I'd been applying and started again.

Boycott Bar is in Phoenix's gayborhood, Melrose, which announces itself with a big, angular arch over the street. The bar is owned by Audrey Corley, and it's the only Latinx-owned lesbian bar in America. It's been open in Melrose since 2017. Boycott Bar is unassuming—a whitewashed, one-story building with a flat roof and a partial facade of what looks like river rocks. There's an endearing rainbow crosswalk leading to its entrance, and swooping, brightly colored murals cover the side of the building. When I'd seen Boycott Bar for the first time that afternoon (we'd driven by it on our way to get coffee), a lifted red truck was parked diagonally across a few of the parking spaces in its small lot. The bar's logo—two touching "female" symbols forming the double Ts of "Boycott"—was emblazoned across the truck's back window. That truck was love at first sight for me. Very few things make me happier than redneck culture reclaimed and repurposed by the queer community. I hoped the truck belonged to the owner.

It does. When I talked with Audrey, she told me the truck's name was "Apollonia, iike Prince's girlfriend." She explained that the brick-

and-mortar Boycott Bar had been open since 2017, but Boycott had been a twice-monthly event she'd been running since 2004.

"Boycott is a funny name," I'd said, and she laughed.

"You either love it or you hate it. I named it in college, way before I ever owned my own bar. I said, 'Someday, I'm going to have a bar called Boycott,' and here we are. I've been in the bar business ever since I was eighteen. That's twenty-eight years now. I was just used to running other people's bars."

When I asked what she thought the vibe of Boycott Bar was, she said, "We have a feel-good vibe where you're able to be yourself, and no one gives a shit. We cater to everyone except assholes, always being aware that we primarily serve women and queer people."

"Can you remember ever seeing something wild at Boycott?"

"Define wild."

"You're saying you've seen a lot."

"It's pretty hard to shock me at this point. Once, on New Year's Eve, we had a customer rip all the mirrors out of the bathroom. All of them. I don't even know how she did it, or why. The next day, she came to the bar to get her phone she'd forgotten, and she had no idea what she'd done. No memory of it. I gave her her phone, and she paid for us to get all-new mirrors. All you can do is laugh. As long as we stay safe here, we're happy. Oh, also, one time we had a U-Haul almost run us down. A U-Haul almost accidentally drove right into the bar. We thought it was funny, maybe an angry lesbian, but it was just some guy. Imagine a U-Haul running down a lesbian bar."

"The jokes alone."

"Right?"

"This is such a rewarding job if you love people," Audrey continued. "You never know how you're getting people when they walk through the door. They could be happy, sad, grieving, going through a breakup, anything, and then you add liquor." She laughed. "I just want to leave you better than I found you when you come in my space."

It was Friday night now, and the little parking lot was full. Shelley and I parked a block away from Boycott and walked to the front. I was anxious. Shelley's first time at a lesbian bar as a person dating women. What if it wasn't fun?

There was no cover. We pulled the door open.

I shouldn't have worried. Inside, lesbians were two-stepping. All around the bar's dance floor, pairs of queers were holding each other's hands or waists, doing the formal little walk-hop steps that mean you know perfectly well how to dance to a classic country song and this is how you do it, goddammit.

"YES," I breathed, ecstatic. This was *exactly* what I'd been hoping for. There are not nearly as many gay honky-tonks in my life as there used to be. Cash Inn Country had closed; Edgewater Lounge in Chicago had also shut down, leaving me with fringed red boots and nowhere gay enough to wear them. Saddest of all: I've never once remembered to get tickets to the North Star Gay Rodeo in time to see the show. There's nothing I want to see more than *Brokeback Mountain* queers yee-hawing on bucking broncos with Pride ribbons woven into their manes, and yet I keep forgetting to write down the gay rodeo dates on my calendar. Assless chaps worn by gay boys but used for their *original purpose*? YES PLEASE.

Keeping to the side of the floor, Shelley and I went up to the bar, which was lit with blue lights. I ordered my usual—a Bombay gin and tonic—and Shelley ordered the same thing. The bartender looked at me and then at Shelley.

"Y'all sisters?"

We nodded in tandem, smiling—we get asked that all the time, we're obviously sisters, our voices are so alike that it's unsettling—but then I was struck by a horrible thought. Maybe the bartender had asked because there was a question of whether we were sisters . . . or *dating*. It could be either. Dykealike couples are real. I suddenly saw Shelley with fresh eyes. She has really short hair. *Oh my god, Shelley looks gayer than me*, I realized.

"Let's find a table," I said grimly. *Fuck. Do we look like we're dating?*

Boycott Bar has silver-painted brick walls hung with several big TV screens and large black-and-white photos of famous women—Amelia Earhart, Marilyn Monroe. The ceiling is black, the floors are cement, and all the tables are high-tops, with metal stools. The whole vibe feels industrial and minimal; colored lights do most of the work for changing the mood. It's a nice bar, and it also looks like it's built for rough use; like, if a fight broke out and there was blood and hair all over the floor, it could be hosed down. There's a DJ area and a cushy booth set on a higher level for VIP seating. I stared at it. *VIP!* Get outta here! This was the first time I'd noticed anything like that in a lesbian bar. (Maybe I just wasn't looking, though? Lesbian bars, do you have secret VIP sections I never saw because I'm an old peasant who says things like, "Bottle service is *how* much? For a Costco bottle of Grey Goose?")

Shelley and I settled into our seats, watching the dancers step-toe around the room. Right away, it was clear who the best dancers in the bar were—an older lesbian couple in western shirts and pressed jeans danced cheek to cheek, eyes closed, their cowboy-booted feet doing fancy things. It looked easy, but that's how you know someone's a good dancer. It's like seeing an Olympic gymnast do a floor routine—you think, *I could do that if I really wanted to, if I really trained for it*, and then you remember you once dislocated your shoulder trying to do a somersault. Other, younger couples trotted past, some carefully watching their own feet, some relaxed and moving effortlessly.

Blake Shelton's "Honey Bee" came on, and anyone who had been sitting out the last song whooped and came back to the floor. A young queer—couldn't have been over twenty-three—was learning how to two-step from an older butch in a purple polo and cowboy boots, mimicking the elder's foot movements shyly, with lots of giggling. I looked around.

There were actually several older couples here; this was the first time I'd seen *such* a varied age group at a lesbian bar. It was so nice. People switched partners nearly every song. Young, rakish queers two-stepped with spruce seventy-year-olds in ironed cotton shirts, hesitantly holding their hands and waists, the older ones nodding encouragingly and moving deliberately, teaching the new generation how to dance.

Shelley smiled happily, toying with her straw. "I like this bar," she said. "I'm gonna go get another drink."

Welp. I knew who the designated driver would be that night. When she didn't come back right away, I went off to explore the rest of the bar. There's a room in the back of Boycott for pool and arcade games. I poked my head in. A lone queer in a navy T-shirt was playing Super Mario, staring up at the screen, their face bathed in greenish light.

Shelley was standing up, talking to three obvious community members, when I got back. I was impressed. She always surprises me at bars and parties; she's good at talking to strangers. And this was her first time at a dyke bar on her own! I had to hold myself back from going over to make sure everything was going smoothly. *Stay out of it*, I told myself, a watchful lezzie helicopter mom. *Let her learn to swim on her own.*

Missy Elliot came on, and every lesbian over fifty sat down immediately. A curvy femme in the kind of cutoffs that are so short you can see the white pockets hanging out the front got up with their partner, and they went to the center of the floor. The rest of the under-fifty crowd followed, and suddenly the dance floor was filled with people grinding. The change from country to hip-hop was startling, but no one seemed to think it was out of the ordinary. I guess when you're the only lesbian bar in Arizona, you have to try to appeal to everyone. It looked like it was working. A bunch of young queers came in, some of them going directly up to the elder queers and saying hello before getting a drink. Polite! Here it all was—the fanny packs worn as front chest purses, the ironic Hawaiian shirts, the septum piercings, the bowl cuts, the chunky gold chains draped over nineties basketball jerseys. In ten minutes,

Boycott Bar

Boycott Bar had turned into a totally different space. A femme in thigh-high black boots strutted through the front doors, two masc-presenting queers following worshipfully behind.

Shelley was back. And a little drunk. "Cupid Shuffle" came on, and people lined up in rows on the floor. She watched them.

"This kinda reminds me of that night with Mom," she said.

"Me too."

It's been five years since our mom died, and we're still figuring out how to talk about it, what it means. Losing a parent—especially a parent you had a very complicated relationship with—is such a strange thing. Everything shifts. Suddenly, after having all this time, so much that you were careless with it, you're out of time. I couldn't call my mom and beg her, *again*, to please, please look for my birth certificate in her filing cabinet (because I'm gay and I *need* to have my astrological chart done and *I can't do it if I don't know what time I was born*). She wouldn't come to visit me ever again, to fuss over my animals and go for walks around the lake and make really, really inappropriate noises in public over dark chocolate gelato. When our mom died, Shelley and I stopped getting family birthday calls, and that was when we figured out that Mom was the one who took care of things like that, that she was the one who had arranged all the smallest details of her children. Recently, after glancing at my phone, Davin said, "Why do you always have, like, one unheard voicemail?" and I had to tell the truth: it was the last voicemail my mom left me, and I can't listen to it.

"Because after I do, there won't be any more, you know?" I teared up immediately. He pulled me in for a hug.

"OK. OK. I get it."

But he doesn't get it. No one gets it, especially me. How close to the surface it is, all the time, even after five years.

I know what it'll say, anyway: "*Hi Krisser, iiiiit's Mom. Just callin' to see if I can try and get ahold of you. You're probably out. Or sleeping. I'll try you tomorrow. Call me back if you get this. Love you, kiddo.*"

Moby Dyke

Because that's what all her messages sounded like.

One year before she died, I was visiting Phoenix alone for once, staying on the living room couch in the pink triplex, when my mom came in. It was late. She often had trouble sleeping. She saw I was up, and motioned for me to scoot over.

"Kris," she said, perching on the edge of the couch and looking serious, "there's something I've been wanting to tell you."

I looked up at her. Did she have cancer? Did I have a secret sibling? "I just wanted to tell you that . . . that I'm sorry."

"What? What are you sorry for?"

"For being . . . for how I treated you when you told me you were gay." Her eyes looked bright and shiny. "I'm so sorry."

"Mom." She began to cry. "Mom, it's OK."

"It's not!"

"Well, no, it's not. But it's OK. It was a long time ago, now. So long. I'm fine."

"We lost so much time."

"We did, and now we have lots more. Mom, it's OK."

I hugged her, feeling her ribs through the back of her robe, and then she went to bed, and so did I. In the morning, we did normal Phoenix things, and time passed, and I found myself feeling angry. *That's it? A decade of my life spent in therapy and she gets to apologize once and it's over?* Letting her calls go to voicemail more often than not. Thinking, *I'll call her back on Sunday.*

When she was first in a coma after her surgery, the doctors told us she could hear us. I sat next to her, held her hand, and said, "Mom. If you can wake up and get better, I will take you to Paris." I couldn't afford something like that, but I'd figure it out. "You and me. We'll eat chocolate croissants and stay in a great hotel, and I will pay for everything." If anything would get her up, that would do it. I was sure of it.

Her chest rose and fell, the machines in control. The cinematic moment I'd been hoping for—the eyelids slowly raising, the confused *"Wha—where am I?"* didn't happen.

I looked at Shelley. I didn't want to think about Mom.

"Wow, I haven't heard *this* in a minute," I said, as Tyga's "Rack City" came on. It wasn't true; I'd heard it a few weeks ago at Sue Ellen's. I'd just wanted to change the subject.

Boycott Bar was openly alternating the music now—hip-hop song, country song; Rihanna, Garth, Usher. It was like two gay teenagers were fighting over the aux cord in 2009. Shelley was shimmying in her chair, the 2.5 gin and tonics having fully hit.

"You wanna dance?" I asked.

"No." Shoulder wiggle.

"Are you sure?"

"Yeah. Actually, it's late. You wanna go soon? I could go to bed."

I love people who want to go to bed. I'm telling you, Shelley is *the* person to bring on your trip. She was the prize, in the end, for the years I spent just trying to be OK, just trying to get through my twenties, just trying to believe that I was worthy of love, anyway. As kids, Shelley and I hated each other, fought constantly. I can remember being five or six, flinging myself at her, deadly serious, not playing, genuinely trying to kill her. Now, as adults, we're best friends, a friendship forged by trying to protect one another.

The older, western-shirted lesbians got up to dance again. I looked at them, a couple, turning around the room like one person, each as sure of the other's next move as they were of their own. They had to be seventy if they were a day. Same age as Mom was when she died. They both looked fairly butch. I wondered what they, as queers, had seen in their lives. Probably a lot. And here they were at Boycott Bar, still two-stepping in a room full of noisy kids, the only people left who really knew how to dance.

Richmond

Babe's of Carytown

◆ ◆ ◆

What's the loudest shriek you've ever heard? Did it come from a human?

All sorts of things can shriek. A fighter jet, streaking across the sky above you, *this close* to breaking the sound barrier. A toddler, when you take away the very chicken nugget she *just said* she didn't want. Your dog, when he sweeps his tail under the foot of your rocking chair moments before you stand up. But what's the most ear-piercing sound you've ever experienced? Which is the shriek you will remember for as long as you live?

I ask because the sound I heard on the beach volleyball courts at Babe's of Carytown was inhuman. It defied physics. I still hear it in the hushed, unreal seconds between sleep and wakefulness.

It was the shriek of a gay boy in skintight jeggings lunging for a spiked ball.

Like an avenging angel, he'd flown in out of nowhere, butting a slow and clumsy teammate out of the way. His scream of rage and fury as he dove through the air and missed—off by millimeters!—caused pigeons, five blocks away, to flock to the air.

I had never seen queers play beach volleyball before, and once I heal my ruptured eardrums, I'd like nothing more than to see it again. I'd actually like to spend every Sunday afternoon the way I spent that sunny Sunday in April at Babe's—with a fruity cocktail in one hand, my bare feet on a warm, sandy deck, and dozens of queers in short-shorts swarming around me.

Babe's of Carytown, in Richmond, Virginia, is the only lesbian bar in America with a full beach volleyball court, and Davin and I were jazzed about it. Especially Davin. He'd been released from working at the Minnesota State Senate for spring break, and he'd come with me on this trip to Babe's. He stood grinning on the back deck, looking like he'd just been sprung from a suit-and-tie cage, a beer in one hand, his grocery store sunglasses hiding his eyes, which I knew were following the back-and-forth volleys like a cat watching a laser pointer. Davin continues to amaze me with how much he likes sports. All sports. I'd been informed only moments ago that he *loves* beach volleyball—that he grew up watching it in Faribault, Minnesota, where his mom and her friends played on a summer bar league for years. "A bar called Bashers," he said.

I tried and failed to picture my mom, who loved to quietly browse fabric store aisles alone, playing on a beach volleyball league at a bar. Davin and I had had different childhoods.

A queer in pink shorts bumped the volleyball to a teammate, and they bopped it over the net. The other side returned the volley neatly, and even though each team had a couple of unserious players (the twink who wandered away midgame to dig through a canvas bag and apply special face sunscreen comes to mind), it was obvious that this was a real game; these people were not just fooling around.

"When we open our dyke bar in Northfield?" Davin began. We'd been fantasizing about having our own bar ever since the Back Door in Bloomington. "We could have a beach volleyball court. Just like this."

"You just want *this* bar."

"It's so cool."

Richmond had been a delight so far. I'd never been there before, and it had been full of brick streets, old, gabled buildings, and really chatty Uber drivers. I had expected Richmond to feel East Coasty, but instead it *looked* like the East Coast and *felt* southern. Strangers ma'amed me here, and the blossoms were already off the trees. These were summer temperatures; everyone was sweating. The crowd at Babe's volleyball courts was as diverse as a carefully cast Target ad. That was how the city felt, too—there didn't seem to be a racial majority. Later, I looked it up and saw that Richmond is almost exactly half Black and half white. It was nice to see that Babe's reflected that.

The fashion happening all around us was peak homosexual. A queer walked by in navy leggings printed with those nineties yellow suns with faces on them. I saw someone wearing socks that said MY DOG RES-CUED ME! (I couldn't tell if they were ironic or in earnest; those socks could really go either way at a dyke bar.) I saw at least ten fanny packs. I even saw a Pin Gay, which is what I call a queer whose entire personal style seems to be based on owning a *lot* of queer-themed enamel pins and wearing them all at once. (Think: an enamel pin shaped like two pairs of scissors scissoring, or a pin shaped like a possum holding a tiny rainbow flag that says GAY TRASH.) Pin Gays buy their pins at queer craft fairs, independent bookstores, and next to the register of the queer-friendly sex toy shop in town (the one that sells the organic, water-based lube that dries a *little* too fast to be helpful but *is* organic, so ::shrug emoji::). They put all their pins on either a backpack or a battered jean jacket that is supposed to look secondhand but was actually $120 at the Levi's store, and then lie in wait for other queers to compliment their pins. This frequently happens, because the pins are great conversation pieces and queers are bad at speaking to people they don't know. Be that as it may, I do not recommend approaching a Pin Gay to say you like a *particular* pin, because if you do, they'll explain their *whole* pin collection. It's like asking a nine-year-old to tell you a little something about *Minecraft*. You could pass out and die waiting for them to finish talking.

More shrieking on the court. A gay wearing a "Slytherin" T-shirt had helped score a point. "*Niiiice*," Davin called. Two sporties stood next to me, chatting in the sunshine. One was wearing an Apple watch and had the kind of front-facing baseball cap over a no-nonsense shiny pony-tail that says, "I make more than six figures and live in a spotless condo without art on the walls." The other was exuberant and a little day drunk, talking about trying to buy a house in Richmond.

"It's impossible," Day Drunk sighed. "Y'know. Especially when you're single." They paused. "Just been me and my pup for a couple months now."

"It can be hard," Spotless Condo agreed. "But not if you know the right people. Whereabouts are you looking to buy?"

I put it together. Day Drunk thought Spotless Condo was hitting on them. Spotless Condo worked in real estate. This was beautiful.

Davin was getting hot. Inside Babe's, it was cool and dim. A group of queers was gathered around the main bar, hooting about a piece of juicy gossip someone was relaying from the night before. The TV was turned to a silent golf tournament nobody was watching. I could not believe we were in the same bar we'd been in last night.

Babe's of Carytown has been in business since 1979, according to Wikipedia, but is thirty-two years old, according to its Facebook page. (Is Babe's catfishing us?) I asked four people on staff how old Babe's was and got four different answers. I do not know. I do know that it's the only lesbian bar in Virginia. Vicky Hester owns it, and it's on a cor-ner in Carytown, a lively part of Richmond full of shops and restau-rants. Babe's is eye-catching. It has a big yellow awning and neon dancing stick figures in its front window. And just fifteen hours ago, at eleven p.m. on a Saturday, the line to get into Babe's had stretched halfway down the street.

"What *is* this," I had hissed, taking my place at the back of the line behind a gaggle of gays. "It's not like this is *Pride*." I hadn't waited in a line to get into a lesbian bar yet on this trip, and the sense of outrage I felt was out of proportion. Davin smiled benignly. Who cared if there was a line? He was on spring break, and it was warm at *night* here.

A commotion ahead. Vax cards were required, and the bouncer had granted entry to all but one of the gay boys. "I left mine at home!" the one barred at the door wailed, his breezy hot-dog-printed button-down flapping in the night wind. His friends looked sympathetic. "Go home and get it!" they urged, but anyone could see from the slump of his shoulders that he knew his night was over.

There was a five-dollar cover, and once inside, I ignored everything and headed straight to the bathrooms. I really needed to pee.

"Sorry, we're waiting," a babyqueer standing near the bar said to me.

"Oh, I'm looking for the bathroom," I said. "Not the bar."

"That's what I mean," the baby said. "This is the line."

I turned toward them then, realizing with a dawning horror that the twenty-person-plus train in front of me was not just a random assortment of people bunched up around the bar. They were *all* waiting for the bathroom.

I was gone for fully thirty minutes. The bathroom situation at Babe's on a crowded Saturday night is out of control, but I had fun bitching about it with the cranky jumpsuited queer behind me, so I guess I can allow it? Bathroom lines at dyke bars are frequently long, *especially if the bathrooms are gendered*, and you can usually make some new bathroom-line friends if you're willing to make the first move, which is generally either a disgusted sigh or a defeated gesture at all the people, paired with, "Can you believe this line? What are they are *doing* in there?" The person standing next to you, if they are at all chatty, will agree that yes, this is outrageous, and then you can both discuss how, when you're in the bathroom, you know how to get things done properly. You're efficient. In and out. Thirty seconds, max. It's not hard!

When I returned from my bathroom odyssey, Davin was tucked away in a high-backed booth on the side of Babe's that serves food. A beautiful woman with the kind of facial bone structure that feels unfair was with him, and they were both beaming.

"This is Maggie!" Davin cried. "She recognized *me*! From your blog! And your Insta!!"

I was flabbergasted. "Seriously?" To recognize Davin from the linked Instagram on a blog that I'd closed in 2017 and only written on sporadically since 2013 seemed impossible.

"Yeah!" Maggie said excitedly. "I saw him at the bar and went up to him and said, 'Excuse me, but is your name Davin?'"

Davin was thrilled, his cheeks smiling so hard they were shiny. He was *loving* this.

"And I said '*Yeah!*'" he half-shouted, bouncing gleefully on the bench seat. "Isn't that NUTS? And get this: Maggie emailed you about this bar! For your book! Weeks ago!!"

Whoops. I had never seen the email. Before I started the bar trips, I set up a special email account to get stories about the bars, but I hadn't checked it in a while.

"And now you're here!" Maggie finished. "What are the odds?"

"WHAT ARE THE ODDS?!!" Davin bellowed.

"Anyway, I live here, and I can show you around if you want," Maggie offered. "I'm kind of new—I moved here a little while ago. I'm married to a cis man and I made friends with my gay neighbor and he brought me here to"—she paused briefly—"explore."

"Oh my god, I would love that," I said. "You sure? I don't want to barge in on your night."

"Please, Babe's is so great!" she said. "I've never felt like I belonged at a queer bar before, but here, it feels so nonjudgmental."

And suddenly, we had a friend at Babe's. Holding my arm, Maggie took us past the bar and through to the dance floor, which was expansive and crammed with queermosexuals dancing to Doja Cat's "Get into It (Yuh)," the song I could not escape on my travels. Everywhere I went, every bar I visited, every city I set foot in, that song was playing somewhere. If it wasn't the actual soundtrack in a room, I heard it streaming from passing cars or being tinnily pulled up on someone's phone as they watched a TikTok.

"There's so many people here!" I yelled, Maggie half-dragging me through masses of flailing arms and popping booties.

"Isn't it great!" she called back over her shoulder. Davin clung to my hand, and we formed a daisy chain across the floor. We entered a skinny hallway, where I saw a couple more bathroom doors, also with significant lines, and I estimated that there were way more than a hundred people at Babe's, and so far, I had only seen four or five toilets. I made a mental note to stick to one drink. Maggie tugged us farther in, and then POOF: We were suddenly in a new bar. A patio-ish kind of bar. Sort of indoors, sort of outdoors, it had white-painted brick walls, with exposed ceiling rafters and a chalkboard drink menu. Wooden stairs led up to a deck above—the rooftop beach volleyball court. This bar was also packed and noisy.

Maggie, bless her, was intro-ing me to people. "THIS IS KRISTA," she called out at a stylish person named Elijah. "SHE'S WRITING A BOOK ABOUT LESBIAN BARS!"

"Ooh, OK!" Elijah said. "I've been coming here every Saturday night for eleven years! What do you want to know? Did you know that Babe's was the first and only bar here for a *loooong* time that required a vax card?"

"I did not!" I said, scribbling in my notebook. "I didn't know about the beach volleyball court, either!"

"The litterbox," joked a pale woman in a bondagey ensemble. I turned to her. "I'm Laura," she said. "And when it gets late enough, you wanna keep an eye on any gay boys standing by themselves around the court."

I told her I'd just waited in a thirty-minute bathroom line, and she nodded sagely. Laura, it turned out, had lived in Richmond for years. "Most people here are transplants," she said. "We have a lot of community, though—there are community fridges; there's a free farmers' market, we have a queer sports league. It's great here."

Maggie took my arm again, and she, Davin, and I went out to the rooftop beach volleyball court. At night, there were metal tables and chairs set up in the sand. You could look up at the dark sky and see down the street into the neighborhood. The air was getting chilly, and the leaves in the treetops rustled. I felt a familiar pang of envy. Richmond was a little-big city stuffed with history and queers, and they all had this *bar*. They could come whenever they liked. (That's what she said.) They could hang out here, they could dance, they could go to one of the drag shows Babe's was locally famous for, they could gloat over the lunch and dinner specials. I'd heard the chicken tenders were incredible.

"You wanna dance?" Maggie asked.

We did. We wove our way down the wooden steps and through the crooked hallways of Babe's. For a second, we stood on the fringes of the mass of dancers, watching the lights flash red, green, blue onto faces shiny with sweat. Then we jumped in, dancing in a little cluster, Maggie and her gay neighbor so much better at dancing than me that I felt self-conscious but decided to just go with it, Davin doing the cute open-arms snapping thing he only does when he's a little bit lit and also very happy. Queers bumped into us on all sides, and no one said sorry because it was so obviously impossible to keep from colliding with one another. Every back I pressed up against was damp; every drink held aloft was beaded and dripping. Like a gay miracle, Robyn's "Dancing on My Own" came on, and as a hundred queers bellowed *"I'm giving it my all / but I'm not the girl you're taking home, oooh-ooh-OOH"* in unison, I realized this was it: This was the moment I had dreamed about during the darkest, loneliest days of the pandemic. The feeling I'd missed more than any other feeling. I was living it now.

"Can you believe this place?" I yelled at Davin. He shook his head, dancing. He couldn't hear me. "Never mind," I hollered, and he smiled, tilting his head back and closing his eyes, pressed in by so many other people, queer like him, queer like us, all of us belting the same words to the same song. This was what we had needed. This was gay therapy. We all deserved it.

A month later, on the first day it was warm out in Minnesota, I caught Davin in the backyard with a tape measure, looking thoughtful.

He was measuring for a beach volleyball court.

Our backyard wasn't big enough. He was crushed.

Washington, DC

A League of Her Own

◆ ◆ ◆

Honestly? It's too much. Everywhere you go in Washington, DC, wherever you look, it's one famous building after another. The Capitol building. The Supreme Court building. The White House. All of them just BAM! at the end of the street, or HI THERE peeking over the tree line at you. There's no escaping these architectural icons. You think you're safe—you're in downtown proper, surrounded by condos, and JK HELLO the Washington Monument's been watching you the whole time.

Coming from small-town Minnesota, where a "famous building" is "that one silo that looks a *little* too much like a dick to not be funny," casually seeing the Capitol building when you're out and about feels outrageous. I'm sure if you grew up in DC, it would feel normal, but to a visitor? Seeing all those buildings takes lot of getting used to. It's maybe like what having Lady Gaga move into your apartment complex would feel like. At first, you'd be like HOLY SHIT LADY GAGA IS IN THE LAUNDRY ROOM and OH MY GOD, THAT'S LADY GAGA GETTING HER MAIL, just everywhere you turn—JESUS CHRIST IT'S LADY GAGA. After a couple of days, though, the novelty would probably wear off a bit; you'd see her around and be like, "Wow, ha, she's everywhere, that's crazy, yeah, Lady Gaga." And after about a week of *that*, you'd be having lunch, looking out the window, and see her sitting in the courtyard, looking up at you, and you'd think, *damn bitch, can I even eat a sandwich?*

That's how I felt in DC. For five days, the Capitol building had watched my every move. Davin and I had taken the train in from Richmond, and, thanks to the parents of our friend Teresa, who own a gorgeous condo they "only use sometimes" in freaking *Capitol Hill*, we were staying for free in DC within easy walking distance of places like the Library of Congress, which you could just *walk right up to*. Same with the Supreme Court—you could just take the stairs right on up to the Supreme Court!

I was floored. I'd never been to DC before, and I'd had no idea you could just, like, take your rented electric Lime scooter up to the US Senate Office Buildings and touch the walls with your sticky ice cream hands if you wanted. Drunk with power, I'd touched every building, every fountain, every bush on the Capitol grounds. "I own this," I'd said each time. "This is mine." Oddly enough, that thought didn't make me want to storm the Capitol while wearing a homemade fur Viking-horn hat, but that's just me.

Davin, who'd been to DC many times before, watched me as we zipped around town, laughing whenever we'd turn a corner and I'd shriek because there was the Capitol AGAIN. Get a life, Capitol building!

And I know I said, way back in San Francisco, that it was a bad idea to rent a scooter, but I'd like to amend that statement to "it's a bad idea to rent a *moped*." Because listen, I have discovered electric rental scooters, the stick kind, and I am never walking anywhere ever again.

"Are you sure you want to do this?" Davin had asked, watching me upload the scooter app on our first morning in America's capital. His face was the picture you would see in the dictionary if you looked up "concerned."

"I'm sure."

"Because we don't have to. We can just walk."

"*Kids* are doing it. Look, those are *kids*."

"Kids heal fast."

"We'll go slow! I promise!"

A League of Her Own

Ten minutes later, I was bouncing across the Washington Monument lawn at top scooter speed, laughing my head off, screaming "THIS IS THE GREATESSSSST!" my hair whipping like a flag behind me. I don't think I walked twenty cumulative steps in DC. Maybe once, in search of another scooter.

Now, because we were staying, for free, in such a classy area of town, and because it was mid-April, with all the cherry blossoms puffing pinkly under cloudless 70-degree skies, and because, thanks to the scooters, I had reduced my own transportation efforts to that of a green pepper on a grocery store conveyer belt, I may have gotten a . . . warped view of DC.

"I could live here," I announced, whizzing past million-dollar townhomes with landscaping details that easily cost what I make in a year to maintain. "Why don't you become the first trans member of the Senate?"

"Because you'd hate that. And we still couldn't afford to live in Capitol Hill," Davin called back over his shoulder to me. His scooter seemed to be much faster than mine.

"Hey, can we get a coffee?" I shouted, suddenly needing cold brew. "At that new queer bar?"

Davin braked, allowing me to catch up.

"That queer bar that just opened," I said, scooting up next to him. "As You Are. The one I was reading about. It's a bar but they have coffee, I think. And food."

"Sure, cutes." Davin already had his phone out. "It's actually really close."

In less than five minutes, we were parking our scooters out in front of As You Are, a two-story, white-painted brick building on Eighth Street SE in Capitol Hill, less than two blocks from Pennsylvania frickin' Avenue (!!). We put our face masks on and walked in, excited to be queers getting special queer coffee in a newly opened space. We were trendy! How often did I get to feel trendy?

"Whoa," I said, taking in a spacious, adorable café with big windows and a bar in the back. Ivy tumbled down from little hanging planters. Toward the rear, there was a wall made of plants, with a green neon sign nestled in the leaves that read PAY IT NO MIND.

"This is so nice!" I said.

"Thank you!" beamed the person behind the bar. "This your first time here?"

"It *is*," I said, spinning around. "Oh my god, are those . . . is that a wall of free condoms?"

It was. And the person behind the bar was Jo McDaniel, one of the owners of As You Are. I explained my book project, and she smiled. "I'm so glad you came to check us out! Did you know I used to be the general manager at A League of Her Own?"

"Get out of here," I said. A League of Her Own was the lesbian bar Davin and I were in DC to visit. A few seconds later, As You Are's co-owner (and Jo's partner) Rach "Coach" Pike bounded in from a back room. A bundle of energy, they welcomed us in, too, and, hearing about my project, mentioned that they used to be both a bartender and head of security for A League of Her Own.

"Why did you open this place?" I asked.

"We had some ideas for how we'd like to do things our own way," Coach said. They locked eyes with Jo for a second. In that single glance, I felt the near-tangible weight of years of DC queer nightlife drama.

It was two p.m., not very busy. Davin and I slurped down an excellent Thai curry and rice noodle bowl and chatted with Jo and Coach about how As You Are works. It's a café during the day and a bar and nightclub at night, and holy shit, is it cute and invested in the work around accessibility and consent within a queer space. They showed us around, contagiously excited. Jo and Coach are doing it right at As You Are—there are signs reminding you that CONSENT IS SEXY. HERE IT'S MANDATORY and the rules for being in the space are clearly posted. Masks are required. There's a ramp to get inside, and the patio is ground-level and accessible. They're working on getting an elevator; working on getting their bathrooms ADA certified. Not only that, but it's fun in there. They have two bars. There's a lounge room with video games and couches and art by local queers. They have events going on almost every night.

Back downstairs, having seen the whole place, I was just so impressed. So, so many spaces within the queer community are not necessarily safe places. So many are simply not accessible to people with disabilities. This was the first permanent queer bar I'd ever been to that was putting safety and inclusion before anything else. It should be standard in all public spaces, but it isn't. As You Are was a beautiful thing to see.

"It's hard to have fun when you're not safe," Coach said. "Safety management is our thing. In here, we've got your back. We believe in calling people in. We want you to be in here. Our standards are clearly posted."

"Our daytime hours are geared toward youth being able to come here. We have sober options, mocktails, board games . . . and the sweaty dance floor is upstairs," Jo grinned.

They specifically hire queer staff, many of whom are young and inexperienced, and train them alongside industry veterans.

"We really want to make sure this is being run well, and people are being held accountable to do a good job," Jo said. "We're here a *lot*."

I was sorry to leave As You Are. Walking out the door, I already knew it would be my working/writing café of choice if I lived in DC. For a second, I imagined myself as a senator's lesbian wife, wearing a red suit with massive shoulder pads and big gold buttons, tapping away on my laptop at As You Are, watching the queers come and go. Will somebody please make an all-queer *West Wing*? The characters could meet at As You Are for their murmured, shifty-eyed conversations! The sexy, good-hearted-yet-stressed trans president could literally jog there from the White House, flanked by booty-shorted members of the Secret Service! Netflix, do we have a deal?

Back on the street, Davin and I kicked off from our scooters again.

"Should we scoot to ALOHO later tonight?" I asked, nimbly nipping into the bike lane.

Moby Dyke

"What?"

"ALOHO. A League of Her Own. That's what people call it."

"I think it's too far to scoot," Davin called back as he passed me. "And we're meeting Teresa and EmJ first."

Teresa, Davin's work-wife at the Minnesota Senate, had arrived in DC that morning to hang out with us at her parents' condo. EmJ (who we'd last seen at Gossip Grill in San Diego) was driving up from Durham to meet us. This was ideal, since EmJ went to college in DC and lived there for years afterward; they were going to take us around town. EmJ was the reason Davin had been to DC so many times.

EmJ remembers spending "a lot of interesting nights" at Phase 1, a locally much-missed lesbian bar that was open in DC from 1970 to 2016. Phase 1 used to be one of the oldest continuously running lesbian bars in the United States. It was also the oldest gay bar in Washington, DC, period. Davin and EmJ used to go to Phase 1 all the time, where they'd sweatily dance and chain-smoke on the patio for hours. Davin remembers once taking one of EmJ's friends home from Phase 1 and discovering that—for the first time in his life—he really was too drunk to fuck. All Phase 1 stories I'd heard from EmJ and Davin sounded sloppy, and it felt unfair to me to have missed the bar entirely before it closed down.

A League of Her Own—Washington, DC's only lesbian bar—was newish in town; its owner, David Perruzza, opened it in 2018 as a companion bar to next-door Pitchers, his gay sports bar in the Woodley Park/Adams Morgan neighborhood. I was eager to see ALOHO. My friend Nellie, who lives in DC, had called it a "dyke dungeon" and then not elaborated, so that was enough for me. I love a mystery!

"Oh," I said, hours later, after we'd met up with Teresa and EmJ. I was standing alone outside A League of Her Own. "It's because it's *actually in a basement.*"

Teresa, EmJ, and Davin were still parking. It was 9:45 at night; they'd dropped me at the front entrance of the bar. We'd all rushed to get to

ALOHO when, after a late dinner, I'd rechecked the bar's hours and discovered, to my horror, that Google said it was closing at ten that night. Ten o'clock! That had *not* been the closing time when we'd booked the trip—I would never have planned to come that night if it was!

"*Drive*," I'd commanded from the back seat of EmJ's car after dinner, my eyes steely. "*We have to get to the bar.*" What if ALOHO was closed? This was the only night we could all go together!

A League of Her Own was not closed. In fact—after I'd descended the steps down from the sidewalk to the entrance and had my vaccination card checked—I saw it was extremely not closed. It was chaos in there. Mayhem. A line stretched from the inside entrance, down the right side of the bar, and up some steps, vanishing into another room. This was thrilling—A League of Her Own was totally open!—and maddening—what the fuck, of course it was.

Two twentysomething queers moved away from a table near the front, and I pounced.

"What's going on?" I asked, hovering over them as they gathered their things, making sure everyone understood this was my table now.

"Drag show," one of them said, turning away with their drink. I stopped them.

"Wait, this is all"—I gestured toward the line—"for a *drag* show? It's *Wednesday*."

"Oh, it's Lady Camden," the other said. "She's meeting people first. That's the line."

I must have looked blank, because they added, "From *RuPaul*?"

Ah. I have seen many, many episodes of *RuPaul's Drag Race*, but always out of order. A season 3 episode here, a four-episode binge of season 10 there. I never have any idea who anyone is, which is why no one wants to watch it with me. "Who's that?" I'll demand, pointing at Trixie Mattel. "Is that Sasha Velour?"

"Shhhh"—everyone in the room.

"I met her once. I think. No, it was that Violet one—you know who

I'm talking about? Violet Chachki. She was in Minneapolis. Wait, why is Sasha mad right now?"

"Just *watch*."

The line to meet Lady Camden was moving slow. I studied A League of Her Own. We really were underground; if ALOHO was an apartment, it would be euphemistically listed as "garden level." The bar had a cement floor and exposed, rainbow-painted wooden rafters. Metal tables and chairs. It definitely felt like a bunker in there, but efforts had been made to cheer it up. Twinkly lights were strung from the ceiling and around the rim of the bar itself; wood paneling made things cozier. A pink neon sign saying GOOD VIBES ONLY crowned a photo wall of famous queers (Frida Kahlo, Samira Wiley, Kate McKinnon, Janelle Monáe). Across from the bar, TV screens hung in a row, two playing a basketball game and three with video games, which were being played by people standing in line to meet Lady Camden, hollering as their race cars buzzed around a track onscreen.

Everyone in the bar looked young. Really young, actually, like "I could have given birth to you" young. A person in a pink-sequined miniskirt and a pink marabou-trimmed cowboy hat that said 21 on the front was sitting at one of the tables with two friends, taking sips of newly legal drinks and looking absolutely elated. Doja Cat's "Get into It (Yuh)" was playing (as it always is now, in my head, when I try to go to sleep at night) and I counted one, two, *three* different babyqueers with Jonathan Taylor Thomas *Home Improvement*–era floppy middle-part haircuts. I sighed. Those who do not learn history are doomed to repeat it.

Davin, EmJ, and Teresa arrived, all just as surprised as I'd been to see that the bar was completely open and not at all closing in five minutes. "Well, what the fuck?" Davin said. He went to get us all drinks. EmJ and Teresa looked at the ever-growing line of people.

"It's Lady Camden, from *RuPaul*," I said, as if I'd known all along who that was. "She's doing a meet-and-greet upstairs."

"What's upstairs?" Teresa asked.

"Pitchers. It's a gay sports bar. You go upstairs and it's the bar next door, I don't really understand it. They're connected but they're different bars."

"The gay men are upstairs and the queers are in the basement," EmJ cracked.

"Yes. Basically."

"That's a look," Teresa said.

It *was* kind of a look. I wasn't sure how I felt about it, but it also didn't matter how I felt about it. At least DC *had* a lesbian bar. Fuck, I'd take a basement lesbian bar in Minneapolis, I'm not too proud! (Listen, I'm on my hands and knees *begging* for a basement lesbian bar in Minneapolis, we'll take *anything*.) I quickly ran up to Pitchers and looked around. I could see there was a lot of crossover between the bars—people kept going up and down the stairs between the two. The bars *were* connected, which was nice. It was just that Pitchers was much nicer. It was roomier. Fancier. Hmm.

I did feel more comfortable downstairs in ALOHO, but that was maybe because I grew up in the Midwest, and lots of people who grew up in the Midwest spent their *entire childhood* in their friends' basements, away from prying adult eyes and as close as possible to the Fla-Vor-Ice slush popsicles buried in the chest freezer. Judging from Pitchers upstairs, the only thing the two bars had in common, besides Pride flags, *was* their connecting staircase.

Heading back downstairs to ALOHO, I went up to the bar. Barbi Larue, the general manager and bartender, smiled amiably at me. Checking to make sure I wasn't causing a traffic jam behind me, I explained the book.

"Nice! I've been here since October," she offered.

"What's it like, managing this place?"

"Oh, it's fun," she said. "I try to do a lot of events here, you know, open mic nights, trivia, speed dating, music nights. I really want this to be a place for everyone to come and just have fun."

"Do you do much with Pitchers?"

"Lots," she said. "There's a lot of back-and-forth with the two bars."

"It's not weird upstairs if people down here want to go up there?"

"Not at all. That's where we go if we want to dance."

"It's nicer upstairs," I observed casually.

"It's a different vibe," she shrugged, and then turned to serve someone. Interesting. I liked Barbi right away. She was friendly while still maintaining the air of someone who was absolutely not going to talk shit, even if there was something to talk shit about. This is a priceless quality in someone who works behind a bar.

I'd kept asking about Pitchers because I was suspicious. I've never been in a bar that caters mostly to cis gay men that didn't feel at least a little frosty toward anyone who *wasn't* a cis gay man. In Chicago's Boystown, you'd be collecting social security checks before you'd get served a drink before a gay man. I simply did not believe that the gay men upstairs willingly shared their space with the queers downstairs at A League of Her Own. But Barbi seemed so matter-of-fact about it.

So did Nika, another bartender I spoke to.

"Nah, we share," she said. This was her second stint of working at ALOHO—she'd left for a while and come back. "I like it here," she said simply. "People are here to have a good time, and we don't tend to get too much bad behavior down here." She grinned. "It's upstairs where people go off a little more."

I walked back to my table. The line to meet Lady Camden had not budged in forty-five minutes, judging by a queer in a sparkly jacket who kept bopping out of the line to see what was taking so long. "We're neeeever gonna meet her," they moaned to their friends.

As I settled back in my seat, EmJ suddenly grabbed my arm, a silent *look at that* warning. A young butch—slicked-back hair, cuffed jeans, and a white T-shirt with the sleeves rolled up—and a long-haired femme in a vintage-looking pink dress had appeared out of nowhere. They were heading out of ALOHO, the femme being led by the hand by the butch, who was cradling a motorcycle helmet with their other hand. Looking at them, I got the strangest feeling. The hairs rose on the back of my neck. It was like seeing the 1950s walk past our table. We all fell silent, watching the door shut behind them. Davin was elated.

"Did you see *that*?"

"Think they were ghosts?" I asked.

EmJ's face was luminous. "I love them."

"They were the coolest people in the bar," Teresa agreed.

Maroon 5 started playing, and the spell was broken. EmJ was glancing around ALOHO with new interest.

"Did you know *Off Our Backs* used to be published right around here?" they said. "On Eighteenth Street!"

"*Off Our Backs* or *On Our Backs*?" I joked. *Off Our Backs* was a super-long-running radical feminist magazine. *On Our Backs* was a women-run lesbian erotica magazine. Big difference. In my earliest babydyke days, I'd once thumbed through one of Pea's dog-eared copies of *On Our Backs* and been absolutely shocked. There was *smut* for *lesbians*?? *Created* by lesbians??? This was *filthy*!!! Did other people know about this? What else didn't I know?

"*Off*," EmJ said, shaking their head at me, laughing.

The line in the bar suddenly started moving. All the kids waiting to meet Lady Camden trooped upstairs, as if on cue. The drag show was starting. I looked around A League of Her Own, which had been almost emptied out.

"I'm hungry," Davin said.

"I don't think they're serving food anymore," I said.

We went outside, where I discovered that in my haste to get inside ALOHO before it "closed," I'd hardly even noticed its exterior. A League of Her Own was housed in the lower level of what looked like a row house, its logo—a rainbow-ponytailed baseball player winding up for a pitch—set over the bar's windows. Cute. I'd loved the original 1992 *A League of Their Own* movie.* Shelley and I had worn the VHS tape out watching it. A League of Her Own, this strange basement bar, was pretty cute.

ALOHO had a patio set out front in the street, and a few knots of queers were out there. Gay men spilled over from the Pitchers patio next door. It all looked busy and fun, Ubers arriving to scoop passengers up, lesbians leaning against doorways to send "u up?" texts to their exes, kids dressed all in black blowing clouds of candy-scented vape smoke as they passed, like little goth dragons vanishing into the night. Davin, EmJ, Teresa, and I walked a few doors down to a place called Jumbo Slice, which sold the jumbo-est slices of pizza I'd ever seen. Davin's slice was the size of his upper body, and he gazed at it with an almost paternal pride and fondness. "Look at this thing," he murmured, cradling it, grease already shining in a line down his arm.

Sometimes I miss living in a city, and this was one of those times, I thought, watching a normal weeknight in Washington, DC, unfold around me. We'd seen the future that day: As You Are bar is what I think the future looks like for queer spaces. We'd seen the past: the ghosts of 1950s butch-femme culture had brushed past us at an underground lesbian bar. We'd also seen something I didn't believe could exist: a lesbian bar and a gay bar sharing space, seemingly gracefully.

And when EmJ rounded the corner in their car to drop us off at the condo, we saw the Capitol building at the end of the street. Again. There it was, a wildly famous American icon of a building, just lurking. And for the first time, I didn't shriek. I was used to it by now.

Eventually, you get used to living among these famous buildings.

---

* And became a huge fan of *A League of Their Own*, the new, queered-up TV series from Abbi Jacobson and Will Graham, when *that* came out.

Eventually, through enough exposure, you get used to seeing Lady Gaga in the courtyard of your apartment complex.

It was just like queer people, really. We were everywhere; no need to shriek. Society was getting used to us. It was one of the clear reasons lesbian bars were closing. The need—the absolute desperate need to be around others like ourselves—had diminished with assimilation.

Fortunately, the *want* is still there. I still *want* to be around others like me; so do millions of other queers. Our remaining spaces are shifting and changing as queer identity shifts and changes. New spaces are opening. It's a beautiful thing to see.

Davin was futzing with the lock on the front door of the condo. It had been notoriously difficult during our visit, refusing to either lock or unlock without many attempts and a lot of swearing. But now, on our last night in DC, the lock clicked easily, and the heavy door swung open. Kicking my shoes off, I walked across hundred-year-old parquet floors, past windows that looked out on hundred-year-old row houses. *These floors, these houses, were built during a time when no one could be out*, I thought, heading for the bathroom. Four blocks away, bills that said things should be different had been signed into law within my lifetime. So much had changed. So much still needs to change.

These bar visits had been a snapshot of a moment in time within queer history. I had a lot of hope for what was coming next.

Tulsa

Yellow Brick Road Pub

• • •

Tulsa felt like the inside of a mouth. By myself—Davin was back in session at the Minnesota Senate—I'd driven my own car from Minnesota to Oklahoma, a nine-and-a-half-hour trip *without* stops. By the time I rolled up in Tulsa at four p.m., I was shocked by the mid-May heat, stunned, my mouth open, the AC gurgling a death rattle.

"This can't be real," I muttered, sticking my arm out the window and hastily pulling it back in, the sizzle from my own seared flesh leaving a plume of trailing smoke behind me. Hot, exhausted, sick to *death* of podcasts, and feeling the kind of gross you can only feel after a really long day spent in the car eating nothing but differently shaped kinds of sodium, I spotted the turnoff for my hotel. Thank god. I inched up to the light. And that's when I saw that the street across from my hotel was called Celebrate Life Way.

"No," I said firmly. "Nope."

Celebrate *Life* Way? This *street*, this street in *Oklahoma*, had the *audacity* to be named Celebrate Life Way *just a few days after the* Roe v. Wade *Supreme Court draft opinion had leaked*? "I think the fuck not," I said aloud, guiding my car's nose over to the side of the road to take a picture. "Unbelievable."

This did not feel like a good start to the Oklahoma section of these trips. Oklahoma was the last leg of my journey. It had *three* lesbian bars, which meant it tied with New York as the state with the most. And while

264

I'd been excited to visit all the bars, all over the country, I'd been looking forward to going to the Oklahoma bars the most. These bars would, I thought, be true islands in the storm. They wouldn't be like in New York, where you step outside the dyke bars and there's little contrast between the patrons and the people walking by. The Oklahoma bars, I hypothesized, would be something magical to see. Spaces that existed in absolute defiance of their surroundings.

I was so excited for the Oklahoma bars, in fact, that I'd saved them for last on purpose, anticipating them deliciously. They were like the Reese's Peanut Butter Eggs I had stashed in my cupboard from last Easter—I knew they were there, but I was waiting until the time felt just right.

I'd finally made it to Tulsa, and I'd been looking forward to this for so long, and so I did not need any chilling reminders from menacing, evil-hearted street signs that I was in one of the worst states in the country to be a woman and/or to be queer. Abortion was *already* illegal in Oklahoma. Queer people didn't have basic antidiscrimination protections at work. Gay people could be turned away when applying to adopt kids. Public school teachers couldn't legally talk about LGBTQIA+ topics in the classroom. Fuck. And I was white! What would it be like to be Black here? Black *and* queer? Oklahoma was the middle buckle-hole of the Bible Belt, one of the reddest of the red states, a Trump-votin', big truck-drivin', anti-sodomy law havin' *state*, one where *enough people to be noticeable* apparently felt fine about flying Confederate flags off their back porches, where they could be seen from the highway.

Celebrate Life Way. Fuck outta here.

There was another reason I'd been excited to see the lesbian bars in Oklahoma. So far, I'd noticed that the farther south I went, the kinder people were to strangers (me) in their bars. People were more willing to chat, less willing to bunch up in cliques and eye nosy outsiders asking bar-related questions with suspicion. *Outside* the doors of lesbian bars in the South, God had been everywhere. The stone Ten Commandments tablets guarding my hotel in Dallas. Store employees working God into small talk ("Have a blessed day!"), Bible quotes running along the bottom of menus, megachurches looming over the highways. *Inside*, the red-state lesbian bars had mostly felt safe and welcoming, tiny oases of protection from the nonconsensual God-phlegm being coughed on me all day. If the Oklahoma dyke bars were in keeping with this southern trend I'd observed of being extra welcoming, I felt sure they were going to be some of the best in the country.

Yellow Brick Road Pub, Tulsa's only lesbian bar, was first. At ten p.m. on a Saturday night, I cruised past it twice, unsure. Was this it? I could see the YBR sign, a four-sided yellow rectangle on a post out on the sidewalk, and Siri was telling me this was it, but . . . mmm. Was it open? The sign wasn't lit up, and YBR looked like an addition built onto an office building. Cars drove past on the otherwise-deserted street, their headlights illuminating a mix of stores and industrial buildings. I pulled into what looked like alley parking next to YBR and got out, uneasy. Could I park here? Was this OK?

I stood out front, hesitating. This was definitely it. It looked too small to be a bar, but I could see now that Yellow Brick Road had two tiny front windows, each with a lighted sign in it. One just said BAR; the other was a lit-up question mark placed over a gay flag. (I interpreted this as "Ya queer somehow? Come on in.") My stomach swooping like it always does before I go inside a new lesbian bar, I opened the door.

Ohhhh. A shotgun building! Super long and not wide, *that's* why it had looked so small from the outside. Got it. Yellow Brick Road, whose walls were painted the signature semigloss bloodred color™ of dyke bars everywhere, stretched out in front of me, with a long row of people seated around a curved wooden bar. Beyond them, I could see pool tables and more seating. It was fairly dark, except for the string of lights along the ceiling, and liquor bottles gleamed softly, illuminated by a mirrored bar back. Cozy. Little gay flags, pictures, and rainbow stickers were posted all over the bar itself, which gave YBR a feeling of age, like it was cluttered with memories, even though it wasn't *that* old—it opened in 2000. People looked up when I came in and then went back to chatting.

"Hi, sweetie," a handsome man behind the counter said. I jumped. I hadn't seen him there. "Welcome in. What can I get you?"

The bartender's name was Tackett, and when I asked, he told me he'd worked at Yellow Brick Road for seven and a half years. "Come with me," he said, leading me over to the end of the bar, where the obvious regulars were sitting in a cluster. "Scoot over, make room for Krista," Tackett commanded. "She's writing a book about the last lesbian bars and everyone has to talk to her."

I turned red, feeling like I was imposing, and a woman named Tracy patted a bar seat. "Come sit here by me," she said. "I work here, too. Part-time, for five years, now."

"Are you working right now?" I asked.

"Nope! Just stopped by to say hello and harass Tackett."

At the end of the bar, someone tapped their cigarette into an ashtray. Thinking about what I wanted to ask people, I watched the ash fall, the tip glow bright again.

Wait a second.

"You can smoke here?" I blurted. "INSIDE?"

Tracy laughed. "Yeah!"

"Are you *serious*?"

I looked around, suddenly realizing that *almost everyone was smoking.* "I CAN'T BELIEVE THIS," I bellowed, my eyes bugging, all shyness gone.

"You can't smoke inside where you're from?" an onlooker asked.

"*No,*" I said. "Oh my god, *no.* Not for like, fifteen years or something." I stared, unable to get over the sight of people lighting up at the bar over a whiskey. It felt like 2005 in there! Queers who smoke: have I got a road trip destination for *you.*

"Hey, you really missed it," Tackett said suddenly. "The original owner of the bar, Kevie, she had a big reunion party here just last Friday. This place was packed with older lesbians, the people who ran this place back in the day."

"Oh no," I said, stricken. This had been such a theme of my lesbian bar travels—finding out I'd missed something great *just* the night before, or had come in a week *after* Shane from *The L Word* was there, or had *just* missed the owner by ten minutes, an owner I'd been unable to get in contact with. *It's OK*, I told myself, channeling what Davin kept telling me when I would freak out about this kind of thing. *You cannot see it all. You're going to miss stuff.*

"There used to be a lot more places for lesbians to go in Tulsa," Tracy said. "We had TNT's for a long time. That was a great lesbian bar."

"TNT's?" I asked, writing as fast as I could.

"Tits and Twat," Tracy deadpanned. "But it's closed now. This is the only bar here now. And it's more of an everyone bar, at this point." She gestured to the room, which, admittedly, did not look like it had many blatantly obvious queers in it. "The clientele here has really morphed over time," she added. "It used to have much more of a reputation for being unfriendly to people who weren't lesbians. Now it's a lot more chill. It's a bar where everyone's welcome."

I nodded, privately wishing that I could get any lesbian bar owner or employee to say *anything* but exactly this, but also knowing that the sentiment was loving and good.

A trans woman on my other side, Bri, joined in the conversation. She'd been coming to Yellow Brick Road for years. "Lesbians were my first allies," she said. "It's sad to see it go this way [be less lesbian-centric], but it was at the cost of more inclusiveness. I think it's good that everyone comes in here. We're gonna sink or swim together."

As if on cue, a group of four people dressed like pirates walked into the bar. They radiated heterosexuality. "We were at a pirate feast!" cried one in a leather-look wench outfit. Tackett waved them over.

"The people who *are* in here are super supportive," Tracy offered.

"The only thing is—because this is a neighborhood bar—we have so many people come in and have no idea this is a gay bar."

"That's why we have the sign," Tackett said.

"Sign?" I hadn't seen a sign.

Tackett brought me over to it. I don't know how I missed it. Right by the door, a sign at YBR says IN CASE YOU DIDN'T NOTICE, THIS IS A GAY BAR.

"I love it," I said, immediately wanting to steal it. I don't know why, but I always think about how easy things would be to steal. I've only stolen two things in my entire life, and one was a Diet Pepsi from Home Depot—I just opened it and drank it as I followed my ex around the power tools department. This was a decade ago, and I still feel bad about it. But that gay bar sign! Imagine that hanging next to your front door. Over your bed!

Back at the end of the bar, the topic of discussion for the regulars I'd been sitting with had changed to "wild sex stuff." I'd clearly missed something good. "I never did nothin' like that before," one of the regulars said, chuckling and shaking their head. "No way."

"Tackett, tell your threesome story," Tracy ordered.

"Which one?"

"You know which one."

"I once had a three-way with [name redacted; very famous basketball player] and [name redacted; very famous porn star]," Tackett said calmly. [Author's note: if you're trying to guess who it might be, the first two people you think of might well be correct.]

The end of the bar erupted.

"No way!"

"That's not true!"

"It *is* true," Tackett said. "It was [famous basketball star]'s birthday, and I was working at a different bar, and [famous basketball star] and [famous porn star] were telling people that they wanted a three-way, and so I said I'd be down. They told me to meet them at their hotel, and I went. It was great. When I told my friends later, no one believed me, and they all used to give me so much shit about it." He paused, a born story-teller. We were all hanging on his every word. "Four years later, [famous basketball player] came to town, and my friends bought us all tickets, just so they could prove it never happened. We were waiting in line for the meet-and-greet later, and [famous basketball player] jumped up and ran toward me, yelling, 'TACKETT!'" He cackled at the memory. "My friends *lost* it."

Sitting at the end of the bar, bookended on either side by regulars who were trying to one-up each other with juicy sex stories? That's a perfect night. People were treating me like I belonged there, like an old friend, and—I looked around—I had met every person in the bar. Every one of them. Even the employees of Pie Hole, the pizza place next door. YBR was their hangout, too.

Watching someone at the bar act out how bad of a kisser their re-cent date had been, I laughed along with everyone else, as chummy as if I'd lived in Tulsa for years. I could just feel it: Oklahoma was going to be incredible.

IN THE DAYLIGHT, YELLOW BRICK Road Pub looked even less like a bar that was definitely open. The base of YBR's signpost was missing big chips of paint; a cracked sidewalk boxed in a patch of bleached, long-dead grass out front. An old hand at this now, though, I parked in the alley like a king, noticing that the side of the building was painted a sunny golden yellow.

YBR was open, and I was going back in.

"Hellooooo," a new bartender greeted me.

"Hi," I said. "I love your outfit." And what an outfit! *This* was Jorhdon, and they were *dressed*. Leopard-spotted hair peeked out from under a wide-brimmed black hat. A sheer lace button-down was open to the navel, tucked into teeny tiny black short-shorts, which clipped to gar-ters, which were holding up black fishnets worn inside knee-high black chunky platform boots. Jorhdon was at least six inches taller than any human being in Oklahoma.

"Oh, thanks," Jorhdon said. "I was feeling casual."

I took a moment to digest this. "Are people any kind of way when they see an outfit like yours in Tulsa? I ask because I'm not from here, and I don't know anything about the queer scene here."

Jorhdon laughed. "Tulsa's just like any city; you can surround yourself in a little queer bubble if you want to. There's a pretty big scene here. I never really have to deal with people who aren't queer."

"That sounds wonderful," I said.

"It is, honey."

"Hi, Krista!" Tracy was at the bar, as were multiple people from the night before. "I was hoping you'd show up! C'mon over here, you gotta meet these two."

She scooted a stool out for me next to two queers sitting at the end of the bar. One had pink hair, they both had baby faces, and I could not tell how old they were, and I mean at *all*. One of the ways you know queers are a chosen people is that when you look at them, you never have any idea if they are even within the *vicinity* of a range of, say, twenty-two to forty-two, and you have to be prepared to keep your face neutral when they tell you their actual age, which is always so far off from your private guess that you fall silent for a second, shocked.

These two were Tori and Ragan, and when they told me their ages, I fell silent for a second, shocked. I had guessed they were both twenty-four. They were married, it turned out, and had met on MySpace (!!!), and had moved to Tulsa recently. I couldn't begin to tell you how we got there, but Tori mentioned she was an ex-Mormon.

"NO," I said. "YOU ARE NOT."

"I am!"

"SO AM I."

"Oh, you'll love this, then! I got with a Bishop's daughter."

"SHUT UP."

Tori grinned. "Back in the day."

"How do you feel about the people who come in this bar?" I asked, looking around. "I was here last night, and I don't know if I saw that many glaringly obvious queers. You know, for a lesbian bar."

"Oh, they're here," Tori said. "But there's a lot of gay-adjacent people who come in here, too. I love this bar. Nobody who comes in here is showing off; it's the working-class gays. Gritty. But we do have a lot of hundred-footers. They're just not here right now."

"Hundred-footers?" I asked.

"You know, people you know are gay from a hundred feet away."

"Yeah, a lot of people come in here," agreed Ragan. "I think everyone feels comfortable here."

"An everyone bar?" I suggested, arching my eyebrows.

"Yeah."

"It *is* a lesbian bar." Jorhdon had joined the conversation. They leaned over the counter. "To not call this a lesbian bar does a disservice to the reason the bar was created. This bar was built decades ago to be a safe space for lesbians. This is not a gay bar. This is a lesbian bar, and to ignore that is an erasure."

My mouth opened and shut, an astounded trout. "Say that again," I ordered, scrabbling for my notebook. "Say exactly what you just said again."

Jorhdon repeated what they'd said, and my heart swelled. They had just put into words the feeling I'd had all this time, that we were sometimes missing something at these bars when we called them bars for everyone. I understood that everyone was welcome; I *wanted* everyone to be welcome. But to gloss over the fact that most of them were historically lesbian bars *did* feel like an erasure.

On my other side, a woman I'd met the night before, now so drunk she'd been nodding onto the counter, suddenly sat up, her eyes wide open. She poked me.

"Hey," she said. I turned to her. "Hey. C'mere." She gestured for me to lean in. "I wanna tell you something. A secret."

I leaned in. She cupped her hand around my ear. "You can't tell anyone, but"—her voice dropped to a stage whisper—"I fucking love Medieval Times."

"You do?"

"I do!" she yelled, turning to face the bar. "I fucking love it!"

I cracked up. Tori looked over, eyebrows raised. She gestured to our surroundings.

"It's just a red-painted hallway filled with cigarette smoke," she said, shaking her head and smiling. "Best bar in the city."

[Author's note: Two months later, I learned that Yellow Brick Road had burned down. They are rebuilding.]

Oklahoma City
Alibi's

◆ ◆ ◆

I t was time to reevaluate everything I knew.

All around me, wall-mounted signs were chattering. DON'T MAKE ME PUT MY FOOT DOWN, warned a tin flamingo standing on one foot. SORRY FOR MY BLUNTNESS, THAT'S HOW I ROLL, explained a sassy hand holding a joint. Above a picture of a curvy fifties pinup girl, a wooden plaque sighed, THE PROBLEM WITH THE WORLD IS EVERYONE IS A FEW DRINKS BEHIND. Over the pool table, a black-and-white photo showed someone surrounded by a crowd, holding a sign that said I CAN'T BELIEVE I STILL HAVE TO PROTEST THIS FUCKING SHIT. There was no escape from the signs, not even on the toilet. THIS IS A BATHROOM, NOT AN INTERNET CAFE—SHIT & SPLIT.

I hate things that say things. Pastel mugs that say NEVERTHELESS, SHE PERSISTED. Water bottles that announce IT'S A GOOD DAY TO HAVE A GOOD DAY. Nightshirts printed with BUT FIRST, COFFEE in that stupid-ass skinny Comic Sans–looking font, you know the one I'm talking about. (It's actually called the Rae Dunn font; I have never had a more powerful enemy.) I lost my fucking *mind* during the Keep Calm & Carry On era, and Davin recently had to escort me out of the notebook aisle at Target, where dozens of options ordered me to DREAM IT. DO IT and BE A NICE HUMAN and WORK IT because I was a BOSS LADY.

"There aren't any ones with blank covers," I seethed. "I just need a blank one, *there is not a single blank notebook here.*"

Alibi's

"OK, cutes, come on," Davin coaxed.

"I JUST WANT A NICE NOTEBOOK WITH A BLANK COVER WHAT THE FUCK IS SO HARD ABOUT THAT."

"Ohhhkay, time to go."

But I was at Alibi's, one of the two (!!!!) lesbian bars in Oklahoma City, and Alibi's was covered in signs, and . . . I loved the signs. Loved them. There were just so many of them. None of them related to any of the others. It was overpowering—there was no use fighting. And for the first time in my life, I succumbed, feeling, I think, what marketers *want* me to feel when a water bottle printed with a fox orders me to DRINK WATER, FOR FOX SAKE. In Alibi's, my brain relaxed, slumping to the side of my skull like a pile of warm grits. I didn't need an inner monologue anymore. The signs would take care of it for me. YOU'RE NOT STUPID, YOU'RE JUST NOT LUCKY WHEN IT COMES TO THINKING, heeyucked a yellow sign in front of me at the bar. *Ha*, I remember thinking as I read it. *That's funny.*

The signs had worn me down.

Alibi's is a gem. It is a little brick box with a maroon awning along the side of the road in a run-down section of Oklahoma City's Shepherd Historic District, and I would not change a single thing about it. It has free parking. It has a back patio painted with deeply lesbionic murals, the kind that feature backlit trees against full moons, or that are lavender and say BE THE CHANGE YOU WANT TO SEE. Alibi's opened in 2003. It's now owned by Krystal and Tiffany McDaniel, who bought the bar in 2013 from the previous owner, Cathy Glover. It has three main rooms—a bar, a raised billiards area, and a big back room that looks ideal for dancing, with a movie screen and garden globe lights all strung around. It is covered, unapologetically covered, in things that say things, and if I could choose a lesbian bar to fold up and put in my pocket and pop open when I feel sad, it would be this one.

Apprehensive as ever to be entering a new queer space alone, I walked through the front door. Immediately, an elderly Great Dane bounded up to me and demanded to be patted, politely putting her nose under my hand and tilting her neck back so my fingers slid along her shining black head.

"Scooby, no *ma'am*," her owner called. "Get back, you let people be."

Scooby ignored this and leaned against me, her warm weight knocking me off-balance.

"Scoooooobyyyyy," I crooned, my eyes adjusting to the light. It was dim and cool inside Alibi's, especially in comparison with the heat and dust outside. Alibi's, I could see, had kind of an industrial-tropical vibe going on. It was like an aqua-painted oasis, the bar made of wood-topped corrugated sheet metal; a floofy bouquet of real pink and yellow roses sitting atop the beer dispenser between two colorful Furbies; so many beach house–vibe signs.

"This is my dream dog," I murmured. I was in a trance, stroking Scooby's ample sides, talking to no one. "I've always wanted a black-and-white Great Dane. Just like this one. Just like you, Scooby. Aren't you a good baby? Aren't you, Scooby? You *are*."

"She is," the bartender said, wiping their hands and coming around from the other side of the bar. "Watch." The bartender held up a treat, and Scooby sat, extending an elegant paw for a shake. I clapped, as enthusiastic as a preschooler clapping after blowing out her own birthday candles.

"Do you always have dogs in here?" I asked, measuring Scooby with my eyes. *Would she wear a children's size 6 or 8 T-shirt? The only way to know would be to put one on her.*

"All the time," the bartender said. "Except not after ten."

"What happens at ten?"

"There are no dogs allowed after ten."

"I've never been here before," I said, quickly explaining my project. "Why aren't dogs allowed after ten?"

The bartender, a cute queer named Lisa with a lying-down pastel pink mohawk, smiled.

"Because there is no reason a dog needs to be in a bar after ten p.m.," she said firmly. "Nothing good can come of it."

I looked at her. There was more to this story.

"We made that rule after an incident," she added.

"Ah." I didn't press any further. She'd said "incident" with a capital "I."

I glanced around. *Beetlejuice* was playing on the TV by the pool table. Beneath the TV was a table graced with—oh my god, my midwestern heart!—a full-size, blue-and-white Crock-Pot.

"Why is there a Crock-Pot in here?" I whirled around to Lisa. "What's in the Crock-Pot?"

"Queso!" she said. "For chips. You want some?" I must have looked dumbstruck. "It's free," she added. A queer in a black baseball hat came up and spooned some out over a bowl of chips. The queso was pale yellow, creamy looking, with little bits and chunks in it—homemade. Unable to resist, the queso queer loaded a heavy, dripping chip into their mouth, chewing as they spooned out a little more over their bowl. "Mmmpf," they said, looking up to see me watching. "S'good. Come get some."

Now, I have been offered free popcorn in bars. I have been offered free nuts, free bags of chips, even BOGO beers when the beers were not technically BOGO. But I have never been offered *free homemade freaking queso in a Crock-Pot someone brought from home*, and I am here to unhesitatingly give Alibi's five stars in this Yelp review.

They were setting up for bingo, too. "I love bingo!" I cried. In Chicago, I used to live a block from St. Gregory the Great, a big Catholic church that held weekly bingo nights in their basement. I used to go fairly often, usually the youngest person there by many decades. I never won anything—I was just there to watch the bingo ladies setting up their lucky talismans around their bingo cards. Stuffed elephants, plastic rabbit figurines, palm-size glass vases filled with tiny glass flowers, troll dolls; Dolores and Barbara would run five or six cards at once, absolutely lethal with their hot pink or neon blue bingo dabbers. I miss really particular things about living in Chicago, and bingo nights at St. Gregory's rank pretty high up on the list.

Unlike at St. Gregory's, bingo at Alibi's was free to play, and tonight— I examined my card—the theme was "Weed Bingo," with boxes that said things like "Dank" and "Chronic" and "Visine."

Customers ringed the bar, but there was an open stool at the counter near the door that led to Alibi's patio. "Can I sit here?" I asked a friendly looking trans man in a brightly printed tank top.

"Sure," he said, gesturing for me to take the stool. I hopped on. "My name's Krista," I said hopefully.

"Hayden," he said, offering his hand. Then: "*What* are you writing?"

"A book about the last lesbian bars in America. I'm here to research this one tonight."

"Well, Alibi's is the greatest," Hayden said promptly. "I love this bar. I always come here." He gazed around the bar with fondness. "You going to Frankie's, too? We have two bars in Oklahoma City."

"Yep, Frankie's is next," I said. "Wednesday night and Thursday night."

Lisa leaned over the bar. "You're going to Frankie's on Thursday?" she asked, raising her eyebrows. "You can't. They're moving."

"What."

"Yeah, they're moving this week! Actually, Wednesday is the big moving day, I think," she said. "So they're closed. How long you staying?"

"Until Friday morning," I whimpered. My pulse quickened. Time to panic. Of course this would happen. Of course the one week of my life that I would be in Oklahoma specifically to visit all three of the state's lesbian bars would be the *same* week that the final bar I was supposed to visit was closed and moving out of the historic space they'd occupied for years, the historic space I'd come specifically to see. *This was all Nellie's fault*, I thought, murder in my heart. After months of being careful, I'd finally caught Covid in early May at a birthday party in Minneapolis. Knowing I'd made it that far and *still* not caught it, I'd stupidly let my guard down; I'd hugged Nellie, who was there visiting from DC. The morning after the party, Nellie texted everyone that she'd tested positive. It was rotten timing; I'd had to postpone my entire Oklahoma road trip, which had originally been scheduled for a week earlier, *when Frankie's would have been open.*

Nellie, I snarled to myself, making the same face Jerry makes on *Seinfeld* when he realizes Newman has gotten him again.

"You might want to extend your trip," Lisa suggested, handing over my mango-spiked seltzer. "They're having their opening-night party on Friday."

"Oh!" *Omg, maybe I could do it.* "They are? OK! Thank you for telling me that!" I sat on my stool, heart racing, doing the panicked mental calculations you get used to when you've spent the last ten months traveling with almost no allotted vacation time on a hilariously tight budget and very, very few things have gone according to plan. *Wait'll I tell Davin,* I thought, shaking my head. *He'll flip.*

OK. It was fine. This was fine. I'd been waiting for something to go wrong on the Oklahoma trip; it was a relief to have it just be this. Really, what was another night spent at the crumbling Courtyard by Marriott across the street from a Boot Barn at this point? We'd maxed out the travel credit card months ago; *everything* was out of pocket now!

Lisa had the ease and skill that all good bartenders have—she was doing five things at once, pulling beers, wiping glasses, opening tabs, pouring shots, all while making it seem like she had nothing but time to talk. She'd worked at Alibi's for seven years. "Working here is the best," she said. "I meet so many great people. We get people from all over stopping in here. You know, Oklahoma City has a big queer scene. You'd be surprised."

"Really?"

"Oh, yeah. Have you been to The Strip yet?"

I had not. "Thirty-Ninth Street," she said. "It's our gayborhood."

"What's Pride like here?"

"At Alibi's?" She grinned. "It's nuts."

"They fill up the patio with sand during Pride and have a beach party," Hayden explained. "They're always doing stuff like that—the owners—always making things fun for the community. During Easter, they fill plastic eggs up with cash and hide them around the bar for an Easter egg hunt."

So wholesome. I had talked with one of the owners, Krystal Mc-Daniel, and she had been wonderful, saying simply, "Alibi's is my whole heart." She'd bartended at Alibi's for four years before buying the bar with Tiffany. "I loved this bar the moment I walked in as a customer," she'd said. "It had this amazing vibe. When I started working here, it just became home, and I wanted to make it better and last forever."

"Being a bar owner is really difficult at times," she added. Krystal doesn't want to close Alibi's, but she mentioned a few reasons why she believes lesbian bars close.

"Women don't have as much disposable income as our male counterparts. I also think eventually, people sell or close because they want more routine in their lives."

I hadn't heard another bar owner mention the lack of routine in their lives as a reason bars sometimes close, but it made a lot of sense. The lifestyle of a bar owner—especially a new bar owner—must be exhausting. The hours alone! I thought back to Jo and Coach at As You Are in DC. They'd told me they pretty much lived at the bar right now.

Krystal and Tiffany cultivate the family feel of Alibi's. "We try to be here for our community and provide a safe space for everybody. I think bars geared toward women, especially lesbian bars, are necessary because it makes us feel safe. We would love to open an Alibi's day center for our LGBTQIA+ youth."

A young queer walked out toward the patio, carefully carrying an enormous ten-dollar fishbowl margarita, vivid yellow. Two friends followed, one holding three straws and looking exultant.

Bingo started. "Kush," bellowed the bingo caller, who was sitting in the back room with a microphone. "Nugget."

My card was not lucky. A pretty femme pulled up a stool next to me. Her name was Reeta, and she shook her head when I asked if she needed a bingo card.

"I'm not playing," she said, ordering a peach-flavored shot. "You want one?"

"I better not, I'm a lightwei—"

"She'll have one, too," Reeta said to Lisa, pointing at me.

Mustn't be rude. We clinked our shot glasses together and knocked them back. I tried to act like this was normal for me—I was not about to tell Reeta that this was only the third real shot I'd ever taken in my life. The other two happened at two different Prides, and both were tequila, and both were to make me feel OK about the fact that I was dancing *and people could see me*. Reeta popped her glass on the counter. "That was delicious!" she said. "I'll have another."

"Let me get yours this time," I said.

"OK, thank you very much!"

I had meant to just get Reeta a shot, but Lisa poured two more and set them in front of us. Oh no.

The rest of the night is a little hazy. I remember talking at great length with Hayden and Lisa about all the creatures in Oklahoma that can kill you (black widows, cottonmouth snakes) or burn huge holes in your flesh (fiddleback spiders). I remember Abbie, another bartender, coming in, and finding out that Abbie was dating Lisa, and squealing over their matching couple's lock-and-key earrings. I remember leaning over to Reeta, saying, "Reeta, I don't want to be weird, but you smell incredible," and Reeta promptly opening her purse and pulling out two (!) full-size (!) glass bottles of perfume, and me screaming over the idea of someone casually carrying two full-size bottles of perfume around with them, just clacking together at the bottom of a purse. The one making her smell like that was Armani My Way, which I'd dismissed, unsniffed, months ago in Ulta's tester aisle for being pink and having a stupid name. "People stop me in the streets over this one," Reeta said, tapping the bottle. "Every day." I remember eventually winning bingo on the word "Doobie." The prize was a twenty-five-dollar bar tab at Alibi's, and I remember giving it to a teacher sitting at the bar whose last day of school was the next day.

"You earned it," I said.

"Yes god, I did," they said, shaking their head. "Thank you."

By the end of the evening, I was drinking lots of water, and Lisa and Abbie were watching to make sure I didn't leave until I'd sobered up. It took a while. I looked around Alibi's. What a wonderful bar. Just like at Yellow Brick Road in Tulsa, I had met every person there, and every person I'd met had been kind and polite and so, so welcoming. I felt like I'd been coming there my whole life. *Should we move to the South?* I wondered. *What about the spiders?*

Above the bar, a wooden sign said ENTER AS STRANGERS, LEAVE AS FRIENDS.

"I like that sign," I said, pointing up.

"That's Alibi's motto," Abbie said.

"It fits," I said.

A few hours ago, I'd never have liked that sign. I was too snotty for it. But Alibi's had knocked something loose in me, and now I saw the sign for what it was: a message to everyone who walked through the door, important enough to nail to the wall.

Oklahoma City

Frankie's

◆ ◆ ◆

The last bar.

I sat in my car, hands on the steering wheel. It was seven thirty p.m. on Friday, May 20, 2022, and I was in the parking lot of Frankie's, the second lesbian bar in Oklahoma City, the third lesbian bar in Oklahoma, and the last lesbian bar I'd be visiting for this book.

It didn't feel like the last bar. It felt like just another night of the new life I'd gotten used to over the past ten months. You know—yet another night where I'd started with an afternoon nap in an anonymous hotel in a strange city, then spoken my bar-visit mantras aloud while leaning over the mirror and putting on eyeliner ("You are allowed to take up space in your own community! No one is gonna talk to you! And that is fine because you are gonna talk to everybody!"), and then headed to another dyke bar where I didn't know anyone, notebook in hand and eyes peeled for cute LHBs.

But *this* time was the last time. I turned the thought over in my head, unable to grasp the concept. The last time. I would never do this again. *I'll miss this*, I thought suddenly. *It all went so fast.*

I shook my head. Time to pull myself together. "It's just another night," I said out loud, applying lip gloss in the rearview mirror and popping one of those horrible Listerine mini-sheets onto my tongue. "Glahhhh." (Why are they *so minty*? Who asked for this kind of pain from a breath freshener?)

283

A car door slammed nearby, and two queers in snapbacks, T-shirts, and cargo shorts got out. *Ah*, I thought, unbuckling my seat belt, *my people*. They made their way toward the entrance of Frankie's. I watched them go, wondering if they were excited to see the new space. Had they been regulars at the old Frankie's?

Lisa from Alibi's had been right—Frankie's had spent the week moving from its old location, and tonight was the opening night of the *new* location. I had driven past the old location several times in the last few days, mostly because I had been dying to see inside, but it had been locked all three times (yes! I'm a creep! and also trying to do research!) I'd tried to get in. "C'monn," I'd muttered like an old pervert, yanking uselessly on the door handle in the middle of the day. "Just let me get a peek."

I was upset I'd missed seeing the old Frankie's—it had such a good backstory. (Well, I thought it did. Something like fifteen people had tried to tell me the backstory and none of the versions completely matched up.) Frankie's, from what I'd heard, used to be called Partners, and used to be owned by a lesbian couple. Long story short, the couple split up, but neither one of them wanted to give up the bar, and so what do you think they did?

You'll love this. They put a *wall* down the *middle of the bar*, dividing it into *two bars*, Partners and PartnersToo, and if that isn't the most lesbian shit you've ever heard, I can't help you. I mean, can you imagine the *pressure*? If you were friends with *both people in the couple*? Which side would you go to if you wanted a drink? The sheer potential for dyke drama made my neck break out in hives when I heard the story.

Somewhere in there, the bar was renamed Frankie's, and eventually, another lesbian couple—Tracey Harris and Ann-Rene Harris—bought it. The other side became a gay bar called Faces. And then Frankie's moved. To this new space—the one I was standing outside.

All I could really see from the parking lot was a tall, new-looking wooden fence. A banner hung on it: FRANKIE'S—WELCOME HOME. I

walked past the fence, and . . . oh wow. *This* was a *front yard*. The new
Frankie's has a big-ass, grassy front patio, studded with colored umbrellas and cornhole boards. (Does everyone remember what cornhole is? A
beanbag toss game. I know we saw the American Cornhole League Kickoff Battle in Denver, but I'm never sure if I'm just assuming everyone
understands midwestern pastimes.) It was full of people, all grouped
cozily around outdoor tables or standing in tight circles, chattering in
the open air. They definitely all knew each other. They looked up when I
walked by. I took a deep breath through my nose, letting it slowly out as
I passed. I was allowed to take up space in my own community. No one
was gonna talk to me. And I was gonna talk to everybody.

Seven thirty was a strange time to be starting my night, but I was at
Frankie's early because I'd checked their Instagram over lunch and seen
a post announcing the Fifth Annual Free Mom Hugs Tour Kickoff starting at seven p.m. I had heard of Free Mom Hugs, but wasn't sure what it
was—was this a nonprofit? Were these the sweet parents who hugged
people during Pride? I definitely remembered *someone* wearing a Free
Mom Hugs shirt hugging me during Pride at some point. Covered in
glitter from the parade, sweaty and gross, I'd been staggered at the level
of love I'd felt in that hug. As I'd pulled back, I'd seen a gay boy wearing
nothing but gold micro shorts and a pair of gold lamé wings also being
enfolded into a hug. His eyes were closed, and he just held completely
still, wrapped in the feeling of a parent loving him. If this was what Free
Mom Hugs was—a group of people giving up their weekend morning to
go offer hugs to queer kids whose parents didn't accept them—I knew I
wanted to meet them.

It was too early for Frankie's to be busy inside. Doing a slow spin, I
took in black walls (not red! a triumph of restraint!), a disco ball, cool
colored LED lighting, and a sound booth. My god, this was a big bar.
Everything looked brand-spanking-new, because it was. It felt strange
to be in a brand-new bar on my last trip, but also fitting. A tangible sign
that a lesbian bar was growing, moving up in the world.

And *wow* was it new. Unbidden, the *Titanic* lady popped into my head: *It's been eighty-four years, and I can still smell the fresh paint. The china had never been used. The sheets had never been slept in.* That was Frankie's on its first night—so shiny. None of the cushioned stools were split yet; there weren't any stains on the floor from years of surprise vomit. *Frankie's was called the Ship of Dreams, and it was. It really was.*

To the left, an abnormal number of electronic dartboards stood in a row. *What* is *it with drunk people and darts?* I wondered. It's hard to think of many things that go together less. Like, here you go: Why don't you take this large sharpened aerodynamic needle designed to fly and throw it as hard as you can in a room filled with people? And how would you like a shot of Fireball to go with that, ya li'l rascal?

I headed back outside, setting my things on the only open table and steeling myself to approach a lot of people. OK: there was someone in a Free Mom Hugs T-shirt.

"Hi," I said. "You're with Free Mom Hugs?"

"Yes!" beamed a lady named Jan Pezant, who turned out to be the secretary of Free Mom Hugs, which, I found out, is a nonprofit that celebrates the queer community "through visibility, education, and conversation." They *were* the people who give out hugs at Pride—Free Mom Hugs had been walking in Pride parades since 2016, Jan explained.

"How did you get involved with this?" I asked, curious.

"I have a gay son," she said, "and, while my husband and I weren't really surprised when he came out, we were worried about what would happen to him. We had seen some of his friends lose their families when they came out, and we wanted it to be different for him."

I looked at Jan's pleasant face, her matter-of-fact explanation that she had wanted her gay son to feel loved, and *ew, fuck*, I was tearing up. Shit, I had been here less than five minutes.

Another woman came over—Karrie Fletcher-Rollins, executive director of Free Mom Hugs. A lesbian, she said, "I spent fourteen years trying to change my sexuality because of my faith." She'd been involved in ex-gay ministry—conversion therapy. My mouth formed a silent O.

"I came out in 2016," Karrie continued. "I'm gay, and a Christian. I joined the board of directors of Free Mom Hugs in 2020. I think queer people need to be included in religion; that's what I work toward. But you should really talk to Sara"—she pointed—"over there. She started Free Mom Hugs; she's why we're all here."

"Every year, except during Covid, Sara and her son Parker take a tour for ten days, to ten cities, with a goal of giving out ten thousand hugs," Jan added. "This year, they're going to Florida. Pulse Nightclub is the final destination. This is the kickoff party for their tour."

Karrie and Jan walked me over to Sara Cunningham, the founder of Free Mom Hugs. An energetic-looking woman with cropped white-blond hair and bright red lipstick, she was wearing a shirt that said DON'T HIDE YOUR PRIDE! and animatedly talking with a big group of people in the yard. She was cheerful about being interrupted and let me interview her and the social media manager for Free Mom Hugs, Katrina Kalb, on the spot.

"Let's go inside," she said. "It's too noisy out here!"

Inside Frankie's, Sara, Katrina, and I settled onto stools at a high-top. Sara tried to buy me a drink, and I had to explain that she was doing *me* a favor.

"Not even a water?"

Huge mom energy. I am positive that if I'd said I was hungry, she'd have pulled a granola bar out of her bag. I asked her how Free Mom Hugs came to be.

"Well, my son Parker, my youngest son, came out to me," she said. "Now, you know, this is Oklahoma—it's conservative!—and I was raised to believe that that's bad. I had a hard time with Parker coming out, but eventually, I took some time to get educated, and we got through it—we repaired our relationship. In 2014, I made a button that said 'Free

Mom Hugs' and wore it to a Pride festival, offering hugs to anyone who wanted one. And I hugged people, and some of them cried, and some told me their stories, and it was heartbreaking. And so I started Free Mom Hugs—a group that offered hugs at Pride. Then I made a Facebook post that said 'I'll stand in at your wedding if your parents won't come,' and the post went viral. I met Katrina, and then we started having chapters pop up."

"We have chapters in all fifty states!" added Katrina, a former chaplain and survivor of conversion therapy.

"Wait a minute," I said. "You'll stand in for parents? At gay weddings?" Uh-oh. My voice was warbly.

Sara nodded. "I have. I do. I've officiated them, too. And there are moms all over who will do it. And dads. You just have to ask, we'll be there."

Welp, this is why I could never be a journalist. I was crying, trying to breathe carefully so they wouldn't notice, but big tattletale tears were running down my face. Sara studied me.

"Would you like a hug?"

I nodded mutely, a child. Sara opened her arms and I hugged her. It was a great hug—huge and enfolding. She rubbed my back for a sec. "I'm so sorry, honey," she whispered. "I'm so sorry." She just knew.

I sniffed and wiped my eyes on my sleeve, hopelessly trying to pull myself together. I was here to research this bar! Goddammit it is *embarrassing* to be a walking open wound about shit like this! *Should I have called this book* Mommy Issues*? Fuck.*

"Why do you both come to Frankie's?" I asked, a little too brightly.

Sara smiled. "Frankie's hosted the first Free Mom Hugs tour fundraiser. They always host us; they've been wonderful. They do all kinds of things like this—fundraisers, charities, events for the community. [Owners] Ann and Tracey are always here. They work so hard. They live over this new space, did you know?"

"I did not."

Frankie's

"Frankie's is safe," Katrina said. "It's not scary; it's just where you hang out. I love it here."

They had to get back to their kickoff party. "There's the owner of Frankie's," Sara said, pointing across the room. "Well, one of them. Tracey."

I thanked them and headed over to Tracey Harris, who was *also* cheerful about being interrupted on Frankie's opening night and willing to be interviewed, right then and there.

"First things first," I said, sitting up in my lawn chair, notebook at the ready. "How do you spell your name?" Tracey told me. "And what are your pronouns?"

Tracey, a butch-presenting person with short silver hair, shrugged and laughed. "She. They. I don't care."

"How long have you owned Frankie's?"

"It'll be five years in October," Tracey said. "I own Frankie's with my wife, Ann-Rene. We both retired from corporate life, and six months after I retired, we got Frankie's. We bought the bar we met in! I've always wanted to run a business. We bought this new building—the whole thing—with the idea of moving the bar. We live above it." Tracey gestured to a modern-looking apartment with big windows over Frankie's.

"Some 'retirement.'"

Tracey chuckled. "I had no idea the amount of labor running a bar would take. Like this patio. I built this patio! Yesterday! But I've met so many cool people here. I love it."

"Tracey, why are there so many dartboards inside?" This had been troubling me.

"Because darts are huge here! This is a dart bar."

"A what."

"We have a ton of people in dart leagues! We host tournaments. We host all kinds of things—fundraisers, queer shows, comedy shows, drag nights. Tonight is Women of Country. Hey, Ann-Rene's singing in the show tonight! You coming?"

"I'll be there."

"Don't miss it."

"I won't," I said.

The sun had set. A big group of people from Free Mom Hugs were gathered in a circle on the lawn, and Jan gestured for me to come over and join them. "Scoot down," she said. "There's plenty of room." I sat next to a woman named Mahkesha, who I'd seen setting up snacks outside for Free Mom Hugs, her flowy yellow maxi dress floating in the breeze.

"Me? My pronouns are she/her/bitch," she laughed. She was straight, she told me, but an ally.

Mahkesha, it turned out, was more than an ally. She was . . . well, shit, she had done more for the queer community than my gay ass had ever even *thought* about doing. Mahkesha does drag. She volunteers at events. In 2011, she'd created the Oklahoma Coalition for Gay Straight Alliances, a 1,200-member private group on Facebook where people could post events. She'd been on the board of OKC Pride in 2013, when they held the first mass same-sex couples' commitment ceremony in Oklahoma. "We had fifteen couples walking down a rainbow aisle!" she said.

Mahkesha knew *everything* about the queer scene in Oklahoma City. "Did you know we have a gay hotel? The District, you should stay *there*," she suggested. Between sips of beer, she gave me an astonishing rundown of the history of Pride in OKC. "At the first Pride in 1988," she said, "the Ku Klux Klan came, but they were met by five hundred queer people and supporters and the KKK ran away."

"Whoa. I have never heard about *any* of this."

I listened to her, the warm night air around us, the lights on Frankie's patio glowing. Mahkesha was now telling me about the drama within the drag community. "Honey, you wouldn't believe it, where do I even begin? OK. One of the queens posted on Facebook . . ."

The show was about to start, and we got up, following the stream of people going into Frankie's. Back inside, the bar was crowded. It was standing-room only, and Mahkesha looked around, saying, "This should be good. New Frankie's, but I've never been to Frankie's and not had a good time."

A lovely older woman wearing an amazing outfit—black cowboy hat, bolo tie, black western jacket, cowboy boots with lucky horseshoes embroidered on them—motioned to us over the noise. "You can stand at this table if you like," she said. "Set your things down."

We did, thanking her profusely. The lights went down and the Women of Country show began.

OK, FIRST OF ALL, I want to say this: *I was not prepared for the level of talent I saw during the Women of Country show at Frankie's*. No offense to anyone, but I hadn't expected anything exceptional. At this point, I'd spent close to a year at lesbian bars watching drag shows and karaoke, and all the shows and singers I'd seen had ranged between "fine" and "hey, this is pretty good." Only one show had blown my mind so far—the drag show at the Back Door.

THE WOMEN OF COUNTRY SHOW BLEW MY MIND.

The emcee was a drag queen, and guess what her first number was? The Chicks' "Ready to Run," because *clearly* someone knows what the queers want to *see*. It wasn't "Goodbye Earl," but it *was* another homosexuelle country banger, and if you've never seen a drag queen do "Ready to Run" at an Oklahoma dyke bar, I am here to suggest you may not have ever really seen a crowd go "apeshit" before. Along with everyone else, I screamed myself hoarse by the first chorus. And then, in the middle of the song, she started fucking CLOGGING. A drag queen *country-ass clogging* while perfectly lip-syncing "What's all this talk about luuuuuuuve?" is something I will remember for the rest of my life, and the show only got better.

The other owner of Frankie's, Ann-Rene, came out in a sueded fringe cape and a black cowboy hat, singing Little Big Town's "Girl Crush," and she was incredible—truly gifted. Someone else came out and sang

Bonnie Raitt's "Angel from Montgomery" and suddenly, there wasn't a dry eye in the house.

"What the fuck," I whispered to Mahkesha. "Why is everyone so good?"

"It's from gospel singing," she whispered back. "Almost everyone in Oklahoma can at least carry a tune—it's because we go to so much church! You get raised here singing."

Someone in the show began singing the Stones' "Paint It Black," and the woman in the western outfit who'd shared her table narrowed her eyes and put her phone down. She'd been filming the entire show.

"This isn't country," she said crossly. Her name was Mary-Anne Shelley, and she told me she used to teach country dancing at the old Frankie's.

"Everyone at Frankie's wanted to lead when they were learning to dance," she said, shaking her head and laughing. "It was a problem." Mary-Anne told me that she'd been around and going out when gay bars were illegal. "They used to do raids in the early seventies in Oklahoma," she said. "Cops would come in and arrest people. They'd just grab you and put you in the paddy wagon."

I looked at her. Another country song had started; it was one I didn't know. Mary-Anne pointed to my notebook. "Did you get all that down?"

"I did." I showed her, and she nodded, satisfied. She picked up her phone and began recording the Women of Country again. "They're wonderful," she said.

They were. Frankie's was wonderful, too. Their new space was wonderful. Oklahoma had been wonderful. My theory had been correct—Oklahoma lesbian bars were some of the best bars in the country.

With a jolt, I realized I had to hit the road early the next morning. Really early. My trip was over.

Feeling suddenly, overwhelmingly calm, practiced in my movements, I walked to the bar, cashed out my tab, said goodbye to Mahkesha, and headed out the door, waving to Tracey, who waved back.

Frankie's

Sara Cunningham stopped me. "You leaving? Well, it was so nice to talk to you, Krista," she said. "Can I give you one more hug?"

She hugged me again, another enveloping hug, and said, briskly patting my back, "Love you, honey. You be safe getting home, OK?"

But I already was home. I'd been home the entire year.

Epilogue

In the six months since I got back from Oklahoma, so much has happened.

Davin and I got *really* married. I say "really" because we'd already been legally married for almost two years. The first time around, in September 2020, we both signed some papers in the backyard with a few face-masked friends as witnesses, and that was that. It was because of Covid—we'd had to cancel our original May 2020 wedding date. In the backyard, I wore a caftan; Davin wore a flowered shirt; we said, "I do," and then we went inside and ordered a pizza. I know that's not a wildly romantic story, but I was tired of saying "my fiancé" and Davin needed insurance, so we got the legal part out of the way.

But Weddinggate wasn't over. Not even close. Sipping his $8.99 champagne in the kitchen after the signing, Davin pointed at me. "This isn't the real one we're going to have anniversaries about, though," he'd said.

"I know."

"We're doing this again. For real."

"I *know*."

The bridezilla of our relationship, Davin had been dreaming of a big wedding his whole life. He wanted it all—the bridal party, the entire extended family invited, the big reception, the photos, the dinner, the open bar, the dancing, all our friends invited for the weekend—all of it. It didn't have to be expensive, but it did have to happen.

"You'll love it," he'd said, so many times, trying to convince me. "You'll see. All the people we love in one place—you'll see."

Epilogue

"Sounds great. Do you know how much that shit costs."

"We'll save up!"

I had wanted none of it. I had always wanted to elope, if I ever found someone to marry, to go to City Hall, and then to never have to talk about table decorations, for any reason, for as long as I lived. Davin and I had been arguing about the wedding pretty much since the day after he proposed.

Standing in our kitchen in my caftan on our legal wedding day in September, I had poured a second glass of cheap champagne and smiled to myself, a bride plotting for evil. I was going to win this. Davin would come around. Now that we were married, it would be stupid to get married *again*.

We got married again on July 23, 2022.

Davin was right. I was wrong. All the people we loved in one spot. It was the best day of my life.

As I walked down the aisle, I looked to my right and saw my dad, an active Mormon, beaming. He looked genuinely delighted to be there; he was taking picture after picture. One of the rainbow hand fans we'd set at everyone's place was tucked into his suit coat pocket. He wanted to keep it. At the reception, as I watched my aunt Carol, another active Mormon, tearing it down on the dance floor, it suddenly occurred to me why she'd flown, at unexpectedly huge expense, from Canada for our wedding. She had come because my mom could not. She was standing in for my mother.

Every one of our closest friends was there. I watched them all on the dance floor, laughing, jumping up and down, reveling in being reunited again while disco lights flashed in the dark and the bartender announced we were all out of whiskey. I thought about how important they each were to me, how many times I had seen those same faces lit up under dance-floor lights at dyke bars as we all navigated our twenties and thirties. We became queer adults together. The backdrop had always been queer spaces. We'd been lucky enough to have them.

Epilogue

The young queers just coming up, just growing into adulthood, will also have them. I'm no longer worried about it. With all the trips for the book complete, it was clear there was one more thing to celebrate: the number of lesbian bars left in America. That's because lots has changed in the time since I began my bar visits and now.

I started writing this book for a few reasons: Because I adore lesbian bars. Because I needed others to experience the joy of these spaces. Because I wanted to see the current state of dyke bars in this country, and to see if I could find out why so many were closing. And, sadly, because I wanted to see every last lesbian bar in America before they vanished. In case they all did.

Based on the trajectory we'd all been experiencing, I just assumed that more bars would close. I assumed that we'd see one depressing social media announcement follow another, and hear *more* queers wailing about a bar they loved that was closing. And then one day, we'd stop seeing announcements altogether, and that would be the end.

Well, guess what, friends? The joke was on me. Not only did *no* bars I visited for this book close, but two old ones *opened back up* (Ginger's in Brooklyn and Hershee Bar in Norfolk, Virginia), and then ... *new bars started opening*. MANY NEW BARS. So many, in fact, that people were constantly sending me articles and announcements they'd seen about new spaces, so often that I was opening my DMs and having a panic attack when I'd see that nine different friends in one morning had sent me the news about a new space that was open in Chicago. *Oh my god, yes, I know about Nobody's Darling in Chicago,* I'd think, heart pounding. *Fuck, how am I going to get to it??*

And—OK. I love these bars. All I want for these spaces is for them to be protected, and for there to be more of them. You know I do. But—

"CAN THESE MOTHERFUCKERS JUST CHILL OUT FOR ONE GODDAMNED YEAR UNTIL I WRITE THIS BOOK?"

Too many new spaces were opening! This book was gonna be out of date the moment it went to print! What do you fucking *mean*, there's a

Epilogue

new bar called Doc Marie's in Portland? "I WAS LITERALLY JUST NEXT DOOR IN SEATTLE, COME THE FUCK ON."

All the media attention surrounding the end of lesbian bars had outraged queers, and if there's one thing queers are good at, it's turning outrage into action. *The trajectory for lesbian bars is finally moving upward.*

I did my absolute best to get to new bars that were opening or were already open. Nearly all of them fell under the category of "queer bars"—not necessarily *lesbian* bars, but queer bars—like As You Are in Washington, DC—but I wanted to see them anyway. For gay science!

Nobody's Darling, for instance. Davin and I went when we were in Chicago, at the end of our midwestern road trip. And frankly? Standing in the middle of Nobody's Darling, I became furious about Nobody's Darling. This perfect, elegant, Black lesbian–owned new queer cocktail bar is exactly *three blocks* from where I lived for *five frickin' years* in Chicago, and I cannot accept that this could have been my regular bar, had I just stayed put. Nobody's Darling, which is named for the Alice Walker poem "Be Nobody's Darling," has cocktails so fucking good, so delicious and creative, that they've been nominated for a James Beard Award. They put a little "(B)" next to alcohol brands that are Black-owned, *and* most of their cocktails are thirteen dollars and under. In Chicago! And our friends Reba and Yo just wandered over and met us there! *And* a hot stranger at the end of the bar sent our friend Jen a drink, just like in a movie! And really, I'm just so FOMO-y about all of this, all the bars that are opening in places I no longer live, all of the queer bars I could not get to in time, that I could just cry.

Jolene's in San Francisco. Babes Bar in Bethel, Vermont. There are two other brand-new bars in Chicago—Dorothy and Whiskey Girl Tavern—that I didn't even hear about until we had already been home for months. There's a group of queers in Minneapolis (!!!!) fundraising so they can open a dyke bar. There's a roaming lesbian party in Queens—Dave's Lesbian Bar—that I've heard is looking for a permanent home.

Epilogue

I am not even going to *mention* the rumor I heard from a *very* credit-able source about *two* new lesbian bars opening soon in Los Angeles, because your dyke-ass mother is too exhausted from tramping around the country all year.

That's all. I hope we meet again soon. I'll be the femme on a bar-stool wearing a dress, surrounded by a sea of flannel and Blundstones. A person who is, I am delighted to report, no longer afraid of approach-ing anyone to start a conversation. If chatting with strangers makes *you* nervous, though, believe me, I understand. And let me offer you a tip, because my friend was right: the best opening line when approaching any stranger at any lesbian bar is "Hi."

It doesn't matter what you wear. It doesn't matter who you came with. What matters is that you're there. The only thing lesbian bars need is you.

See you there.

Acknowledgments

Thank you to my wonderful agent, Valerie Borchardt. You contacted me the first time you ever read something I wrote, which shocked the hell out of me. You encouraged me, nudged me, and waited patiently for years as I got my shit together. I am so grateful for you.

To my editor, Sean Manning: You are so talented I was humbled; your knowledge of which cuts and additions needed to happen made me whisper "wtf how does he do this?" dozens of times as I worked on my drafts. You insisted that I talk about my own story, even though I very much just wanted to make lesbian jokes for 299 pages. This book is a million times better because you edited it.

Jenifer Prince: Thank you for your amazing artwork on the cover. When I saw it for the first time, I shrieked and waved my phone around in the kitchen, refusing to even let Davin see it until I'd stared at it for a full two minutes.

Thank you to the team at Simon & Schuster who worked on this project. This was probably your 803rd time working on a book, but it was my first time, and you made the process incredibly easy.

Dr. Rae Rosenberg: Thank you for doing the sensitivity reading of this book. I'm so glad you were just a text away anytime I woke up, panicked, in the middle of the night, certain everyone was going to hate everything I said about the bars, and then also hate me because of it. Having your eyes on my words helped more than I can say.

Thank you to Teresa Mozur—your enthusiasm is contagious, and your insistence that other people wouldn't be appalled if I did a GoFundMe for the book trips saved us from financial ruin.

Acknowledgments

Speaking of which: Thank you to everyone who donated to the GoFundMe for this book. You are all kind and generous; I was amazed and so grateful you donated. Y'all are the only reason I made it past Phoenix.

To the Lesbian Bar Project: Thank you for bringing so much media attention to the closure of lesbian bars. (And thank you for making the list of bars!) May all the lesbian bars stay open for years to come.

To Jennifer Parker, from whom a direct line can be drawn to this book, and to the *New York Times*: thank you.

Thank you to Tavi Gevinson, who asked me to write for *Rookie*. You, and all the writers and editors at *Rookie*, changed my life.

I want to thank anybody who ever read my blog, *Effing Dykes*. I started it to kill time at my job and make my friends laugh, and to have it eventually lead to the book you're holding is mind-boggling.

To all my friends who were in any way involved with this project—if you let me stay at your apartment during a bar visit, if you came to meet me at a dyke bar, if you asked me how I was even though you knew full well I would immediately start talking about this book and only this book—you know who you are, and I love you, and I appreciate you so much. You are the reason I have anything to say about dyke bars. We were there together.

To EmJ, Stephen, Rae, Janet, Cole, George, Isabel, Jim, Clare, Shelley, Kelly, Tawnya, and Seven: When the primaries for Davin's election were happening and he was managing another campaign and the magazine I write for my job was due and my first draft of this book was due and Davin and I were about to get married in front of 130 people, all within the span of the same two weeks in summer 2022, you made the wedding happen. You cleaned our house, bought all the flowers at grocery stores three hours before the wedding, decorated the reception hall, made the tiniest, fiddliest crafts, and acted like it was no big deal. It was a big deal to us, and I love you. I don't know how to thank you enough.

Acknowledgments

To my dad, Bruce Burton: Thank you for being the first person in my life to tell me I should be a writer.

To Shelley Burton, my sister (and one of my beta readers): You're the first person I called when I found out I got to write this book, and you're the last person I texted, just now, about some dumb shit, like I do dozens of times every day. Thank you for being there, through everything. I would not have made it without you.

I want to thank absolutely everyone I approached at a lesbian bar who did not back away slowly. If you talked to me at a dyke bar, included me, made me a drink, or simply moved over to make space for me, I am unbelievably grateful to you. I was so nervous, and you helped me so much.

Do you own a lesbian bar? I love you, you are the reason we still have these spaces, you can't imagine the difference you make in queer lives. Thank you.

And finally, to Davin, my husband, who also happens to be the most attractive person alive: You're the best person I've ever met. Thank you for dealing with me while I wrote this book, whether I was obsessively calling you from the Atlanta airport while you were leading a meeting, or snarling at you about deadlines when you wanted us to go to Pride (or out to dinner or to a friend's house or to do literally anything that did not involve me sitting cross-legged on the couch, scowling into my laptop). You planned out every detail of every bar trip I took, you remained calm when we maxed out the travel credit card and our bank account was down to $9 four days before payday, you read the first and second and third drafts of this book, and you never once made me feel like my dream was a burden. Not only that, but you are very fucking fun to travel with. It goes without saying that I could not have done this without you. I love you.